Freud's Dream

of

Interpretation

❧

*SUNY Series in Modern
Jewish Literature and Culture
Sarah Blacher Cohen, Editor*

Freud's Dream of Interpretation

Ken Frieden

Foreword by Harold Bloom

STATE UNIVERSITY OF NEW YORK PRESS

Published by
State University of New York Press, Albany

© 1990 State University of New York

For information, address State University of New York
Press, State University Plaza, Albany, NY 12246

Library of Congress Cataloging-in-Publication Data
Frieden, Ken, 1955–
    Freud's dream of interpretation / Ken Frieden.
        p.   cm.—(SUNY series in modern Jewish literature and
    culture)
        Bibliography: p. 143
        Includes indices.
        ISBN 0-7914-0124-3.—ISBN 0-7914-0125-1 (pbk.)
        1. Dreams—History.   2. Freud, Sigmund, 1856–1939.
    3. Dreams—Religious aspects—Judaism—History of doctrines.
    4. Dreams in the Bible.   5. Judaism and psychoanalysis—History.
    I. Title.   II. Series.
BF1078.F82   1990
154.6'34'092—dc20   89–4597
                                                                        CIP

10   9   8   7   6   5   4   3   2   1

It will not be easy for any reader of this book to put himself in the emotional position of the author—who does not understand the holy language, is completely estranged from the paternal religion, as from every other, and who cannot share nationalistic ideals; yet who has never denied belonging to his people, feels his particularity as Jewish and does not wish it otherwise. Were one to ask him: What is still Jewish about you, if you have given up all these mutualities with your fellow people? he would answer: Very much, probably the main thing. But he could not at present express this essential part in clear words. Sometime later it will certainly be accessible to scientific inspection.

—Sigmund Freud, Preface to the Hebrew edition of *Totem und Tabu*

How wonderful and new and at the same time how frightful and ironic I feel, directed toward the whole of existence with my knowledge! I have *discovered* for myself that in me ancient humanity and the animal world, even the entire primeval age and past of all sentient being continues to invent, love, hate, conclude—I have suddenly awakened in the midst of this dream, but only to the consciousness that I am dreaming and that I *must* go on dreaming, in order not to perish: as a sleepwalker must go on dreaming in order not to fall.

—Friedrich Nietzsche, *Die fröhliche Wissenschaft*

Contents

Foreword   ix
Preface   xi
Introduction   1

1.   **Freud: Interpreter and Seducer**   9
Freud's Path to Dreams • Against the Past •
Interpretation by Correspondence and Displacement •
"Free" Association • Revisions of Secondary Revision •
Freud's Monopoly and the Dream Facade •
Occupation and Resistance

2.   **Joseph and Daniel: Disguises and Interpretive Power**   47
"Will You Rule Over Us?" • "Do Not Interpretations
Belong to God? Tell Me" • "As He Interpreted to Us,
So It Was" • "This Is Your Dream" • "Worship the
Image of Gold" • "Mene Mene Teqel Upharsin" •
"Your God . . . Will Deliver You"

3.   **Bar Hedia and R. Ishmael: Battles of Interpretation**   73
"A Dream That Is Not Interpreted . . ." • "All Dreams
Follow the Mouth" • "Your Father Has Left You Money
in Cappadocia" • "Because of Your Mouth . . ."

4.   **Freud: Demystification and Denial**   95
Dreams of Prophecy and Telepathy • The Prophetic
Interpreter • Languages of Dreams • Dreams of
Wordplay • An Absurd Decree • The Grand *Verneinung*

Conclusion   133
References   139
Indices   151

Foreword

In Ken Frieden's first book, *Genius and Monologue* (Ithaca and London: Cornell University Press, 1985), the dilemmas of our current sense of textuality are not allowed to strand us in the deconstructive abyss. Frieden concludes by offering us a wary way out from an endless rhetoricity: "The new transcendence is a transference, a *metapherein* that surpasses the present, transforms past figures through imaginative obsessions, and constitutes the self in endless dialogues" (p. 194).

Freud's only transcendence, his perhaps unknowing vestige of Platonism, was his worship of the Reality Principle. But since reality testing, for Freud, was pragmatically the constant acceptance of our mortality, such transcendence borders uneasily upon the Death Drive, beyond the Pleasure Principle. Part of Freud's interpretive heroism was his own refusal to yield up Eros or transference to Thanatos or the Death Drive, even though transference, in Freud, is one of the masterworks of emotional ambivalence, together with the taboo and the Oedipus complex.

Frieden's second book, *Freud's Dream of Interpretation,* is the best exegesis I have encountered of one of the ultimate sources of Freud's moral heroism, located by Frieden in the repressed Judaic aspects of Freudian dream interpretation. Partly, Frieden studies the intertextual relation between Freudian and ancient Jewish modes of reading, but more cunningly his book investigates the complexities of Freud's Jewish self-identity. Scientism, Freud's defense against anti-Semitism, led Freud to distance himself from the prophetic mode of such ancient seers of the dream as Joseph and Daniel. By placing all reality in the past, except for the dreamer's death, Freud had to abandon the dream's intuitive quarrying of the future. And yet, as Frieden shrewdly demonstrates, Freudian "free associationism" is the dreamer's future. To dream, and even more to interpret the dream, is to postpone or to modify reality, to ward off or at least to perspectivize the necessity of dying.

Freud's Jewishness had its equivocal or ambivalent elements, but this is hardly unique, whether in our era or in previous times. Like Kafka, Freud became a dominant and permanent figure in Jewish culture, without altogether intending such an achievement. Frieden's own conclusion is a crucial clue to Freud's hesitation: "The dream work is ultimately indistinguishable from the interpreter's work." Such a realization of the arbitrariness of his interpretations was not acceptable to Freud, though the realization is deeply founded in Talmudic tradition. The authority of science, such as it was, was a psychic necessity for Freud.

One of the many values of Frieden's study is that it reminds us of the curious status of psychoanalysis today, at once an inescapable element in our intellectual lives, and yet also a rather literal-minded church, as it were, founded upon Freud's tropes. What Freud teaches is the freedom of interpretation, even though he himself was perhaps the most tendentious interpreter in all of Western intellectual tradition. His most Jewish quality was his deep conviction that there is sense in everything, and that such meaning could be brought up to the light. He read the unconscious as Judaic exegesis read the Hebrew Bible, with every nuance, every omission, being made to show an extraordinary wealth of significance. But, if everything has an ascertainable meaning, then all meaning is overdetermined, which amounts to affirming that everything has happened already, and is in the individual's past. Freud's theory of repression depends upon this belief that there never can be anything new. It is our responsibility, and our therapy, to learn and accept what has happened to us, even though so much of that is dreadful, indeed is *the* dreadful.

Dream interpretation became Freud's royal road to the Unconscious, and he could not accept the notion that anyone had walked that road properly before him. A master of evasions, Freud once joked that he had invented psychoanalysis because it had no literature. It had a vast literature, literature itself, and Ken Frieden demonstrates precisely how the Bible and the Talmud were part of that literature.

Harold Bloom

Preface

Sigmund Freud's dream of interpretation arose from his wish to sever all ties between himself and ancient dream interpreters. Much remains concealed, past and future, in *The Interpretation of Dreams,* for Freud evaded his forerunners and produced distortions analogous to those of the dream work. Freud's specific rejections of Judaic dream interpretation also recall psychoanalytic "denial," by which intellectual judgment represents yet disavows a repressed thought.

This book interprets disparate traditions of dream interpretation and situates them in relation to broader issues of interpretation. It does not follow a linear path from the Hebrew Bible to Sigmund Freud, but rather constructs a space defined by three concentric spheres. The innermost core contains readings of biblical and Talmudic dream interpretations; the intermediate sphere reflects on Freud's approach to dreams; the exterior surface places Freudian, biblical, and Talmudic interpretation in the context of current literary theory. Ambivalent, Freud's writings mediate between ancient and modern realms.

The opening chapter examines Freud's attempts to decipher his patients' dream reports. After he renounces prior methods, Freud attempts to establish his own scientific approach. He both relies on philological assumptions about interpretation and introduces the radical practice of free association, which alternatively stabilize and destabilize the relationship between dreams and their meaning. Torn between conflicting demands, Freud's language suggests that psychoanalysis resembles war, a staged battle, or a seduction, and is—in any event—a risky venture.

Chapters 2 and 3 return to biblical and Talmudic narratives, which emphasize the prophetic component of dream interpretation. Biblical stories imply that God communicates through dreams; rabbinic sources combine respect toward and mistrust of dream visions. Like secular narratives, dreams sometimes vie with Scripture, and certain dream interpreters stand in competition with rabbis. The debate over interpretive activity revolves around the extent to which interpretations may determine the future they predict.

The final chapter reinterprets Freud in connection with haunting questions of prophecy and telepathy. Freud dismisses claims for prophecy in dreams, admitting only the familiar mechanisms of transference and the dream work. Nevertheless, when he derives the meaning of dreams from dreamers' associations, Freud cannot entirely exclude elements of suggestion and prophetic influence. Freudian practices are closer to Judaic tradition than Freud chose to admit.

This discussion is not a comprehensive survey of psychoanalytic and Judaic dream interpretation. It provides literary readings of the relationship between the Bible, the Talmud, and Freud, which appears precisely through Freud's recurrent denials. In spite of his elusiveness, Freud is a link between ancient traditions and postmodern trends. Freud's repression of biblical and Talmudic examples has enabled recent critics to rediscover these veiled precursors—not in theory, but in the actual practices of Midrash.

For influential discourses and dialogues over the past fifteen years, I am indebted to Harold Bloom, Daniel Boyarin, Leslie Brisman, Edward Casey, Brevard Childs, Jacques Derrida, Avner Falk, Shoshana Felman, Peter Laderman, Jean-Luc Nancy, Paul Ricoeur, and Heinrich Weidmann. Special thanks go to my wife Joan and to the members of my family, for their patience with countless visions and revisions. I also thank the students who participated in my Emory University course on "Jewish Dream Interpretation." Finally, Patricia Stockbridge has provided invaluable assistance with word processing.

All translations in this book are my own, except where otherwise indicated. Citations refer the reader to the most accessible German and English editions.

* * *

He dreamed of ancient hieroglyphics that resembled nothing he had seen before. But the meaning was transparent: I know, I am in the know.

He dreams of a modern script that is absolutely lucid. But the meaning is ineffable: I know nothing, I am not.

The interpretation of a dream always creates a new dream.

INTRODUCTION

1

Without tracing a direct line of influence, these pages bring together Freud's writings and ancient Jewish traditions of dream interpretation. This intertextual field has been misunderstood, in part because Freud himself vehemently renounced the early interpreters of dreams. Freud's disavowal provokes reexamination of what he so insistently denied.

Numerous writers have commented on Freud's Jewish identity.[1] Their

---

1. See David S. Blatt, "The Development of the Hero: Sigmund Freud and the Reformation of the Jewish Tradition," *Psychoanalysis and Contemporary Thought* 11 (1988), 639–703; Dennis Klein, *Jewish Origins of the Psychoanalytic Movement* (Chicago: The University of Chicago Press, 1985); Susan A. Handelman, *The Slayers of Moses: The Emergence of Rabbinic Interpretation in Modern Literary Theory* (Albany: State University of New York, 1982), pp. 129–52; Avner Falk, "Freud and Herzl," *Contemporary Psychoanalysis* 14 (July 1978), 357–87; Martin S. Bergmann, "Moses and the Evolution of Freud's Jewish Identity," *The Israel Annals of Psychiatry and Related Disciplines* 14 (March 1976), 3–26; Paul Roazen, *Freud and His Followers* (New York: Alfred A. Knopf, 1975), pp. 22–27; Léon Vogel, "Freud and Judaism: An Analysis in the Light of His Correspondence," trans. Murray Sachs, *Judaism* 24 (1975), 181–93; Robert Gordis, "The Two Faces of Freud," *Judaism* 24 (1975), 194–200; Marthe Robert, *D'Œdipe à Moïse: Freud et la conscience juive* (Paris: Calmann-Levy, 1974); in English, see Robert, *From Oedipus to Moses: Freud's Jewish Identity*, trans. Ralph Manhein (Garden City, N.Y.: Anchor Books, 1976); John Murray Cuddihy, *The Ordeal of Civility: Freud, Marx, Lévi-Strauss, and the Jewish Struggle with Modernity* (New York: Basic Books, 1974); Max Schur, *Freud: Living and Dying* (New York: International Universities Press, 1972), pp. 22–27; Peter Loewenberg, " 'Sigmund Freud as a Jew': A Study in Ambivalence and Courage," *Journal of the History of the Behavorial Sciences* 7 (1971), 363–69, and "A Hidden Zionist Theme in Freud's 'My Son, the Myops . . . ' Dream," *Journal of the History of Ideas* 31 (1970), 129–32; Earl A. Grollman, *Judaism in Sigmund Freud's World* (New York: Appleton-Century, 1965); David Bakan, *Sigmund Freud and the Jewish Mystical Tradition*, (1958; repr. Boston: Beacon, 1975); Ernst Simon, "Sigmund Freud, the Jew," *Leo Baeck Institute Year Book* 2 (1957), 270–305; Karl Menninger, "The Genius of the Jew in Psychiatry"

observations tend to conceive Freud's "Jewishness" too narrowly, however, in predominantly biographical terms. The present analysis turns from Freud the individual to Freud's works, and from personal influences to textual interrelationships between Freudian dream interpretation, the Bible, and the Talmud. In *The Interpretation of Dreams,* Freud admits to identifying with the biblical Joseph. Yet as a modern interpreter, he rejects what he takes to be Joseph's archaic methods, and Freud's work on dreams stands in an ambivalent relationship to biblical and Talmudic sources. Freud may not have known the central Talmudic passages on dream interpretation until *Imago* published a relevant article in 1913.[2] Nevertheless, he did study Scripture at an early age, and remarked on its importance for his development; Freud's dreams, letters, and occasional comments reflect his linguistic awareness of Hebrew and Yiddish.[3] Freud knew enough of Judaic traditions to be uneasy about his knowledge.

Freud might have responded more fully and consistently to biblical sources. In order to counter the skepticism of modern science, he repudi-

---

(1937), collected in *A Psychiatrist's World: The Selected Papers of Karl Menninger,* ed. Bernard H. Hall (New York: The Viking Press, 1959), pp. 415–24; and A. A. Roback, *Jewish Influence in Modern Thought* (Cambridge, Mass.: Sci-Art Publishers, 1929), pp. 152–97. For a dissenting view, see Peter Gay, *A Godless Jew: Freud, Atheism, and the Making of Psychoanalysis* (New Haven: Yale University Press, 1987).

2. Chaim Lauer, "Das Wesen des Traumes in der Beurteilung der talmudischen und rabbinischen Literatur," *Internationale Zeitschrift für Psychoanalyse und "Imago"* 1 (1913), 459–69. More recently, Gérard Haddad juxtaposes Freudian and Talmudic theories in *L'enfant illégitime: Sources talmudiques de la psychanalyse* (Paris: Hachette, 1981). He observes that Freud "sought to leave this relationship in obscurity" (p. 14).

3. See Willy Aron, "Notes on Sigmund Freud's Ancestry and Jewish Contacts," *YIVO Annual of Jewish Social Science* 11 (1956/57), 286–95, and Régine Robin, "Le yiddish, langue fantasmatique?" *L'écrit du temps* 5 (1984), 43–50. Concerning Freud and the Philippson Bible, see Eva M. Rosenfeld, "Dream and Vision—Some Remarks on Freud's Egyptian Bird Dream," *International Journal of Psycho-Analysis* 37 (1956), 97–105; Théo Pfrimmer, *Freud: Lecteur de la bible* (Paris: Presses Universitaires de France, 1982), part 2; and William J. McGrath, *Freud's Discovery of Psychoanalysis: The Politics of Hysteria* (Ithaca, N.Y.: Cornell University Press, 1986), pp. 26–58. Freud discusses his relationship to Judaism in his Address to the B'nai Brith Society (*GW* 17, 51–53/*SE* 20, 273–74). Among other passages, see Freud's *Autobiographical Study* (*GW* 14, 33–35/*SE* 7–9), his letter to the *Jüdische Presszentrale Zürich* (*GW* 14, 556/*SE* 19, 291), and his prefaces to the Hebrew editions of *Introductory Lectures on Psychoanalysis* and *Totem and Taboo.*

ated Joseph and Daniel, who approach dreams as bridges to the future. Freud opposed prophetic dream interpretation and ignored the potential legitimacy of its future orientation. Determined to trace the dream report to prior causes, then, Freud underrated the dreamer's wish to have the dream turned toward a future. Wishes do not merely precede dreaming; they often color the commitment to interpretation. Because Freud convincingly established new methods, few commentators have recognized that the prophetic dimension of ancient dream interpretation was at once suppressed by Freud and implicit in his practices.

From the beginning, men and women have sought their fortunes in the enigmatic images of dreams. Interpreters respond by shedding light on the darker realm where elusive laws of fiction give birth to infinite possibility. To dream is to deceive oneself: English *dream* and German *träumen* derive from *dreugh,* to deceive. A dream text is a tale told by a dreamer, full of equivocations, signifying everything and nothing. Dreams veer away from reality, and the lost dreamer seeks a guide to a more certain world. But the interpretation of a dream is always subject to revision.

One pragmatic thesis of this book is that no interpretation is intrinsically true, because a present truth depends upon the future reality that confirms, alters, or gives meaning to the interpretive act. Meaning does not stand waiting to be uncovered behind a dream or text, but evolves in front of it, actualized by readers and interpreters who produce new possibilities. It follows that while some commentaries are self-contradictory and demonstrably false, others can only be measured against the way in which they modify the future. When Pablo Picasso was told that Gertrude Stein did not look like his portrait of her, he responded: "That does not make any difference, she will."[4] Picasso's portrait has indeed become the predominant image of Stein. This story illustrates the power of the interpretations performed by art, literary criticism, and psychoanalysis.

Meaning is made, not discovered. Freud's analogies to adventure and archaeology deceptively suggest that the meaning of dreams lies buried in an objective ground. Since the medium of dream texts and interpretations is always language, strategies of interpretation have little in common with an archaeological dig. Language leaves its traces in elusive patterns of collective and individual rhetoric. Freud's basic approach to oneiric meaning—in the correspondence between a dream and the childhood wish that motivates it—is incomplete and awaits a supplemental future orientation.

---

4. Gertrude Stein, *The Autobiography of Alice B. Toklas* (New York: Random House, 1961), p. 12.

2

If "all the world's a stage," then psychoanalysis revises personal dramas in a scenario of remembering, repeating, and working through. The patient's dream performances reveal typical roles. The dream interpreter, who never merely translates the text of a dreamer's fading past, facilitates a rewriting of the future.

Arthur Schopenhauer writes that "everyone, while he dreams, is a Shakespeare."[5] C. G. Jung also employs the dramatic metaphor and calls the dream "a theater, in which the dreamer is scene, player, prompter, director, author, audience, and critic."[6] The psychoanalyst may also assume these roles. Psychoanalysis is a drama in which the patient tries on masks, playing opposite the analyst's feigned neutrality. To the experienced analyst this proceeding resembles child's play, a game of presence and absence in which the subject creates an imaginary world. Whether we reposition our objects in the world or dream of a new order, one primary impulse is to attain or maintain control. Playing, the child strives against an unpredictable world, as does the dreamer who stages a drama of chaos and order. Some authors assert that Freud manipulated his patients, but it is more accurate to say that the "talking cure" manipulates a patient's fictions.

The dream in itself is a fiction. Because no dream is ever directly conveyed, dream interpretation relies on the retelling of a dream that displaces whatever may have inspired it. To recall a dream is to generate a narrative based on heterogeneous materials; waking associations situate the dream text in a broader linguistic framework. Interpretation translates the dream text into new texts and contexts. The dreamer creates fictions, and the interpreter acts as a literary critic. The meaning of a text is always expressed through another text, and consequently every interpretation is in turn open to interpretation. While no dream is ever fully transcribed or understood, an interpretation may serve limited ends when it incites a patient to change.

The play of inventive associations has linked dreams to prophecy, to sexuality, and to death. According to a Talmudic source, "sleep is one sixtieth of death; dream is one sixtieth of prophecy."[7] The dream interpreter

---

5. Arthur Schopenhauer, "Versuch über das Geistersehn und was damit zusammenhängt," in *Sämtliche Werke,* 2d ed., ed. Wolfgang von Löhneysen (Stuttgart: Cotta-Insel, 1963), vol. 4, p. 279.

6. C. G. Jung, "Allgemeine Gesichtspunkte zur Psychologie des Traumes," in *Über psychische Energetik und das Wesen der Träume,* 2d ed. (Zürich: Rascher, 1948), p. 200. In English, see "General Aspects of Dream Psychology," in *Dreams,* trans. R. F. C. Hull (Princeton: Princeton University Press, 1974), p. 52.

7. The Babylonian Talmud, tractate Berakhot 57b.

discerns unexpected similarities. The Greek author Artemidorus reports, for instance: "I know of a man who dreamt that he went into a brothel and could not leave. He died a few days later, this being the quite logical result of his dream. For a brothel, like a cemetery, is called 'a place men have in common,' and many human seeds perish there. In a natural way, then, this place resembles death."[8] As a figure for death, the brothel is a commonplace, a *communis locus* in the symbolism that associates eros and thanatos.

Aristotle states that "the most skillful interpreter of dreams is he who has the faculty of observing resemblances."[9] Because dreams employ distorted images, like reflections on moving water, they do not superficially correspond to what they represent. In connection with poetic style, Aristotle writes that "the greatest thing by far is to be a master of metaphor . . . since a good metaphor implies an intuitive perception of the similarity in dissimilars."[10] Hence, according to one traditional view, the dream interpreter's task is to return from the metaphorical expression to the literal meaning. Like the poet, the interpreter works freely with metaphors: the dream content is not literally its meaning, but represents meanings figuratively.

Dream interpretation is a variant of textual commentary,[11] and two opposed strategies compete within Freudian interpretation. Freud often indicates that the interpreter perceives symbols that enable him to reconstruct the authentic image from its distorting fragments; at other moments, he follows the more radical demands of free association, giving meaning to dream elements by allowing them to be successively displaced.

The Aristotelian model of resemblance is based on the figure of metaphor. The more radical Freudian method of association reverts to unfamiliar figures of difference, and is unsettling, even to its originator. Freud conceives symptoms and dreams as figurative distortions, framed beyond the conscious intentions of a subject. Although he strives to liberate the dream from its figuration, in his most original phase Freud also accredits every associative displacement and approaches a realization that the dream has no literal meaning. It remains difficult to determine whether dream interpretation is high drama or a comedy of errors.

---

8. Artemidorus, *The Interpretation of Dreams*, trans. Robert J. White (Park Ridge, N. J.: Noyes, 1975), p. 59.

9. Aristotle, *Prophesying by Dreams* 464b. In *The Basic Works of Aristotle*, ed. Richard McKeon (New York: Random House, 1941), p. 630.

10. Aristotle, *Poetics* 1459a. In *The Basic Works of Aristotle*, p. 1479.

11. Compare James Kugel's comments and references in "Two Introductions to Midrash," in *Midrash and Literature*, ed. Geoffrey H. Hartman and Sanford Budick (New Haven: Yale University Press, 1986), p. 101n.

3

Scripture has predetermined both the collective dream and the communal reality of the Jews. To the extent that personal dreams represent a nonscriptural imagination, they threaten this textual state. Interpretation of private dreams contends with interpretation of Scripture; to dream or to interpret at a distance from divine language may be to distance oneself from God. Although Jewish life submitted to Mosaic law for centuries, at every moment—even at the reception of the decalogue—this textual mosaic was threatened by the possibility of idol worship. Idolatry displaces writing by imagery, and substitutes forbidden fantasies for the language of God.

Judaic sources insist that Scripture (written Torah) must be understood together with the Talmud (oral Torah). This tradition gives rise to contradictory expectations. On the one hand, rabbinic interpreters sometimes efface themselves before a biblical passage, as if allowing God's text to speak for itself. On the other hand, Jewish interpreters also revise God's words by embedding quotations from Scripture in new contexts.

Twentieth-century psychology has been marked by analogous tensions in connection with the dream text and its interpretation. Freud searched for the meaning of dreams in the past, as if to say that the dreamer's psyche interprets itself by exposing its underlying causes. Yet post-Freudian psychotherapists have recognized that the demands of cure lead beyond thoughts that may have inspired a dream—toward future effects. In consequence, some analysts have shifted their focus from past causes to present conflicts and future possibilities.

Freud was divided between disparate interpretive outlooks. While his fundamental conception of textual and psychological meaning is consistent with the nineteenth-century hermeneutics of Friedrich Schleiermacher and Wilhelm Dilthey, certain psychoanalytic strategies anticipate contemporary literary theory. In particular, Harold Bloom and Jacques Derrida advance aspects of Freud's work that elude European hermeneutics, reading otherwise and obliquely reflecting rabbinic precursors. No thorough comparison between poststructuralism and rabbinic commentary is possible, however, since rhetorical critics and rabbinic authors have employed highly diverse methods.[12] Rather than attempt to demonstrate analogies between Midrash and contemporary criticism, the present study considers a specific point of contact in psychoanalytic dream interpretation.

---

12. For a sober critique of recent efforts to juxtapose ancient Midrash and current literary studies, see Robert Alter, "Old Rabbis, New Critics," *The New Republic*, 5–12 Jan. 1987, 27–33.

Freud's debt to nineteenth-century interpretive views cannot be traced to specific forerunners, because his fundamental assumptions were typical of an entire milieu. Chajim Steinthal paraphrased Schleiermacher's views in a way that characterizes the interpreter's Freud: "The philologist understands the speaker and poet better than he himself and his contemporaries understood him. For he brings clearly into consciousness what was actually, but only unconsciously, present in the other."[13] Freud often assumes that the deeper meaning of verbal expressions is linked to unconscious ideas.

Yet aspects of Freudian psychoanalysis overstep the limits established by nineteenth-century hermeneutics. Freud's interpretations do more than illuminate a realm of conscious, preconscious, and unconscious thoughts. Freud's attention to puns, wordplays, and verbal associations—beyond subjective agency—allies him with both current trends in literary criticism and ancient rabbinic practices.

Freud emerges as an intermediate sphere between ancient and modern Judaic commentary, despite his efforts to forestall such associations. He never acknowledges the pseudorabbinic elements of his work, and his silence forms a resonant space in which his repressed precursors echo.[14] Reading Freud in relation to the Bible and Talmud reveals his importance as a *topos* in Judaic thought.

The rabbinic and poststructuralist attention to language is symptomatic of larger concerns: like many rabbis in the Talmudic period, current authors sometimes write ahistorically about the textual universe. One unmistakable rabbinic quest has been to live in the margins of divine language, like marginal commentaries on the Bible or Talmud. Every question that arises, the Talmud suggests, can be resolved in the proper scriptural context. Dreams potentially pose a threat if they follow nonbiblical sources or employ materials foreign to the rabbinic world.

In Vienna, the imagination of Freud and his patients obviously transgressed the boundaries of biblical literature. Scripture no longer provided the key to dreams; associations of all kinds became admissible. With this

---

13. Cited by Hans-Georg Gadamer in *Wahrheit und Methode: Grundzüge einer philosophischen Hermeneutik,* 4th ed. (Tübingen: J. C. B. Mohr, 1975), p. 181. In English, see *Truth and Method* (New York: The Seabury Press, 1975), p. 170.

14. Compare Jacques Derrida's references to evasions in his Jerusalem lecture "Comment ne pas parler: Dénégations," in *Psyché: Inventions de l'autre* (Paris: Galilée, 1987), pp. 535–95. In English, see "How to Avoid Speaking: Denials," trans. Ken Frieden, in *Languages of the Unsayable: The Play of Negativity in Literature and Literary Theory,* ed. Sanford Budick and Wolfgang Iser (New York: Columbia University Press, 1989), pp. 3–70.

expansion of potential meaning, as the relevant intertexts become conspicuously more diverse, interpretation loses its appearance of dependability.

Rhetorical criticism follows the Freudian lead in observing the dynamics of textuality and intertextuality; in so doing, it also responds to ancient precursors. Like manifest dream contents in Freud's estimation, every text appears "overdetermined" by possible meanings. Recent poststructuralist authors—for whom both the biblical canon and conscious intentions have lost their primacy—share rabbinic assumptions about textuality, and are acutely aware of the hazards presented by a failure of grounds.

Freud's relationship to biblical and Talmudic dream interpretation is characterized by denial. Ancient dream interpreters are Freud's repressed precursors, constantly present in his works by being systematically excluded.

1

FREUD: INTERPRETER AND SEDUCER

Freud was intrigued by the Roman god Janus.[1] As a dream interpreter, Freud was also two-faced, divided between orientations toward the past and toward the future. He looked back in time for causes of mental events, but his method of free association inspired the creation of new meanings and guided his patients forward. The father of psychoanalysis was ill at ease with his own hints at fulfilling a prophetic role, and made efforts to disguise this aspect of his work.

One of Freud's basic psychoanalytic strategies is to hide his face and act as a blank screen. This self-effacing performance encourages the patient to transfer his or her emotional attachments onto Freud in a first step toward working through childhood complexes. The analytic psychodrama leaves Freud's image an enigma, because within the walls of his office he surrenders his identity to the phantoms that haunt his patients. Freud also eludes the reader, who invariably projects personal concerns onto his texts. In diverse contexts, Freud figures as the scientist, the clinician, the philosopher, the cultural critic, the demystifier. His blank expression may adapt itself to every available mask.

Behind his masks, Freud is always an interpreter. His practices of interpretation are both radically new and burdened by traditional assumptions, producing a conflict that complicates but does not diminish the force

---

1. See Freud's letter to Fliess of 17 July 1899 (*BWF* 397/*CL* 361). A discussion of Freud's interest in Janus is provided by Peter Gay's *Freud, Jews, and Other Germans: Masters and Victims in Modernist Culture* (New York: Oxford University Press, 1978), p. 42. For a key to abbreviations, see pp. 139–40, below.

of Freud's methods. At the same time, his hermeneutics cannot be entirely separated from the transference, and reveal a seductive potential. Psychoanalysis is never simply true to existing reality; Freud changes the subject of analysis in accordance with his interpretations.

Freud's Path to Dreams

Near the middle of his life's way, Freud strays from the familiar paths of neurological science: he awakens from a vivid dream and tries to grasp its meaning. To make his inventions appear more credible, Freud tells this tale. The wanderer follows a long line of spiritual travelers, yet he experiences a disconcerting isolation in the byways of nineteenth-century medicine. When Freud emerges from darkness onto his "royal road," the light of a sudden recognition overwhelms him: "The dream is a wish fulfillment." Freud's autobiographical references suggest that this discovery inspired the writing of his dream book.

The initial task for *The Interpretation of Dreams* is to establish dream interpretation as a valid field of scientific inquiry. This topic had not so much been neglected as consigned to the realm of popular nonsense. During the latter half of the nineteenth century, dozens of books in German and French purported to explain the nature of sleep and dreams; Freud carefully refers to those scanty aspects of prior theories that lead toward his own.[2] The first chapter of *The Interpretation of Dreams* simultaneously undermines earlier beliefs about dreams and insists that dreams are valid objects of inquiry.

Freud compares his work to a journey through a forest, both in *The Interpretation of Dreams* and in a letter to Wilhelm Fliess. After Fliess complains that the opening chapter of his book might discourage readers, Freud explains that "the whole thing is planned on the model of an imaginary walk (*Spaziergangsphantasie*)."[3] His letter describes a stroll that is also a hike through an imaginative realm. Freud explains: "First [comes]

---

2. For Freud's immediate purposes, the most important previous works on dreams are Karl Albert Scherner, *Das Leben des Traums* (Berlin: Heinrich Schindler, 1861) and Johannes Volkelt, *Die Traum-Phantasie* (Stuttgart: Meyer and Zeller, 1875).

3. Letter to Fliess of 6 August 1899 (*BWF* 400/*CL* 365; cf. *Td* 141n/*ID* 155n.) Throughout this book, except where otherwise indicated, all translations are my own and differ from the English versions that are cited. Freud also uses the travel metaphor in *The Interpretation of Dreams* (*Td* 141, 489–90/*ID* 155, 549. Compare Leonard Shengold, "The Metaphor of the Journey in *The Interpretation of Dreams*," in *Freud and His Self-Analysis*, ed. Mark Kanzer and Jules Glenn (New York: Jason Aronson, 1979), pp. 51–65.

the dark forest of the [previous] authors (who do not see the trees), without prospects, rich in false paths (*aussichtslos, irrwegreich*). Then a hidden gorge (*verdeckter Hohlweg*) through which I lead the reader—my dream specimen with its peculiarities, details, indiscretions, bad jokes—and then suddenly the summit, the view, and the inquiry, 'Which way would you like to go?' " (*BWF* 400/*CL* 365). Freud alludes to his dream of Irma as the concealed gorge leading to a newly attained height.

The dream of Irma's injection ("the specimen dream of psychoanalysis") holds a privileged place both in *The Interpretation of Dreams* and in Freud's intellectual autobiography.[4] Although he does not fully analyze the wishes and conflicts it reveals, Freud traces his theory of dreams as wish fulfillments to this example, and adds in a later footnote: "This is the first dream that I submitted to a thorough interpretation" (*Td* 126n/*ID* 139n). References to Freud's dream report are printed in italics (originally in spaced type), as if to accord them special status and to establish the norm for dream texts. Even the punctuation, employing dashes and ellipses, seems designed to reflect the dream experience or the halting process of fixing it on paper.

Dream of 23–24 July 1895

A large hall—many guests, whom we are receiving. —Among them

---

4. Increasingly skeptical of Freud's interpretation, commentators have returned again and again to the dream of Irma's injection. The two seminal essays are Erik Erikson, "The Dream Specimen of Psychoanalysis," *Journal of the American Psychoanalytic Association* 2 (1954), 5–56, and Max Schur, "Some Additional 'Day Residues' of 'The Specimen Dream of Psychoanalysis,' " in *Psychoanalysis—A General Psychology: Essays in Honor of Heinz Hartmann*, ed. Rudolph M. Loewenstein et al. (New York: International Universities Press, 1966), pp. 45–85. See also: Harry C. Leavitt, "A Biographical and Teleological Study of 'Irma's Injection' Dream," *Psychoanalytic Review* 43 (1956), 440–47; Alexander Grinstein, *On Sigmund Freud's Dreams* (Detroit: Wayne State University Press, 1968), pp. 21–46; Heinz Politzer, "Freud als Deuter seiner eigenen Träume," in *Der unbekannte Freud: Neue Interpretationen seiner Träumen*, ed. Jürgen vom Scheidt (Munich: Kindler, 1974), pp. 56–71; Didier Anzieu, *L'auto-analyse de Freud et la découverte de la psychanalyse*, 2d ed. (Paris: Presses Universitaires de France, 1975), vol. 1, pp. 187–217; Marianne Krüll, *Freud und sein Vater: Die Entstehung der Psychoanalyse und Freuds ungelöste Vaterbindung* (Munich: C. H. Beck, 1979), pp. 37–40; in English, see Marianne Krüll, *Freud and His Father*, trans. Arnold J. Pomerans (New York: W. W. Norton, 1986), pp. 21–24; Janet Malcolm, *In the Freud Archives* (New York: Alfred A. Knopf, 1984), pp. 44–50; Jeffrey Moussaieff Masson, *The Assault on Truth: Freud's Suppression of the Seduction Theory* (New York: Farrar, Straus and Giroux, 1984), pp. 55–106 and 233–50; and Shoshana Felman, "Postal Survival, or the Question of the Navel," *Yale French Studies* 69 (1985), 49–72.

Irma, whom I immediately take aside, as if to answer her letter, to rebuke her for not yet accepting the "solution." I say to her: If you (*du*) still have pains, it is really just your fault. —She answers: If you only knew what pains I feel in my throat, stomach, and abdomen; they're tying me into knots. —I am frightened and look at her. She appears pale and bloated; I think, in the end I must be overlooking something organic. I take her to the window and look down her throat. She shows some recalcitrance, like women who wear false teeth. I think to myself, she really doesn't need to. —Then the mouth opens wide, and I find a white spot to the right, and in another place I see extensive white-gray scabs on remarkably curled structures, which are apparently modeled after the turbinal bones of the nose. —I quickly call Dr. M. over, who repeats and confirms the examination. . . . Dr. M. looks completely different than usual; he is pale, limps, and his chin is beardless. . . . My friend Otto now also stands beside her, and my friend Leopold percusses her through her bodice and says: She has an area of dullness on the lower left, points to an infiltrated skin area by her left shoulder (which I perceive, as he does, despite the garment). . . . M. says: No doubt, it is an infection, but no matter; dysentery will follow and precipitate the toxin. . . . We also know immediately whence the infection comes. Recently when she felt unwell, my friend Otto gave her an injection with a propyl preparation, propyls . . . propionic acid . . . trimethylamin (the formula of which I see printed in bold type before me). . . . One does not make such injections thoughtlessly. . . . Probably the needle wasn't even clean. (*Td* 126–27/*ID* 139–40)

Freud's interpretation of his prototypical example is punctuated by refusals to tell the full story.[5] In a cynical footnote, Freud observes that he "was probably right not to place so much trust in the reader's discretion" (*Td* 125n/*ID* 138n). Like the relationship between Freud and his patient, the relationship between Freud and his reader is characterized by combative tensions and suspicions. The repressed sexual dynamics in Freud's dream are especially evident at the moment when "I take her to the window and look down her throat. She shows some recalcitrance (*sträuben*), like women who wear false teeth. I think to myself, she really doesn't need to [resist]"

---

5. E.g., *Td* 125, 133, 137n, 139/*ID* 137–38, 146, 151n, 153–54. One obviously curtailed feature of Freud's self-analysis is the dimension of his own sexuality. Freud notably omits information necessary to show that the dream of Irma represents the fulfillment of infantile wishes.

(*Td* 127//*ID* 139). As one reinterpreter of Freud's dream points out, "these phrases, then, are a link between the associations concerning patients who resist 'solutions,' and women (patients or not) who resist sexual advances."[6] Freud's actions in his dream are "intrusive" and "phallic";[7] this scenario represents one direction of the psychoanalytic cure. Freud views dreams as disguised (*verkleidet*) fulfillments of repressed wishes, and he wishes to examine and undress his patients, if only to demonstrate the correctness of his theories.

Freud explains that the dream "fulfills several wishes" by transferring the blame for Irma's suffering from him to Otto. He traces the dream to his discomfort over Otto's veiled criticism of his treatment of Irma, and thus the dream appears to avenge itself on the betraying friend, determining that the accuser is himself guilty. As one who administers a dirty injection, Otto becomes guilty of a disguised sexual transgression. Yet Freud's analysis makes light of both the suppressed sexual content and the dream's aggressive treatment of his friends.[8] While Freud writes that Otto and Dr. M. are "competitors," he does not dwell on their competitive struggle. From this complex of unexplored meanings, he distills only his conclusion that "the dream is a wish fulfillment." The prototypical dream of wish fulfillment receives only partial analysis, for Freud discloses neither the biographical context nor his concealed wishes.

Recent authors have emphasized the "day's residues" that helped to produce the dream of Irma's injection. In his cautious letter to Fliess of 8 March 1895, Freud does not retell the full story, but he does provide a clearer picture of what he felt obliged to suppress from his published analysis. "Irma" is almost certainly a fictitious name for Emma Eckstein, who was Freud's patient and the victim of malpractice by Fliess in a questionable nose operation Freud advised. Because of the condensations and displacements that characterize dreams, we cannot determine the full cast of characters behind Freud's famous dream text. One author indicates that Fliess is represented by the friend Leopold, while Otto and Dr. M. stand for Oskar Rie and Josef Breuer. This would mean that Fliess was "put in the exalted role of the knowing, understanding, superior friend," and "the blame had to be displaced to Rie (Otto), while M. (Breuer) had to be

---

6. Erikson, "The Dream Specimen of Psychoanalysis," 25.

7. Ibid., p. 30.

8. Compare Jacques Lacan, *Le Séminaire*, ed. Jacques-Alain Miller (Paris: Editions du Seuil, 1975), vol. 1, p. 296, and *Le Séminaire*, ed. Jacques-Alain Miller (Paris: Editions du Seuil, 1978), vol. 2, chaps. 13–14.

ridiculed.'"[9] One could also argue that Freud played out his negative transferences by explicitly blaming Fliess, in the figure of the negligent Otto. Dr.
M. and Leopold might then represent the physicians Gersuny and Rosanes,
who took charge after the postoperative care of Emma Eckstein became
unaccountably complicated.

A few months before the date Freud gives to his Irma dream, in the
letter to Fliess dated 8 March 1895, Freud makes this reference to the dis-
astrous treatment of Emma:

> There was still moderate bleeding from the nose and mouth; the fetid
> odor was very bad. Rosanes cleaned the area surrounding the open-
> ing, removed some sticky blood clots, and suddenly pulled at some-
> thing like a thread, kept on pulling. Before either of us had time to
> think, at least half a meter of gauze had been removed from the cav-
> ity. The next moment came a flood of blood. The patient turned
> white, her eyes bulged, and she had no pulse. . . .
>
> I do not believe it was the blood that overwhelmed me—at that
> moment strong emotions were welling up in me. So we had done her
> an injustice; she was not at all abnormal, rather, a piece of iodoform
> gauze had gotten torn off as you were removing it and stayed in for
> fourteen days, preventing healing; at the end it tore off and provoked
> the bleeding. That this mishap should have happened to you; how you
> will react to it when you hear about it; what others could make of it;
> how wrong I was to urge you to operate in a foreign city where you
> could not follow through on the case; how my intention to do the best
> for this poor girl was insidiously thwarted and resulted in endanger-

---

9. Schur, "Some Additional 'Day Residues' of 'The Specimen Dream of Psychoanalysis,' " ed. Loewenstein, p. 70. In the context of Freud's waning friendship
with Fliess, Schur argues, Freud still sought to "exculpate Fliess from responsibility for Emma's nearly fatal complications" (ibid.). Max Schur expresses a more
complex view in his *Freud: Living and Dying* (New York: International Universities
Press, 1972): "Freud unconsciously knew very well that Fliess was responsible for
the critical complications and blamed him for them, so that his trust in Fliess had
been deeply shaken. . . . At that time Freud could not afford to abandon his positive relationship which had to be protected by denial and a displacement of the
accusation. Torn between needing and blaming Fliess, Freud's actions were highly
revealing throughout the period of crisis" (p. 81). See also Schur's "The Background of Freud's 'Disturbance' on the Acropolis," in *Freud and His Self-Analysis*,
ed. Kanzer and Glenn, which refers to Freud's "desperate need to deny his ambivalence towards Fliess" (p. 118). Compare Anzieu, *L'auto-analyse de Freud et la
découverte de la psychanalyse*, vol. 1, pp. 200–204.

ing her life—all of this came over me simultaneously. I have worked it through by now.[10]

Freud would have privately acknowledged that his dreams expose repressed sexual wishes, which he understandably excludes from his published analysis. While he admits elements of sexuality, aggression, and ambition, Freud declines to discuss ways in which the dream responds to a specific event in his recent experience.[11] Current knowledge of the Emma Eckstein fiasco, however, forces us to consider other meanings of the seminal dream. In short, the "Irma dream" returns to the traumatic discovery that Emma's complaints were the result of Fliess's professional incompetence. This is, presumably, one meaning of Freud's dreaming accusation of Otto: "The needle wasn't even clean." It was not a wish fulfillment for Freud to blame this mishap on his friend, except to the extent that by transferring blame in this way he satisfies competitive wishes.

The dream of Irma appears to have replayed one of the most problematic case histories in Freud's career and a decisive moment in his waning friendship with Fliess. Rather than conceive it in accordance with Freudian theory, as the "(disguised) fulfillment of a (suppressed or repressed) wish" (*Td* 175/*ID* 194), we may understand this dream as an attempt to resolve a difficult problem. This means taking the manifest content seriously and recognizing its direct response to recent events in Freud's life. Freud himself suggested that the dream was a wish fulfillment because it shifted guilt from himself to "Otto," but his letter of 8 March 1895 makes clear that Emma's problem had in reality been exacerbated by Fliess. Freud maintained that dreams always express unconscious wishes, and sometimes declined to see the more immediate significance of dream texts. In addition to fulfilling wishes, dreams and their interpretations may revise the life history of the dreamer and aim toward future "solutions" to conflicts.

After discussing his dream of Irma, Freud reviews the path he has traveled: "When one has passed through a narrow gorge and has suddenly arrived at a summit, after which the ways part and the richest prospect opens in different directions, one may linger for a moment and consider

---

10. *CL* 116–17; for the German original see *BWF* 117–18. See also Schur's earlier publication of this letter in "Some Additional 'Day Residues' of 'The Specimen Dream of Psychoanalysis,'" pp. 56–57.

11. In a letter of 8 January 1908, Karl Abraham requests further details concerning the Irma dream; Freud evades his inquiry by responding, in his own words, "hastily, formlessly, impersonally." See Sigmund Freud and Karl Abraham, *Briefe 1907–1926*, ed. Hilda C. Abraham and Ernst L. Freud (Frankfurt am Main: S. Fischer, 1965), pp. 32–33.

which way one should turn first" (*Td* 141/*ID* 155). In this published statement, Freud omits his unflattering image of the previous authors as a dark forest, referring only to his narrow escape route that leads to the summit. When Freud arrives at the conclusion that "the dream is a wish fulfillment," it remains to be seen whether his inspiring dream of Irma typifies all dreams, and what new clarity it provides.

In his metaphorical journey, Freud represents the previous authors on dream interpretation as a "dark forest" that easily leads the traveler astray. *The Interpretation of Dreams* elaborately repudiates all past dream theorists, researchers, and interpreters. This insistent gesture eliminates all competitors from the scene and permits Freud to expound his practice of dream interpretation at a somewhat exaggerated distance from other methods. His disavowals conceal other associations, as becomes clear from his additions to later versions of the dream book.

Against the Past

Freud's metaphor of adventure indicates that he abandons the pathways of earlier neurological science. He arrives at a new terrain by means of his detour through an unexpected crevice, the dark tunnel of a mysterious yet subsequently interpretable dream process.[12] When Freud awakens and emerges into the light, he proposes to explore the previously obscure cavern of dreams; first, however, Freud dismisses the familiar routes. He asserts that dreams are not, as a forerunner suggests they are, "comparable to the irregular sounding of a musical instrument struck by the blow of an external force instead of by the player's hand."[13] Freud insists that the dream is "not senseless, not absurd," but instead "a completely valid psychical phenomenon" (*Td* 141/*ID* 155). His problem is to introduce the terms that will enable him to demonstrate this validity. Freud does not represent his discovery as a simple attainment of the truth, but as a dynamic resolve to place dreams "in the context of comprehensible waking mental acts." Dreams are not merely wish fulfillments; they are expressions of "an extremely complex mental activity" (ibid.). Without as yet naming this activity the "dream work," Freud raises questions that follow from his hypothesis that dreams have meaning.

The dream work is analogous to Freud's imaginary journey through a

---

12. *BWF* 400/*CL* 365. In his *VEP* 106/*ILP* 88, Freud identifies the dark cavern of sleep with the mother's womb.

13. See L. Strümpell, *Die Natur und Entstehung der Träume* (Leipzig: Veit, 1874), p. 84. Compare *Td* 100, 141, 230/*ID* 110, 155, 256 and *UTT* 12/*OD* 14.

hidden gorge. After Freud arrives at the summit of his metaphorical hill, he examines the distortions of the dream work as he retraces his steps through the tunnel of dreams. This image expresses his general notion of dream interpretation: "In waking interpretation, we follow a path that leads from dream elements back to the dream thoughts" (*Td* 509/*ID* 571). It is, however, impossible to simply reverse the path of the dream work. Freud moves in the light of day, peering down at the darker products of mind: "During the day we drive shafts above new thought connections," and these probes "make contact with the intermediate thoughts and with the dream thoughts, now at one point and now at another." As a result of the investigative process, "fresh thought material from the day inserts itself into the interpretive sequence" (ibid.); Freud assures us that these "collaterals" need not disrupt our search for the concealed dream thoughts. If there occur elisions, condensations, displacements, or even "interpolations and additions" (*Td* 471/ *ID* 527), it remains to be seen whether the dream interpreter can distinguish between dream thoughts and thoughts that arise during interpretation.

The opening chapter of *The Interpretation of Dreams* reviews "the scientific literature on dreams." For the most part, this literature is irrelevant to Freud's work, since it deals with dreaming and sleeping without regard to questions of interpretation. From the earliest times until Aristotle, diverse authors discussed the causes and characteristics of dreams. Freud's own sympathies evidently lie closest to Aristotle, who (according to Freud) believed that dreams "follow the laws of the human spirit" (*Td* 30/ *ID* 37). Freud quickly dismisses all prescientific conceptions of dreams, describing them as superstitious projections (*Td* 32/*ID* 38). He subsequently turns to nineteenth-century, scientific theories, and rejects them from the outset with the comment that "no foundation has been laid" on which later researchers might build. In short, Freud appears completely at odds with his forerunners.

The second chapter of *The Interpretation of Dreams,* however, shows Freud to be significantly closer to some of his precursors. After outlining nineteenth-century scientific dream theories, Freud surveys the history of "lay" dream interpretation. Paradoxically, he strives to establish a science of dream interpretation that conforms with some elements of what previously existed on the plane of superstition. Although Freud renounces the earlier methods, then, in some respects he does identify with his ancient precursors Joseph and Artemidorus.[14] Apart from their common interpretive activity, Freud may also have identified with Joseph as a result of their similar position in the family romance. As favored, first sons

---

14. Compare *Td* 466n/*ID* 522n and *Td* 119n–120n/*ID* 130n–131n.

of Jacob's second wife, they received special privileges.[15]

Freud admits that popular opinion anticipated his belief that dreams have meaning (compare *UTT* 12/*OD* 15), yet he questions two basic methods traditionally employed to uncover this meaning. Both methods attempt to replace the dream content by a corresponding sense. Symbolic dream interpretation "views the dream content as a whole and tries to replace (*ersetzen*) this through another, comprehensible and in certain respects analogous content" (*Td* 117/*ID* 129). Freud cites the example of Joseph's interpretation of Pharaoh's dream: "Seven fat cows, after which come seven thin cows that devour the others; this is a symbolic substitute (*Ersatz*) for the prophecy of seven years of famine in the land of Egypt that devour all the abundance created by seven fruitful years" (*Td* 117–18/*ID* 129). Freud objects that Joseph's method depends solely on the interpreter's intuition, and can only develop as an art.

The second popular method of dream interpretation is a process of deciphering (*Chiffrierverfahren*), which at first sight represents the opposite extreme. Rather than rely on the interpreter's intuition concerning the entire dream, the method of decoding "treats the dream as a kind of secret writing (*Geheimschrift*), in which every sign will be translated into another sign with a known meaning, according to a fixed key" (*Td* 118/*ID* 130). This conception leads to a mechanical approach that employs a code to decipher individual dream images.

In spite of his criticisms, Freud acknowledges that "lay opinion" provides the closest analogues to his own work on dreams. He favors the related and slightly more sophisticated practices of Artemidorus, who takes the circumstances of the dreamer into account (*Td* 119/*ID* 131). All too quickly, however, Freud tries to dispense with both Joseph and Artemidorus by discounting their "symbolic" and "decoding" methods. Freud suggests a preference for the latter, while striving to keep his distance.

Freud's subsequent additions to this discussion attest to his discomfort in relation to his predecessors. A footnote of 1909 mentions a third form of popular dream interpretation that employs neither symbolism nor decoding: "oriental dream books" perform interpretations based on homonymic wordplay.[16] Two years later, Freud adds "the most beautiful" ancient ex-

---

15. On Freud's identification with Joseph, see Leonard Shengold, "Freud and Joseph," in *Freud and His Self-Analysis*, ed. Kanzer and Glenn, pp. 67–86, and Ernest Jones, *The Life and Work of Sigmund Freud* (New York: Basic Books, 1953), vol. 1, p. 4.

16. *Td* 119n/*ID* 131n. Concerning relevant similarities between Greek and rabbinic dream interpretation, particularly in their use of paronomasia, see Saul Lieberman, *Hellenism in Jewish Palestine* (New York: Jewish Theological Seminary, 1950), pp.

ample of this kind—from Artemidorus, whose work thus seems to escape the category of interpretation by decoding (*Td* 120n/*ID* 131n–132n). In a footnote of 1914, however, Freud insists on the difference between his methods and those of Artemidorus. Basing his remarks on a study by Theodor Gomperz, Freud withdraws his earlier praise. Artemidorus works on the basis of association: "A thing in a dream signifies what it recalls to the mind. Of course, what it recalls to the mind of the dream interpreter!" (*Td* 119n/*ID* 130n). Artemidorus' processes of interpretation betray an inevitable arbitrariness; Freud sets himself apart from Artemidorus by noting that the psychoanalytic use of associations "assigns the work of interpretation to the dreamer" (ibid.). Over the years, Freud's dream interpretations increasingly rely on familiar symbolic relations, and the claimed distance between his dream book and ancient dream books becomes less tenable. Freud's later compilation of symbols with standard meanings, especially in chapter 6 of *The Interpretation of Dreams,* is in some respects comparable to the ancient dream books; Freud dismisses his precursors by understating the similarities between their techniques and his own.

Freud continually looks back over his shoulder, nervously eyeing his forerunners. He escapes from the confines of prior methods by telling another story. During his studies of hysteria with Josef Breuer, Freud writes, he began to treat the dream as a symptom, or at least as a link in the individual's psychical chain (*Td* 121/*ID* 133). His challenge was to expose the underlying links methodically.

Interpretation by Correspondence and Displacement

In order to account for the strange form assumed by dreams that purportedly represent wishes, Freud differentiates between latent thoughts and manifest dream contents. He wonders: "What alteration took place with the dream thoughts, until out of them the manifest dream was formed, as we remember it on awakening?" (*Td* 141/*ID* 156). Assuming that the latent contents or dream thoughts are expressed by the manifest dream, Freud examines the developmental relationship between these elements. Freud postulates that dreams represent wish fulfillments, and he retrospectively confirms this postulate with the help of his opposition between the dream thoughts and the manifest dream (see *Td* 152, 161/*ID* 168, 179).

Freud achieves his solution to the riddle of dreams through the method of free association. He models this technique after a letter in which

68–82. Heinrich Lewy demonstrates broader similarities between the dream interpretations of Artemidorus and the Talmud in "Zu dem Traumbuche des Artemidorus," *Rheinisches Museum für Philologie,* N. F. 48 (1893), 398–419.

Schiller urges a frustrated writer to free himself from mental obstacles:

> The ground for your complaint lies, it seems to me, in the constraint
> which your understanding imposes on your imagination. . . . It seems
> bad and disadvantageous for the creative work of the soul, if the un-
> derstanding inspects the ideas that are streaming in, as it were, at the
> very gates. Considered in isolation, an idea can be quite inconsider-
> able and overly adventurous, but perhaps it will, in a certain connec-
> tion with others that perhaps appear equally tasteless, furnish a very
> purposive link:—All this the understanding cannot judge, if it does
> not persevere long enough to view the idea in connection with oth-
> ers. . . . Thence [come] your complaints of unproductivity, because
> you discard too soon and discriminate too stringently. (Letter of
> 1 December 1788; cited in *Td* 123/*ID* 135)

Freudian psychoanalysis establishes conditions under which every patient
may speak and invent freely, following the example of creative writers.
Freud himself finds that he can achieve "uncritical self-observation" when
he writes down his associations (*Td* 123/*ID* 136).

Freud's interpretive method thus calls for a further process of text
creation rather than an intuitive guessing of symbols or the passive manipulation of the key to a code. Out of the dream the dreamer must create new
links or narratives until a coherent story emerges. For psychoanalysis the
meaning of a dream or text is always another text, as reconstructed from
associations, except when Freud reverts to the ancient notion that certain
symbols are interpretable independently of the dreamer's associations. In a
footnote of 1925, Freud asserts that he can interpret dreams without reference to the dreamer's associations "when the dreamer has employed *symbolic* elements in the dream content" (*Td* 247n/*ID* 274n). Freud initially
dismisses his precursors by commenting on the "uselessness of both popular practices of interpretation" for a "scientific treatment of the subject"
(*Td* 120/*ID* 132). His subsequent footnotes show, however, that he cannot so
easily supersede the methods of Joseph and Artemidorus, which play some
role in his own practices. Interpretive models compete within Freud's
works.[17]

---

17. Compare Paul Ricoeur, *De l'interprétation: Essai sur Freud* (Paris: Editions du
Seuil, 1965), p. 36–44. In English, see *Freud and Philosophy*, trans. Denis Savage
(New Haven: Yale University Press, 1970), pp. 28–36. Ricoeur ascribes to Freud a
"hermeneutics of suspicion" in which the interpreter seeks out hidden meanings;
Ricoeur also discusses a mode of interpretation as recollection or restoration of
meaning. Both models figure into Freud's methods. See also Philip Rieff, *Freud:
The Mind of the Moralist* (New York: Anchor Books, 1961), chap. 4, and Donald P.

Freud's dream theories rely on the basic opposition between manifest and latent dream contents, between actual dream images and concealed meanings, explicit and implicit layers, surface and depth structures. To elucidate the distortion of the latent dream wish and dream thoughts, in the manifest dream content, Freud postulates the agency or process of the dream work (*Traumarbeit*).[18] One-third of *The Interpretation of Dreams*, all of the wide-ranging sixth chapter, is devoted to this phenomenon. In his effort to facilitate dream interpretation, Freud studies the ways in which dreams are formed. If it is possible to discover the mechanisms of dream distortion, Freud hopes, this discovery should enable him to return from the dream to the repressed wish it obliquely represents, using the materials of the manifest content in relation to the day's residues (*die Tagesreste*).[19] Freud's coinage implicitly belittles these "residues," which evoke something that is left over from the day and remains unwanted, like dregs at the bottom of a bottle, in mental life. This derogatory terminology of the word

---

Spence, *Narrative Truth and Historical Truth: Meaning and Interpretation in Psychoanalysis* (New York: W. W. Norton, 1982). Jürgen Habermas, in *Erkenntnis und Interesse* (Frankfurt am Main: Suhrkamp, 1973), states: "Psychoanalysis at first appears as only a particular form of interpretation. . . . But the interpretive work of the analyst . . . demands a specifically amplified hermeneutics" (p. 263). For the English edition, see Habermas, *Knowledge and Human Interests*, trans. Jeremy J. Shapiro (Boston: Beacon Press, 1971), pp. 214–15.

18. On the difficult distinction between latent dream thoughts and dream contents, see *Basic Psychoanalytic Concepts on the Theory of Dreams*, ed. Humberto Nagera et al. (London: George Allen and Unwin, 1969), pp. 28–39. An early work that considers the instinctual forces behind dreams is Alfred Maury's *Le sommeil et les rêves*, 2d ed. (Paris: Didier, 1861), pp. 334–38.

19. Dieter Wyss shrewdly questions Freud's hermeneutics in his *Die tiefenpsychologischen Schulen von den Anfängen bis zur Gegenwart*, 3d ed. (Göttingen: Vandenhoeck & Ruprecht, 1970): "To recognize the latent thoughts in the manifest dream content means to follow the reverse path from the irrational, manifest dream appearance back to the (apparently) original, logical intention. *The apparent intelligence, the often admired refinement with which the dream expresses latent dream thoughts, is without question the intelligence of the analyst, who on this reversed path sees his own purposive thinking in the irrational dream products*" (p. 372). In English, see Dieter Wyss, *Psychoanalytic Schools from the Beginning to the Present*, trans. Gerald Onn (New York: Jason Aronson, 1973), p. 501. See also Michel Foucault's introduction to Ludwig Binswanger's *Le rêve et l'existence*, trans. Jacqueline Verdeaux (Bruges: Desclée de Brouwer, 1954), especially pp. 24, 37–38; the English translation by Forrest Williams and Jacob Needleman entitled *Dream and Existence* is contained in a special issue of the *Review of Existential Psychology and Psychiatry* 19, no. 1 (1984–85).

Tagesreste accords with Freud's frequent devaluation of the manifest dream content.

Attributing the distorted relationship between manifest and latent dream contents to operations of the dream work, Freudian theory assumes an essentially bipartite model of interpretation.[20] The drawback of this dual framework lies in its tendency to cast the manifest dream as a mere facade that conceals the true dream thoughts (e.g., *Td* 221, 472/*ID* 245, 529). Freud is consequently inclined to undervalue the manifest contents, despite the fact that a dream report is the necessary starting point for interpretation.[21]

Freud's practices conceal subtle tensions between a hermeneutics of correspondence and a method of association or displacement.[22] On the basis

---

20. Compare Georges Politzer, *Critique des fondements de la psychologie,* 3d ed. (Paris: Presses Universitaires de France, 1968): "The analysis comes back to positing, anterior to the dream, a conventional thought expressing the meaning of the dream in giving to the significative intentions their adequate signs." According to Politzer, this involves postulating a prior "narrative which never occurred" (p. 180).

21. For a revaluation of the manifest dream content, see Wilhelm Stekel, *Die Sprache des Traumes* (Wiesbaden: J. F. Bergmann, 1911): "Freud places the greatest weight on the material which is piled up behind the dream facade. I have been concerned to show that the *manifest* dream content already discloses to us the most important aspect of the content, of the *latent* dream thoughts" (p. 14). Compare Wilhelm Stekel, *Fortschritte und Technik der Traumdeutung* (Vienna: Weidmann, 1935): Freud's basic mistake was that "he neglected the *manifest* dream content and overestimated the associations, which were supposed to convey the *latent* dream thoughts" (p. 9). Another psychoanalytic study that emphasizes the manifest dream is Samuel Lowy's *Psychological and Biological Foundations of Dream-Interpretation* (London: Kegan Paul, Trench, Trubner, 1942), e.g., pp. 1, 19, 77. Menard Boss, in *Der Traum und seine Auslegung* (Bern: Hans Huber, 1953), pp. 28–48, reviews theories that dispute Freud's views of the manifest dream.

22. This analysis focuses on two central, though not all-encompassing, interpretive modes. Correspondence and association, which are perhaps akin to Freudian *Verdichtung* and *Verschiebung,* to some extent also parallel *Rücksicht auf Darstellbarkeit* and *sekundäre Bearbeitung.* But this does not mean that only two modes of figuration and two competing models operate in Freud's work. The opposition has heuristic value here, as does the related distinction between metaphor and metonymy. See Roman Jakobson and Morris Halle, *Fundamentals of Language,* 2d ed. (The Hague: Mouton, 1975), pp. 72–76, 90–96. For a discussion of the unstable interactions between metaphor and metonymy, see Paul de Man, *Allegories of Reading: Figural Language in Rousseau, Nietzsche, Rilke, and Proust* (New Haven: Yale University Press, 1979), pp. 12–15.

of the correspondence theory, the interpreter searches for similar dream thoughts that lie behind dream contents in a condensed yet homologous form. Drawing from the associative approach, the analyst uses connections provided by the dreamer, which relate to the dream contents by contiguity, not by resemblance. The two interpretive models stand opposed, yet they also tend to blur into each other.[23]

The characteristic overdetermination of dream contents inspires but ultimately opposes a simple correspondence theory.[24] Overdetermination of dream contents means, first of all, that "each of the elements of the dream content shows itself to be . . . multiply represented in the dream thoughts" (*Td* 286/*ID* 318). This must be the case, Freud reasons, in light of the disparity in length between the laconic dream text and the elaborate interpretation. He concludes that the dream results from a condensation of dream thoughts, which involves a relation of similarity and is thus comparable to the poetic figure of metaphor.[25] Freud sometimes writes as if the tenor of the metaphorical equation could be definitively adduced from its vehicle, but at other points he observes an incommensurability between the two terms.

The dream work also entails a displacement, a relationship by contiguity. Freud writes that "the individual dream thoughts are represented in the dream by multiple elements" (*Td* 286/*ID* 318). Moreover, "the elements in the dream content which stand out as the essential components by

---

23. Samuel Lowy hints at the essential interdependence of correspondence and association theories in his *Psychological and Biological Foundations of Dream-Interpretation*: "The dream is not simply a condensed, abbreviated formation, which is essentially identical with the total [*sic*] of its 'latent' content. I should say that the dream and its parts *correspond* to a multitude of original elements, like two things which belong to each other, yet which are not identical and even not necessarily similar. *Dream-interpretation, then, is essentially a conclusion* a posteriori. We cannot say definitely that the various elements and relations which we find in the associations, are really contained in the dream image, *really* make up the 'content' of the dream" (p. 195).

24. Johannes Volkelt's *Die Traum-Phantasie* (Stuttgart: Meyer and Zeller, 1875) is an unmistakable precursor to the Freudian discussion of *Verdichtung* (see pp. 24, 87, 135), *Verschiebung* (see pp. 86, 117–18), and *Rücksicht auf Darstellbarkeit* (see p. 31). But in connection with associative dreams, Volkelt observes that "one can no longer speak of such a fixed kernel" of meaning (p. 118).

25. See Volkelt's *Die Traum-Phantasie*, pp. 24, 86–87, 117–28, 135. Compare Jacques Lacan, "L'instance de la lettre dans l'inconscient," in *Ecrits* (Paris: Editions du Seuil, 1966), p. 511. In English, see *Ecrits: A Selection*, trans. Alan Sheridan (New York: W. W. Norton, 1977), p. 160.

no means play the same role in the dream thoughts'' (*Td* 305/*ID* 340). Disparities are even more compelling when the dream contents have been displaced and have received a completely new center of interest.

On one level, Freud adheres to the bipartite model according to which reported dream contents correspond to dream thoughts hidden in the depths of the psyche. On another level, he does not rely on a conjunction of the dream and its meaning, but refers to a textual difference (*Textverschiedenheit*) (*Td* 307/*ID* 343). The latter conception diverges from hermeneutic practices based on the recovery of mental acts that give meaning to texts. Although Freud frequently resorts to dream thoughts revealed by dream contents, insisting on their sexual character in connection with infantile wishes, he is also aware of an alternative paradigm.

"Free" Association

Freud's interpretations employ a procedure that substitutes a text for a text. Starting from each segment of the dream report, Freud's self-analysis and psychoanalytic dream analyses generate additional materials. Freud admits to some uncertainty as to whether these associations may be identified with mental concomitants that produce the dream: "In view of the superabundant number of associations which the analysis brings to every single element of the dream content, in some readers the basic doubt will be aroused whether all that occurs to one subsequently in the analysis may be counted among the dream thoughts'' (*Td* 283/*ID* 314).[26] This doubt stands at the crossroad between Freud's competing correspondence theory and associative approach to meaning. Does the dream analysis directly correspond to the dream thoughts, or does the analysis produce associations that have no equivalent in the dream? The final chapter of *The Interpretation of Dreams* elaborately rephrases the problem, and rescues the correspondence model from a threat of ruin: interpretation retraces the path of the dream work until by an indirect route it reattains the dream thoughts (*Td* 509/*ID* 571). Yet intervening displacements unsettle the security a correspondence theory might promise.

Freud's method works from individual elements of a dream, noting associations at each point and seeking a return to the dream thoughts behind the dream (*Td* 504/*ID* 565). Freud anticipates a criticism: "Something can be associatively linked with every idea; it is only remarkable that one is

---

26. Compare Ludwig Wittgenstein's pointed remarks on psychoanalysis, contained in *Wittgenstein: Lectures and Conversations*, ed. Cyril Barrett (Berkeley: University of California Press, 1966), pp. 42–52.

supposed to attain precisely the dream thoughts in this aimless and arbitrary flow of thoughts'' (ibid.). This critical voice haunts Freud's conclusions.[27]

Elaborating on the method of free association in his lectures of 1916, Freud explains that his technique encourages us to "ask the dreamer what his dream signifies" (*VEP* 116/*ILP* 100). As in *The Interpretation of Dreams*, nevertheless, it remains uncertain whether the dreamer's associations lead back to thoughts that produced the dream; ideally, the work of analysis recapitulates the paths of the dream work, yet there is no guarantee that this is always the case. Freudian interpretation wavers between confident substitutions and doubtful displacements.

In his lectures, Freud argues more forcefully that the dreamer's associations are not random, but instead strictly determined (*VEP* 121/*ILP* 106). This determinate character is in part the consequence of mental "complexes" (*VEP* 124/*ILP* 109). Freud takes the example of attempting to remember a forgotten proper name as analogous to the situation of dream interpretation: in the effort to recall a name, one may spontaneously produce a series of substitutions, much as the dream work produces its manifest content, or as the dreamer produces associations retrospectively. Similar to a substitute name, "the dream element is also not the right thing (*das Richtige*), but only a substitute (*Ersatz*) for something else, for the authentic thing (*das Eigentliche*), which I do not know and shall discover through the dream analysis" (*VEP* 124/*ILP* 110). In German rhetoric, the *eigentliche Bedeutung* is also the literal meaning, while figures are *uneigentliche Gebräuche*. Thus the manifest dream is characteristically linked to "inauthentic" usage, to tropes. Freud concludes that "what is possible in connection with forgetting a name must also be able to succeed in dream interpretation: to start from the substitute (*Ersatz*) and through connective associations make the elusive genuine thing accessible" (*VEP* 126/*ILP* 112). Freud's analogy takes for granted that the dream is "inauthentic," a distortion of something else, and that the "authentic" dream content may be known. Whereas a forgotten proper name (e.g., "Monaco") clearly exists apart from mistaken memories of it, however, there may not be any single "proper meaning" behind the dream report.[28]

---

27. In *Psychological and Biological Foundations of Dream-Interpretation*, Lowy suggests that the dream is essentially inseparable from the free associations it inspires (p. 105n). From a methodological standpoint, there is no firm line between the hypothetical dream in itself and the dream as it is reconstructed by a sequence of mental acts.

28. Compare Frederic Weiss, "Meaning and Dream Interpretation," in *Freud: A Collection of Critical Essays*, ed. Richard Wollheim (New York: Anchor Books, 1974), pp. 56–69.

Freud insists that the manifest dream is inauthentic, for "the recalled dream is indeed not the authentic thing, but rather a distorted substitute for it" (*VEP* 129/*ILP* 114). By a sequence of further substitutions, Freud hopes to arrive at the authentic meaning, the "unconscious of the dream" (ibid.). Yet in setting up this dichotomy, Freud makes an interesting slip of the pen. What was unconscious to the dreamer, he writes, is "concealed, inaccessible, inauthentic" (*VEP* 128/*ILP* 113). Freud's editors note that one would expect him to write "authentic" here. A reversal begins to disturb the clearer opposition Freud attempts to establish. The recalled dream itself is inauthentic, he repeatedly argues, and its interpretation returns to the authentic sense. But Freud upholds this bipartite model only with utmost difficulty.

On the basis of resistances that block an understanding of the manifest content, Freud concludes that "something significant must be hidden behind the substitution" (*VEP* 131/*ILP* 116).[29] The dream is like a child that refuses to open its hand because something is hidden there (ibid.). How can Freud be so certain that something authentic stands behind the dream? He continues his metaphor by considering children's dreams throughout the entire following chapter. Again, however, his discussion implicitly reverses itself. While typical infantile dreams are supposed to be free of disguise, Freud has just mentioned an instance of childhood dissimulation.

Beyond the manifold deceptions of the insidious dream work lies an imagined realm of innocence and truth: the undisguised dream of wish fulfillment. At decisive moments in both *The Interpretation of Dreams* (chapter 3) and the *Introductory Lectures on Psychoanalysis* (lecture 8), Freud resorts to the dreams of children as literal wish fulfillments (*Td* 145–49/*ID* 160–64 and *VEP* 139–47/*ILP* 126–35). When Freud's daughter or nephew dreams of eating desired foods, the dream thought is, as it were, nakedly exposed. With this as the standard of an authentic dream content, Freud can point to the distortions that complicate the interpretation of all other dream types. The idealized, infantile dream appears as a literal representation. But in practice every dream deviates to some extent from this ideal, since dream images result from figurative distortions by the dream work. If a dream is

---

29. Contrast John Brenkman's remarks in "The Other and the One: Psychoanalysis, Reading, *The Symposium*," in *Literature and Psychoanalysis: The Question of Reading: Otherwise*, ed. Shoshana Felman (Baltimore: Johns Hopkins University Press, 1982): "Psychoanalytic interpretation does not seek to restore a hidden center of meaning or some original signified but rather reconstitutes the process of the dream's production" (p. 439). Brenkman alludes to Freud's associative approach, recalling the insight that the dream cannot be strictly distinguished from the associations it generates.

analogous to a matrix of tropes, or "inauthentic" expressions, one can hardly expect to translate it into a secure plane of corresponding meanings. This difficulty intensifies Freud's interest in childhood dreams that appear to lack distortion.

The discussion of children's dreams furthers the myth of childhood as an age of innocence, without deceptions: "These dreams dispense with the dream distortion, and for this reason also they require no work of interpretation" (*VEP* 141/*ILP* 128). According to Freud's construct, infantile dreams illustrate a literalism in which "the manifest and the latent dream coincide" (ibid.). At this point, Freud wavers on the subject of the dream work; if some dreams can exist without it, "therefore the dream distortion does not form a part of the essence of the dream." Freud immediately withdraws this surprising revelation as soon as he offers it, for he grants that even in the dreams of children we perceive "a small piece of dream distortion, a certain difference between the manifest dream content and the latent dream thoughts" (ibid.). Freud hopes to preserve both his theory of dream distortion and the reassuring recourse to relatively straightforward dreams of children.

There is no absolute equivalence between a wish and a dream, except when, if ever, the wish is identical to the manifest content.[30] Thus the literalist approach to childhood and erotic dreams as wish fulfillments is untenable. The dream work assures that dreams are always characterized by figuration, and never correspond exactly to repressed wishes. The final agency of overdetermination and ambiguity, secondary revision, is especially elusive.

Revisions of Secondary Revision

In what sense is "secondary revision" (or elaboration) secondary? Freud's accounts leave obscure the processes of revision implied by *sekundäre Bearbeitung*. Its name suggests a verbal parallel to the other three components of the dream work ("*Traumarbeit*"), but it never fits easily into the Freudian schema. Like an unacceptable dream thought that opposes rational ideas, secondary revision challenges Freud's emerging theories of dream interpretation.

---

30. Responding to the work of Peter Rosegger, in 1911 Freud adds a discussion of dreams that may not qualify as wish fulfillments. Rosegger suffered from recurring traumatic dreams of failure, and Freud admits to having experienced analogous dreams (*Td* 456–58/*ID* 511–13). But in a footnote of 1930, Freud corrects himself by observing that dreams of punishment (*Strafträume*) may be understood as wish fulfillments of the *Über-Ich* (*Td* 459n/*ID* 514n).

Secondary revision names a mental agency or process that modifies the dream contents formed by condensation, displacement, and considerations of representability. From a developmental standpoint, this fourth operation appears secondary in that it follows the other three components of the dream work. Freud defends against the associated uncertainties, however, by asserting that the fourth component of the dream work seldom rises to new creations (*Td* 471/*ID* 528).[31] Secondary revision does not show itself in the generation of materials, Freud says, but in an ordering tendency: "Its influence expresses itself," Freud writes, "like that of the others, primarily in the preferences and selections from the already-formed psychical materials in the dream thoughts" (*Td* 472/*ID* 529). The dream is a conglomerate held together by the ordering work of secondary revision (*Td* 407, 434/*ID* 455, 486); dream interpretation severs the pieces that have been so artfully joined.

The relationship between the initial three components of the dream work and the fourth is analogous to the relationship between poets and a philosopher. Freud comments that, like Heinrich Heine's comic professor who "patches the gaps in the cosmos,"[32] secondary revision takes away the appearance of absurdity and chaos that would otherwise typify the world of dreams. As a result of this process, certain dreams appear to have "already been interpreted once, before we subject them to waking interpretation" (*Td* 472/*ID* 528). The work of secondary revision is thus variable, evident to different degrees in different dreams.

Freud compares the operations of secondary revision to the fantasy work of daydreams. This is a potentially radical turn because it threatens the strict division between waking and sleeping dream processes. Freud has, in fact, already referred to secondary revision as a feature of dream formation that "cannot be distinguished from our waking thinking" (*Td* 471/*ID* 527). Once he grants this element of the dream work, he can hardly maintain the dream report and analysis at a level entirely distinct from the dream.[33]

---

31. Consequently, some interpreters of Freud underestimate the importance of secondary revision. See, for instance, Roland Dalbiez, *La méthode psychanalytique et la doctrine freudienne* (Paris: Desclée de Brouwer, 1936), pp. 194–96.

32. "Die Heimkehr," LVIII. Freud alludes to this phrase in *Td* 471n/*ID* 528n, and quotes it in *VEP* 588/*NIL* 141.

33. In this context, Freud symptomatically introduces a rare dream specimen for which he does not possess careful notes; he seems to disturb the unquestioned hegemony of the dream report (*Td* 475/*ID* 532). Throughout, the italicized (or widely spaced) dream texts have the aura of factual evidence, unmodified in relation to the

Despite his explanation of secondary revision in connection with day-dreams, Freud strives to show its inner relationship to the other aspects of the dream work. He casts aside the previous notion that secondary revision retrospectively modifies the results of condensation, displacement, and considerations of representability. In so doing, he makes secondary revision appear equally primary in the dream work, writing that this process operates simultaneously with the others (*Td* 479/*ID* 537). Freud resists his own suggestion that secondary revision is a later moment in dream production, and proposes that it may be the fourth component of a contemporaneous order; he compares it to the ways in which our waking thoughts process perceptual impressions. But this establishment of order is obviously distinct from the distorting processes that generate dreams. The situation of secondary revision in Freud's theory of dreams remains enigmatic, because it appears to both accompany and follow the other aspects of the dream work.

Freud's discussions of secondary revision do not resolve its equivocations; this act in the drama of the dream work eludes stable treatment. Freud concludes his chapter on the dream work by resorting again to a bipartite model, according to which "the mental work in the formation of a dream is divided into two accomplishments: the production of the dream thoughts and their transformation into the dream content" (*Td* 486/*ID* 544). In one sense, unconscious thoughts are the essential motives for dreams, yet in another sense the transforming dream work is even more characteristic of dream life (*Td* 486/*ID* 544–45). *On Dreams* maintains that secondary revision operates "retrospectively (*nachträglich*) on the already formed dream content" (*UTT* 36/*OD* 73). Specifically, "its accomplishment consists in ordering the components of the dream in such a way that they approximately join together in a continuity, in a dream composition" (*UTT* 36/*OD* 73–74). Freud asserts in general that "the dream work is not creative" (*UTT* 37/*OD* 76); it only modifies the given materials as does a writer or editor working from a rough draft.

Freud refuses to identify secondary revision with the literary processes of revision its name evokes. His later writings on dream interpretation consistently reject every step in this direction.[34] At the center of the

---

argument at hand. Now this convention suddenly fails, in the midst of a discussion that makes such a view appear problematic. If a dream memory is indistinguishable from retrospective contributions, then the dream report cannot claim a pristine, privileged status.

34. In a letter, Freud criticizes Karl Abraham's description of secondary revision, which is "too limited to its last part, distortion while narrating, whereas its essential matter is the false centering of the entire content." See Freud and Abraham, *Briefe 1907–1926*, p. 56.

resulting blind spot is the patient's dream report, the status of which Freud seldom questions. What differentiates a dream text from a novelist's fiction? Only in one extended discussion of the forgetting of dreams does Freud grant the textual problematics involved in dream interpretation. He admits a possible objection: "We have no guarantee that we know the dream as it actually occurred" (*Td* 491/*ID* 550). Apart from the familiar difficulties encountered in remembering dreams, Freud admits that "our memory does not only reproduce the dream fragmentarily, but even untruly" (ibid.).

Freud shifts his sights when he chooses to associate secondary revision with the process of retelling a dream: "It is correct that we distort the dream in trying to reproduce it; here we again find that we have designated as the secondary (and often misleading) revision of the dream through the agency (*Instanz*) of normal thinking" (*Td* 493/*ID* 552). Where previous authors have observed an arbitrary "modification of the dream in being recalled and conceived in words," Freud finds regular and significant patterns. If the dream report is not directly valid as a transcript of the dream, its distortions are themselves significant. Since Freud assumes that there are no accidents in mental events, he willingly counts the patient's dream report as a further, analyzable aspect of the dream work.

Freud sometimes asks patients to recount their dreams a second time and determines key moments by observing the modified passages, where censorship has continued its work (*Td* 493/*ID* 553). The manifest dream is like a dictatorship from which previously deposed rulers (the dream thoughts) have been banished.[35] Rather than strive for an ideal, adequate account, Freud accepts that the report is inevitably distorted and assumes the task of learning the codes necessary in order to make sense of indirect disclosures. Thus Freud subsequently discourages his followers from asking patients to write down dreams immediately after awakening: it is not necessary to exaggerate efforts to arrive at a "faithful preservation of the dream text" (*SA* Supp. 155/*TT* 102). The mind follows creative paths of distortion, in any event, and the problem is to recognize these paths, not to prevent or correct them.[36]

---

35. Compare John Murray Cuddihy, *The Ordeal of Civility: Freud, Marx, Lévi-Strauss, and the Jewish Struggle with Modernity* (New York: Basic Books, 1974), pp. 17–68, and see Carl E. Schorske's political reading of Freud's dreams in *Fin-de-Siècle Vienna: Politics and Culture* (New York: Alfred A. Knopf, 1980), pp. 181–207.

36. Freud later expresses contradictory opinions on secondary revision, as when he questions whether it is part of the "authentic" dream work. "A Dream Which Bore Testimony" treats secondary revision as an element of the dream work, but Freud

Freud's Monopoly and the Dream Facade

On one occasion, Freud referred to another author's work as a "secondary revision" of his own.[37] Notoriously unreceptive to the revisions proposed by competing psychoanalytic theorists, however, he was particularly unimpressed by alternative dream theories. Not only his ancient precursors were dismissed after receiving cursory treatment. In a passage that offended his contemporaries, Freud complained that contributions to the study of dreams had diminished of late: "The analysts act as if they had nothing more to say about dreams, as if the theory of dreams were closed" (*VEP* 452/*NIL* 8). After his own theoretical framework had become more rigid, Freud may have unwittingly projected his wish to have the last word. In spite of this wish, authors such as Wilhelm Stekel, Alfred Adler, Alphonse Maeder, Herbert Silberer, Ludwig Binswanger, and Carl Gustav Jung suggested advances during his lifetime.[38] Freud rejected all but the most minor adjust-

---

grants that one might also consider it separately: "Then one would have to say: the dream in its psychoanalytic sense includes the authentic (*eigentliche*) dream work and the secondary revision of its product" (*UTT* 82/*TT* 201). The *Introductory Lectures on Psychoanalysis* carefully limit the range of secondary revision (*VEP* 188/ *ILP* 182). One of Freud's encyclopedia articles comments that reordering by secondary revision "properly speaking (*eigentlich*) does not belong to the dream work" (*GW* 13, 217/*SE* 18, 241). *Totem and Taboo* suggests that secondary revision creates new meanings, which cannot be identified with those of the dream thoughts (*SA* 9, 382–83/*SE* 13, 94–95).

37. See Sigmund Freud, *Zur Geschichte der psychoanalytischen Bewegung* (Leipzig: Internationaler Psychoanalytischer Verlag, 1924), p. 55. In English, see *On the History of the Psychoanalytic Movement*, trans. Joan Riviere (New York: W. W. Norton, 1967), p. 52. See also Samuel Weber, *The Legend of Freud* (Minneapolis: University of Minnesota Press, 1982), pp. 9–10.

38. See Stekel, *Die Sprache des Traumes*, and especially *Fortschritte und Technik der Traumdeutung:* "The dream searches for a solution of the life conflict or of the day's conflict" (p. 11; cf. p. 92); Alfred Adler, "Träume und Traumdeutung" (1912), in *Praxis und Theorie der Individualpsychologie: Vorträge zur Einführung in die Psychotherapie für Ärzte, Psychologen und Lehrer*, 3d ed. (Munich: J. F. Bergmann, 1927), p. 153–61; in English, see "Dreams and Dream-Interpretation," in *The Practice and Theory of Individual Psychology*, 2d ed., trans. P. Radin (London: Routledge and Kegan Paul, 1929), pp. 214–26; A. Maeder, "Über die Funktion des Traumes," *Jahrbuch für psychoanalytische und psychopathologische Forschung* 4 (1912), 692–707, and "Über das Traumproblem," *Jahrbuch für psychoanalytische und psychopathologische Forschung* 5 (1913), 647–86; Herbert Silberer, *Der Traum: Einführung in die Traumpsychologie* (Stuttgart: Ferdinand Enke, 1919); Ludwig Binswanger, "Traum und Existenz" (1930), in *Ausgewählte Vorträge und Aufsätze*,

ments of his hypotheses, which had gradually attained the status of doctrines. As symbolism took on an increasingly important role in his theories, Freud only repudiated the related work of Stekel and Jung (*Td* 551n/ *ID* 618n).

Freud was particularly uncomfortable with the view that a dream is open to distinct levels of interpretation; he often mentions the work of Silberer and rejects his "anagogic" dream interpretation. According to Freud's paraphrase, Silberer theorizes that "every dream allows two interpretations . . . the so-called psychoanalytic, and another, the so-called anagogic, which turns away from the drive stimuli and aims toward a representation of the higher psychical accomplishments" (*VEP* 239/*ILP* 237). Freud admits that some dreams may signify in this dual way, but "most dreams require no over-interpretation (*Überdeutung*) and are in particular not susceptible of an anagogic interpretation" (*Td* 501–2/*ID* 562).[39] The anagogic level, according to Freud, is only an abstract thought that conceals aspects of the repressed instinctual life. He comments cynically that the opposition "is not always that of high anagogic and common analytic, but rather that of repulsive and decent or indifferent" (*UTT* 108/*SP* 84). Freud argues that the supposedly higher dream content only obscures its connection to repressed unconscious wishes. When Adler and Maeder question this premise, he counters by observing that his critics ignore the difference between manifest and latent contents.

Although later editions of *The Interpretation of Dreams* emphasize recurring symbols, Freud's interpretive approach is fundamentally at odds with an allegorical method. Individual images in dreams may have predictable meanings, but entire dreams generally do not fall into an allegorical pattern. The method of free association, in particular, opposes efforts to discern a coherent allegory behind the manifest dream. By association,

---

vol. 1 (Bern: A. Francke, 1947), pp. 74–97. By Carl Gustav Jung, see: "Allgemeine Gesichtspunkte zur Psychologie des Traumes" and "Vom Wesen des Traumes," in *Über psychische Energetik und das Wesen der Träume,* 2d ed. (Zürich: Rascher, 1948), pp. 147–257; and "Über die praktische Verwendbarkeit der Traumanalyse," in *Wirklichkeit der Seele,* 4th ed. (Zürich: Rascher, 1969), pp. 53–76. In English, see C. G. Jung, *Dreams,* trans. R. F. C. Hull (Princeton: Princeton University Press, 1974), pp. 23–109. See also Emil A. Gutheil, *The Language of the Dream* (New York: Macmillan, 1939); and Lowy, *Psychological and Biological Foundations of Dream-Interpretation.* Theories of problem resolution in dreams provide important post-Freudian alternatives to Freud's wish-fulfillment theory. One pre-Freudian discussion of problem resolution in dreams is a chapter entitled "Die Denkformen im Traume," in Volkelt's *Die Traum-Phantasie,* pp. 140–50.

39. *SA* 3, 185n/*GPT* 157n offers a slightly earlier, and a somewhat more favorable, commentary on Silberer's views.

each dream element gives rise to additional narratives; the analyst then retraces the distortions enacted by the dream work in order to approximate the repressed dream thoughts. Freud's associative model disturbs the correspondence model that seeks a single wish beyond diverse manifest contents. Free association is a process of intertextual substitution and displacement: rather than replace each symbol by its meaning, Freud encourages the patient to transform the dream text into new texts.

Freud does recognize different kinds of dreams when he distinguishes between those that are "from above (*von oben*)" and those "from below (*von unten*)": "Dreams from below are those that are aroused through the strength of an unconscious (repressed) wish. . . . Dreams from above are comparable to daily thoughts or daily intentions, which during the night have succeeded in being strengthened by the repressed material which is debarred from the ego" (*SA* Supp. 261/*TT* 207–8). Freud continues this line of thought in discussing the well-known dreams of Descartes.[40] He is careful to observe that "above" and "below" refer to the surface and depth of consciousness, not to extramundane and mundane influences. Nevertheless, like Silberer, Freud recognizes disparate senses of Descartes' dreams. On the one hand, the dreams represent a conflict between metaphysical good and evil, while an associated feeling of sin hints at repressed sexual ideas. In essence, then, Freud only repeats his familiar tactic of demystification. The dream is supposed to have some kind of exalted, rational meaning, which Freud traces to unconscious wishes.

Several post-Freudian authors concentrate on dream interpretation "from above" in connection with experiential conflicts.[41] Freud's followers

---

40. See "Über einen Traum des Cartesius," in *UTT* 113–15/*SE* 21, 203–4.

41. Stekel, Jung, and Adler have been followed more recently by Thomas French and the cognitive therapists. French argues that dreams "have sense and meaning, similar to and continuous with the wishes and thoughts of waking life," and concludes that the dream work, "like the thought processes directing our ordinary waking activity, is dominated by the need to find a solution for a problem." See Thomas French, *The Integration of Behavior* (Chicago: University of Chicago Press, 1952), vol. 1, chapter 16 on "Dreams and Rational Behavior," pp. 69–75. See also French's earlier "Insight and Distortion in Dreams," *International Journal of Psycho-Analysis* 20 (1939): "We have interested ourselves not so much in the transformations undergone by the latent dream thoughts, but rather with the ego's dynamic problem of reconciling conflicting wishes. We have been interested in the dream work not as a distorted intellectual process, as a peculiar mode of thinking, but rather as an attempt by the ego to solve a practical problem" (p. 292). The fullest discussion of dreams by Thomas French is contained in his *The Integration of Behavior*, vol. 2 (Chicago: University of Chicago Press, 1954). Compare Aaron T. Beck, "Cognitive Patterns in Dreams and Daydreams," in *Dream Dynamics, Sci-*

differ markedly, but many believe that he underestimates the importance of the manifest dream content. Their revaluation of manifest elements is sometimes linked to pragmatic concerns over the place of dream analysis during treatment. To avoid the dangers of suggestion and focus attention on the dream as a symptom of the past, Freud tries to separate the interpretation from its employment in the cure. When the manifest content receives new recognition, this facilitates wide-ranging dream interpretations in terms of future prospects, fears, ambitions, impending choices. The dream report commands greater respect when it is not viewed merely as a shell that conceals repressed wishes, but is perceived as part of a narrative process that may influence future life decisions. One should not blindly follow the actions suggested by a dream, of course, accepting its surface as advice "from above." Within the analysis, a dreamer must confront and revise the mysterious dream narratives concerning past, present, and future. Dreaming is a universal phenomenon of fiction making, a nightly experience during which every individual directs a play of illusions. To the extent that we recall and interpret our dreams, we are literary interpreters of our own texts or life stories.[42]

Freud describes the relationship between the dream and its meaning by analogy to a facade and the church behind it.[43] This architectural comparison is as complex as the phenomenon it metaphorically describes. Freud refers to particular Italian facades that were added in a later style

---

ence and Psychoanalysis, vol. 19, ed. Jules H. Masserman (New York: Grune & Stratton, 1971); Richard M. Jones, *Ego Synthesis in Dreams* (Cambridge, Mass.: Schenkman, 1962); and Rudolph M. Loewenstein, "The Problem in Interpretation," *Psychoanalytic Quarterly* 20 (1951), 1–14.

42. See Wolfram Luders, "Traum und Selbst," *Psyche* 36 (September 1982): "Dream interpretation . . . opens up for the dreamer access to his real self, confronts him with the psychic frame of mind which the dream interpreted" (p. 826–27). Luders summarizes: "Creative capacity is the true definition of the self. If dreams are interpreted accordingly, the dreamer experiences his potential and his strategies for dealing with the subjective and objective reality. Interpretations of the self facet [*sic*] confront the patient with his own way of producing and reproducing his self" (p. 829).

43. Jung's "Die praktische Verwendbarkeit der Traumanalyse," in *Wirklichkeit der Seele,* rejects notions of the dream as "a mere facade, which conceals the actual meaning. For most houses, the so-called facade is . . . by no means a fraud or a deceptive distortion, but rather corresponds to the interior of the house. . . . Thus also is the manifest dream image the dream itself, and contains its complete sense. . . . We are dealing with something like an incomprehensible text, which has absolutely no facade, but which simply cannot be read by us. Then we do not need to interpret behind it, but must rather learn to *read* it" (p. 63).

than the rest of the construction. The dream fantasy is "like the facade of Italian churches, placed in front without any organic connection to the building behind it" (*Td* 221/*ID* 245). A basic difference, Freud admits, is that the dream is chaotic and full of gaps. Modifying his architectural metaphor, Freud writes that dreams stand to childhood memories "approximately in the same relation as some baroque palaces in Rome to the ancient ruins, whose slabs and columns have provided the material for the construction in modern forms" (*Td* 473/*ID* 530). Dreams, like these baroque edifices, employ spoils from an earlier period. In the construction of dreams as of some buildings, moreover, there is a temporal gap between work on the supports and on the facade. Even if the manifest content appears well ordered, "this has arisen through the dream distortion and can have as little organic connection to the inner content of the dream as does the facade of an Italian church to its structure and plan" (*VEP* 187/*ILP* 181). By alluding to the temporal gap between stages of an architectural construction, Freud reinforces his conception of dreams as combinations of childhood materials and recent events.

The architectural analogy is itself like a dream image that requires interpretation. Whereas some Italian churches harmonize external and internal forms, others show stylistic incoherence. Both the main body and the facade of a church are artistic creations; the dream work is comparable to an architect who retains a previous construction while imposing a new style. (For example, Leon Battista Alberti massively transformed the facade of the Church of S. Maria Novella in Florence, reconciling Gothic and Renaissance motifs. The dream work, like a skillful architect, manages to conceal discrepancies.) Hence Freud sometimes indicates that "the process of the dream work is the essential thing about the dream" (*VEP* 452/*NIL* 8); one key to the dream is its work of revision, similar to the advance by which a later architect incorporates and supersedes an earlier design. The dream is a form produced by the dream work from latent materials (*VEP* 189/*ILP* 183). In a footnote of 1925, Freud even suggests that not what stands behind a dream, but the way it conceals, is essential: "The dream is at bottom nothing but the particular *form* of our thinking, which is made possible by the conditions of the sleeping state. It is the *dream work* that produces this form, and it is the only essential thing about the dream, the explanation of its peculiarity" (*Td* 486n/*ID* 545n). Similarly, one might say that an architect's achievement lies in his subtle combination of available materials in accordance with current styles. The dream work, like an artist, reworks perceptions or concepts into a representing form. A problem with this analogy stems from the Freudian presupposition that the dream work is common to all people, regardless of cultural and historical determinants, whereas artistic styles obviously evolve. In either case, Freud confronts difficulties. If the functioning of the dream work changes at different times and in different cultures, then he loses the supposedly immutable, essential characteristic of dreaming. If the dream work remains constant, it seems to transcend the individual, psychological level Freud assumes for the purpose of his scientific research.

Freud hesitates between a formal approach to the dream work and a substantial approach to contents of the dream thoughts. On one level, he adheres to the bipartite model according to which reported dream contents correspond to dream thoughts hidden in the depths of the psyche.[44] On another level, Freud does not presuppose a conjunction of the dream and its meaning, but notes a textual difference (*Textverschiedenheit*) (*Td* 307/*ID* 343). The latter conception diverges decisively from hermeneutic theories based on recovery of mental acts behind a dream or text. Although Freud frequently returns to the dream thoughts revealed by dream contents, insisting on their sexual character in connection with infantile wishes, his works also hint at an alternative paradigm. Some authors note that every patient's report of a dream is linked to strategic considerations in the analysis.[45]

---

44. Sarah Kofman, in *L'enfance de l'art: Une interprétation de l'esthétique freudienne* (Paris: Payot, 1970), remarks that the architectural analogy "must prevent one from interpreting dreams and art as translations of memories or fantasies: a new structure which has its own laws builds itself up on an ancient one, without ever substituting itself totally for it" (p. 52).

45. See Sandor Ferenczi, *Bausteine zur Psychoanalyse*, 2d ed. (Bern: Hans Huber, 1964), vol. 3, pp. 47, 53, 218–19; Otto Isakower, "Spoken Words in Dreams," *The Psychoanalytic Quarterly* 23 (1954), 1–6; Charlotte Balkanyi, "On Verbalization," *International Journal of Psycho-Analysis* 45 (1965), 64–79; and Alan Roland, "The Context and Unique Function of Dreams in Psychoanalytic Therapy: Clinical Approach," *International Journal of Psycho-Analysis* 52 (1971), 431–39. Compare Frederic Weiss, "Meaning and Dream Interpretation," in *Freud*, ed. Wollheim: "But if, as I have argued, the point of dream interpretation is to discover something that the subject means, . . . then whether or not the meaning-for him which is established through his 'associations' is the meaning-for him that is the meaning-of his report is a question that is totally inconsequential in psychoanalysis. The dream *is* a matter of no importance: the analyst need not even be concerned with any meaning it may have in the way that he is concerned with the meaning-of, or the non-meaning-of, other sorts of objects to which the subject may give a meaning-for himself" (p. 68). Weiss concludes that Freud illegitimately claims "to be establishing a meaning, which can tell him something about a patient, dependent on the equivalence of the meaning established through 'associations' with the meaning-of the 'manifest dream'; and he legislates the legitimacy of this equation by taking away the role of 'associations,' giving it to 'latent dream thoughts,' and from them reconferring it on the 'associations.' He is having his cake and eating it too" (p. 69).

Occupation (*Besetzung*) and Resistance (*Widerstand*)

Once Freud questions whether the interpreter can provide a neutral statement of a dream's meaning, he implicitly acknowledges the hazards of interpretive manipulation. Because the dream report invariably distorts and revises, Freud can hardly maintain his bipartite model. Even before interpretation begins, the dream report already modifies the dream.

The analogy between dreams and (censored) texts encourages an application of Freud's methods of dream interpretation to his own writings. His bipartite model of meaning conceives the manifest contents as an outer layer that conceals the latent contents; Freud's psychoanalytic approach implies, at the same time, that the dream work is itself essential. For a literary analysis of Freud, this would mean privileging the modes of figuration and conceiving Freud's texts neither as a set of explicit propositions (for example, "The dream is a wish fulfillment") nor as a complex of hidden thoughts (the personal ambition and sexual dynamics revealed by his self-analysis), but as figures, examples, the turns and detours in Freud's particular rhetoric of war and love.

In many respects, the talking cure resembles a battle and a seduction.[46] Freud encourages the transference neurosis while concealing his own emotions. By presenting the mask of a blank screen, he allows full play to the man or woman who mis-takes him for another; by avoiding any concession to the countertransference, Freud assures that he will emerge from the emotional drama unscathed. Freud is thus a seducer in the tradition of Don Juan, who characteristically dominates the passions of others without allowing his own passions to becomed enslaved. His seductions entail a lack of mutual feeling, in which misguided men and women perceive a nonexistent mutuality.[47] In order to rechannel the patient's (impatient) passion, Freud exploits the authority of the analyst. If the frequency of the sessions and the intimacy of their dialogue is not sufficient to assure that the analysand will fall in love with the analyst, Freud discourages the formation of other emotional bonds during analysis.

---

46. A striking post-Freudian illustration that psychoanalysis may resemble a seduction is contained in Emil A. Gutheil, *The Handbook of Dream Analysis* (New York: Liveright, 1951). Gutheil takes the example of a frigid woman and shows how he undermines her "unconscious hypocrisy" (pp. 49–54). See also Gutheil, *The Language of the Dream*, pp. 108–9, 162–65.

47. Viktor von Weizsaecker, in his "Reminiscences of Freud and Jung," describes Freud's style in terms of "a charm which verges on seduction." See *Freud and the 20th Century*, ed. Benjamin Nelson (New York: Meridian Books, 1957), p. 61.

Figures of war predominate at certain stages in Freud's discussion of psychoanalysis and dream interpretation.[48] According to one early assertion, psychological normalcy may be determined by the degree of suppression (*Unterdrückung*) of the unconscious by the preconscious; the unconscious must be subjugated to the dominion (*Herrschaft*) of the conscious and preconscious mind (*Td* 553/*ID* 620). Freud's language introjects a metaphysical battle between the forces of light and darkness, good and evil, heaven and hell. A skeptical age transforms the opposition between life and death—or the worldly and the otherworldly—into that of waking and sleeping. The divine and daemonic mechanisms are within us. "Flectere si nequeo superos, Acheronta movebo": Freud cites Virgil's *Aeneid* (VII, 312) on the title page of *The Interpretation of Dreams*. "If I cannot bend the powers above, I will move those of the underworld." He later attributes this drive to the repressed impulses.[49] But Freud ultimately proposes to mobilize and conquer the unconscious powers by delivering them to the rational control of the higher powers, the I.[50]

Another essentially military metaphor is *Besetzung*, typically translated as "cathexis" but more aptly translated as occupation, deployment, or investment.[51] This is one of the key metaphors that date from Freud's *Project* of 1895, although the range of this term shifts in accordance with other developments in psychoanalytic terminology. The early passages refer to "cathected neurons (*besetzte Neurone*)" (*AP* 382, 408/*OP* 358, 385, passim); assuming an energetics of the psyche, Freud accounts for alterations

---

48. Compare V. Volochinov [Mikhail Bakhtin], *Au délà du Social: Essai sur le freudisme*, in *Ecrits sur le freudisme*, trans. Guy Verret (Lausanne: Editions l'Age d'Homme, 1980), pp. 65–66. In English, see V. N. Vološinov, *Freudianism: A Marxist Critique*, trans. I. R. Titunik and ed. Neal H. Bruss (New York: Academic Press, 1976), p. 75.

49. Sigmund Freud, *Gesammelte Schriften* (Leipzig: Internationaler Psychoanalytischer Verlag, 1925), vol. 3, p. 169 (also cited in *Td* 577n/*ID* 647n).

50. See *Td* 577/*ID* 647. Compare Walter Schönau, *Sigmund Freuds Prosa: Literarische Elemente seines Stils* (Stuttgart: J. B. Metzler, 1968), pp. 61–73; Carl E. Schorske, *Fin-de-Siècle Vienna*, p. 200; Bruno Bettelheim, *Freud and Man's Soul* (New York: Alfred A. Knopf, 1983), pp. 68–69; and Jean Starobinski, "*Acheronta Movebo*," trans. Françoise Meltzer, *Critical Inquiry* 13 (Winter 1987), 394-407.

51. *Besetzung*, if rendered as "cathexis," loses the relevant associations, while French *investissement* captures its economic range of meaning. Freud does occasionally employ economic metaphors. He writes, for example, that every entrepreneur needs a capitalist to back his venture; in the same way, the waking thought combines forces with an unconscious wish in creating the dream (*Td* 534–45/*ID* 599–600 and *VEP* 229/*ILP* 226). Capital is analogous to libidinal energy.

in quantity by writing of full and empty neurons. After he has explained general psychological events in terms of neural energy transfers, Freud can account for dreams in relation to the emotional investment or wish fulfillment they represent. This terminology continues to operate in *The Interpretation of Dreams*, when Freud discusses the energy transfers and deployments associated with regression and wish fulfillment (*Td* 519, 523, 189–90/*ID* 582, 587, 209–10).

The patient's *Besetzungen* (''cathexes'')—charged with love and hate, eros and thanatos, positive and negative transferences—suggest an economic model, but Freud's heart is not merely a neutral cipher on which the patient places a wager. His deceiving heart cannot be conquered. *Besetzen* means to lay siege, to deploy one's psychical forces around another, perhaps even to cut off supplies and force a surrender. A reversal occurs: at first, the patient's *Besetzungen* resemble a military encirclement of the analyst. But Freud slips out of the trap, demonstrating that the campaign was really a battle within the psyche, between the patient's present desires and past affects. The theory of transference insists that all emotional investments in the analyst are irreal, displaced from prior emotions. The patient's laying siege around the analyst turns into an encirclement of the patient by the past. Freudian *Besetzung* implies a military campaign in which the patient is always conquered, occupied (*besetzt*) by the transference neurosis, in a kind of demonic possession or passion play. To become emotionally attached to a person or thing is, in Freud's implicit rhetoric, to engage in strategic warfare. The psychoanalytic patient's surrender is hastened by the imposed condition of abstinence during cure. Deployment and the overcoming of resistance are central to the Freudian method of treatment; the cure mimics a battle of the sexes.

Besetzung is further related to a matrix of terms that Freud does not explicitly consider. The root verb is *setzen*, to set or posit; emotional life, Freud's choice of words implies, is a kind of self-positing. An *Einsatz* is a wager or bet; we place ourselves on the line when we invest in people and objects. The root noun is *Satz*, a sentence (in grammar) or movement (in music); our psychical energy plays itself out by transferring earlier commitments to new positions. The *Satz* does not merely rule over the *Setzungen* by which we posit our work and our passion. To the extent that love repeats previous patterns of emotion, it is a carryover (*Übertragung*) or repetition (*Wiederholung*) that brings back the past in order that we may relive it. The error behind every transference lies in the fiction of replacement, when we act as if another figure could stand in the place once held by the original. The dream itself is an *Ersatz* for hidden thought processes (*Td* 117/*ID* 129). But *Ersatz* is always a lie that ultimately betrays its counterfeit nature; and the other resists our transferences. *Besetzung* also names the cast of characters in a dramatic production. Wearing a mask of impassive, free-floating attention and sitting beyond the patient's range of vision like a stage director who observes and intervenes in a rehearsal, Freud oversees the play of passions during which the patient remembers, repeats, and (perhaps) works through former emotional commitments. These linguistic resonances lead toward a conception of love and hate as translations (*Übersetzungen*), positive and negative transferences or carryovers (*Übertragungen*) of words and affects. Beyond conscious control, our *Besetzungen* speak a language of desire inside us, or in our relations with others.

The most revelatory essay in this metaphorical field is "On the Dynamics of the Transference," which employs the terms *Besetzung* and *Libidobesetzung*. Freud argues that transference, when it arises during psychoanalysis, can be enlisted in the service of treatment. He opens by observing that every human being develops a particular cliché in the experience of love. Freud could have called it simply a repetition, but he chooses to frame this peculiarity in the linguistic terms of "a cliché (or even several), which in the course of life is regularly repeated, newly printed out (*abgedruckt*)" (*SA* Supp. 159/*TT* 106). Life follows the literary patterns of a printed and reprinted cliché. Childhood relationships are the prototypes, and adults—like belated authors in literary tradition—are exposed to the danger of simply reproducing their exemplars.[52]

Freud's novel method of cure allows the patient to transfer his or her love cliché onto the analyst within the confines of the analytic session. This transference is immediately associated with resistance to the treatment (*SA* Supp. 160/*TT* 107), and so necessitates a shift in the metaphoric texture, from the image of energy transfer to that of libidinal occupation or deployment (*Libidobesetzung*). Initially, when the patient transfers emotions or linguistic clichés onto the analyst, Freud becomes the object of unexpectedly intense emotional attachments. He strives to remain a blank screen on which the patient's past is projected and analyzed (*SA* Supp. 178/*TT* 124), but countertransference threatens to destroy the illusion of neutrality. The cure searches for blocked libido, and in so doing engages in a mutual struggle. The deployed forces of both patient and analyst maneuver to attain their ends: "Where the analytic research comes upon the withdrawn libido in one of its hiding places, a battle must break out" (*SA* Supp. 162/*TT* 108). This battle is highly sexualized, both in its origins and in the metaphors Freud uses to describe it.

---

52. Cultural traditions similarly recapitulate the achievements of preceding ages. For example, the Five Books of Moses might be construed as the collective childhood of the Jews; rabbinic commentators have often interpreted subsequent events in terms of the earlier narratives.

The scenario is essentially one in which a man struggles to overcome a woman's resistance to his sexual advances. The scene of *Besetzung* thus reverses, for the patient's initial investment in the noncommitted analyst has become a full-fledged war. Freud elaborates the metaphors of war at the close of his essay: "This battle (*Kampf*) between doctor and patient, between intellect and the life of the drives (*Triebleben*), between recognition and the desire to act (*Agierenwollen*), plays itself out almost exclusively in connection with the phenomenon of transference" (*SA* Supp. 167/*TT* 114). Noting the great difficulties entailed, Freud adds that nevertheless "on this field the victory must be won" (ibid.).

Freud's great initial discovery, which shocked his collaborator and senior colleague Josef Breuer, concerned the sexual etiology of hysteria. Freud explained neuroses as the consequence of sexual disturbances. If health resembles a freely flowing hydraulic system, illness appears to result from dammed energies. In the complex drama now called psychoanalysis, a neurotic returns to the points of resistance and blockage in order to overcome these obstacles to health.

The libido cannot be freed unless it is first engaged. Hence, after Freud discovers the phenomenon of transference, he enlists its aid in the treatment. From one point of view, therapy begins as does a gambling session in which the house calls to the patron: "Place your bets!" And the patient places more than a monetary fee on Freud's desk. The serious wager is emotional: the patient makes a bid for love; desire errs. To lose, in this context, is to facilitate a discovery of the mechanisms of erotic error. Pokerfaced, Freud insists that he is merely a blank screen or mirror, the empty illusion onto which the neurotic projects desire, and he proceeds to show that the patient has mistaken the object of love. In Freud's office, desire comes to learn the unreality of its objects; the repetition of emotions is replaced by analytic working through. Place your bets! Not with any prospect of winning the game, but only to discover that your strategies are insufficient and that the house always wins.[53] Accumulating capital throughout the twentieth century, the house that Freud built has become an increasingly potent institution.

At the start of a psychoanalytic treatment, Freud seems to say: invest in me, bet on me, occupy me, bring your abandoned dreams or hidden

---

53. The hour begins. A young woman enters Freud's office for the first time. "Bitte setzen Sie sich," Freud says. Please be seated, posit yourself, declare your place. Why am I here? the patient wonders. What does he expect me to do?

In fact, the situation is even worse for the neurotic who is nowhere at home. "Bitte legen Sie sich hin," Freud says. Please lie down. What is he going to do to me? The analysis centers around the overcoming of resistances.

wishes, and throw your past loves into the cure. The scene of battle is full of surprises, however, for Freud feigns a weak position in order to provoke an effort at conquest. From a position of illusory weakness, Freud turns the tide of the battle, craftily redirecting the patient's deployments back toward their source. After Freud conquers the patient's heart, he points the subdued psyche to the hidden cause of its ignominious defeat. The patient is necessarily the loser—unless a victory over the past ensues.

The repressed paradigm is defeat at the hands of parental figures. Suddenly Freud urges a revolutionary alliance, a joint overthrow of the mother country (or *Vaterland*). Psychoanalysis makes forgotten loves actual, "for ultimately no one can be slain in absentia or in effigy" (*SA* Supp. 168/*TT* 115). This concluding metaphor oddly typifies psychoanalytic treatment, because the distinction between real and imaginary slaughter does not obviously correspond to the difference between repeating and working through.[54] Analysis does, nevertheless, attempt to "slay" parental figures in their absence. Freud suggests that the transference is necessary in order to reawaken slumbering affects that may then be re-educated. Continuing the prior images, a part of the patient appears to capitulate; the working through of repressed libido is figured as a murder. At best, a memory trace of the parental cliché has been destroyed, freeing the repressed energies for new investment. But if the cure appropriates and destroys the patient's love cliché, how can this mangled narrative be replaced? Like a totalitarian regime, psychoanalysis succeeds when it rewrites the history of its subjects, and when the conqueror convinces the conquered that figurative seduction is beneficial.

Out of the metaphorical battles between Freud and his patients arise questions concerning the relationship between psychoanalysis and power. Despite his efforts to maintain scientific neutrality, Freud's methods evidently involve him in rather irregular maneuvers. The founder of psychoanalysis not only engaged in symbolic battles with his patients; he also fought endlessly against his rebellious disciples, and in so doing he expressed his ambition to remain the absolute father of his figurative children.

Freud most explicitly discusses power and ambition when he interprets a minimal dream of "R." that also raises issues concerning the Jewish condition. His preparatory account refers to Jewish doctors in Vienna who have been denied the title of Professor because of "denominational considerations" (*Td* 154/*ID* 170). Prior to the dream, Freud writes, he was nominated for this title, but the experience of his senior colleagues led him to fear the worst. Freud observes somewhat irrelevantly that he is, as far as he

---

54. See "Remembering, Repeating, and Working Through," in *SA* Supp. 207–15/ *TT* 157–66.

knows, "not ambitious" (*Td* 153/*ID* 170). Yet his interpretation of the dream of R. centers around a mixture of positive and negative feelings, tenderness and hostility, toward this colleague. By distortion into its opposite, the latent hostility is transformed into manifest tenderness.

Freud explains this dream distortion by analogy with the social situation of two people in which "the first possesses a certain power, and the second must show respect because of the power" (*Td* 158/*ID* 175). He observes that this condition is rather the rule than the exception: "The politeness which I exercise every day is in large part such a dissimulation; when I interpret my dreams for the reader, I am obliged to make such distortions" (ibid.).[55] Ambition and hostility seethe beneath the surface of Freud's scientific persona; Freud conceives dream distortions on the model of social pretenses. Freud also compares the dream work to the activity of a political writer, who "has to tell unpleasant truths to those in power," and disguises his opinions to escape censorship (*Td* 158/*ID* 175). Freud suggests that every individual psyche operates as does a political regime. Long before writing his metapsychological essays on the tripartite psyche, Freud postulates the efficacy of distinct mental powers: "The first forms the wish that is expressed in the dream, while the second exercises censorship on the dream wish and through this censorship forces a distortion of its expression" (*Td* 160/*ID* 177). The self internalizes social hierarchies that assure a disparity between its deepest intentions and manifest expressions.

Freud relates a revealing episode of humiliation at a train station.[56] That Freud was sensitive to such experiences is evident from his memory of an affront to his father—as a Jew (*Td* 208/*ID* 230). A certain Count Thun haughtily passes him on the platform while traveling to see the kaiser. Freud denies that he envies the count, for he is on vacation and pleasantly conceives himself to be the real Count Nichtsthun ("Do–Nothing"). Yet Freud is preoccupied by the evident social hierarchies. Full of "revolutionary thoughts" that oppose social divisions (*Td* 218/*ID* 242), Freud resolves to protest any signs of favoritism. In fact, a certain government official does claim a half-price, first-class seat, and Freud receives an inferior compartment without a lavatory. Freud's uneasy reactions, and the dreams that

---

55. Compare Margaret W. Ferguson, *Trials of Desire: Renaissance Defenses of Poetry* (New Haven: Yale University Press, 1983), p. 180.

56. Jews on trains provided a definite genre of humor, one instance of which Freud mentions (*Td* 206/*ID* 227–28). See also *Jokes and Their Relation to the Unconscious*, discussed by John Murray Cuddihy in *The Ordeal of Civility*, p. 21. A slightly later example from Yiddish literature is Sholem Aleichem's "On Account of a Hat." See Isaac Rosenfeld's translation in *A Treasury of Yiddish Stories*, ed. Irving Howe and Eliezer Greenberg (New York: Schocken Books, 1973), pp. 111–18.

result, show the significance of the issues involved in this experience. Social hierarchy has found its way into the recesses of the psyche, and this anecdote might be read as an allegory of tensions within Freud the individual.[57]

Freud the interpreter cannot be entirely separated from Freud the seducer. Janus-faced, he looks back in time with a pretense to uncovering past causes that explain the meaning of dreams; through transferences and free associations, he simultaneously engages the dreamer's imagination in ways that project toward future possibilities. Provoked by Freud, the dreamer invents variations on the dream text. The transference ensures that, to some extent, Freud's interpretation of these inventions will be realized or enacted.

The recognition that Freud sometimes employed self-fulfilling prophecies does not disqualify his results. Medical standards forced him to deemphasize this aspect of the analysis, at least in his public statements; he knew that transference was the strongest "weapon" of cure, and had good reason to exploit the power of his interpretive influence. At the same time—to meet the expectations of scientific method—he dissimulated this influence. His ancient precursors provided the prophetic model he felt obliged to reject, since he was closer to them in practice, if not in theory, than he could admit.

Freud uncovers the psychological and rhetorical mechanisms that facilitate thematic awareness. Neither themes nor figures, taken alone, constitute his texts; meaning arises out of the interaction between manifest and latent elements. Freud's discussions themselves show distortions analogous to those of the dream work: his examples, allusions, reversals, qualifications, denials, censorships, revisions, metaphors, and analogies all resemble the processes he discusses. This recognition does not justify a moralistic critique. Freud's diction is unusual only in its eloquence; as with all authors, the rhetoric of his manifest contents appears to distort and recast elusive, "authentic" meanings. Authenticity and literal meaning are retrospective illusions fostered by an awareness of tropes and transferences.

Psychoanalysts have pragmatic reasons for borrowing and systematizing certain Freudian concepts while revising and rejecting others, but Freud discouraged his followers from conceiving psychoanalysis as a system.[58] A

---

57. For detailed discussions of Freud's Count Thun dream, see Grinstein, *On Sigmund Freud's Dreams*, chapters 4 and 5, and Schorske, *Fin-de-Siècle Vienna*, pp. 193–97. Schorske also sketches the political background, including the Dreyfus affair and the rise of Karl Lueger (p. 185).

58. Freud, *Zur Geschichte der psychoanalytischen Bewegung*, p. 55. In English, see *On the History of the Psychoanalytic Movement*, trans. Riviere, p. 52.

literary approach takes Freud at his word, or takes seriously the ways in which his words signify, by considering the varied forms of his theories, figures, disavowals, and concealed polemics. According to Freud, the tensions expressed by symptoms, slips of the pen or tongue, and transferences characterize everyday life. To read Freud as Freud read is to observe the distortions or disfigurements that are essential to expression and to discern the movement of texts rather than the congealed meanings they seem to produce. This undertaking runs counter to the forms of psychoanalytic practice that demand routines and standardization: while Freud strives to develop scientific techniques, he also associates dream interpretation with the unpredictable methods of art criticism.

The Interpretation of Dreams is at once a treatise, an episodic novel, and a collection of case studies in which theories, confessions, and fantasies compete. Applied to his own texts, Freud's methods of dream interpretation reveal a system in flux, distorted by condensations, displacements, graphic illustrations, and revisions. Freud searches for concealed wishes, and his own writings acknowledge moments of censorship that veil hidden meanings.[59] As the manifest content of a dream is no random husk behind which the kernel of meaning may be found, however, so Freud's particular dream examples, and the poetic structures of his work, are significant.

Freud's psychological theories are inseparable from the verbal texture of his essays. Recent studies observe some flagrant distortions that have resulted from translation of Freud into English.[60] Yet the present goal is not prescriptive, because no fully adequate translation of Freud into another language is possible. Freud himself anticipated the difficulties that would beset the translator of *The Interpretation of Dreams* (*Td* 120n/*ID* 132n). Rather than work toward a better English version of Freud's texts, we may modestly observe linguistic pathways through which his texts operate. The metaphorical range of Freud's ideas cannot be controlled or reduced to a univocal system; at best, the interpreter attends to meaning on multiple registers.

Critics of Freud have repeatedly questioned the scientific status of psychoanalysis.[61] They argue that Freud fails to impose the highest experi-

---

59. At some points Freud admits the necessity of dissimulation by everyday censorship (e.g., *Td* 158/*ID* 175). At other times, however, Freud indicates that science need not dress up its results in any special form; the conclusions themselves should be sufficient (*VEP* 118/*ILP* 102). For evidence of Freud's careful editing of his dream book, see *BWF/CL*, letters of 9 June 1898, 20 June 1898, and 7 August 1901.

60. See, for example, Bettelheim, *Freud and Man's Soul*, pp. 49–108.

61. See, for instance: *Psychoanalysis, Scientific Method, and Philosophy*, ed. Sidney Hook (New York: New York University Press, 1959); *Freud*, ed. Wollheim; and Adolf Grunbaum, *The Foundations of Psychoanalysis: A Philosophical Critique* (Berkeley: University of California Press, 1984).

mental standards upon his nascent science; some current researchers seek to show that psychoanalytic ideas may be verified or falsified, at the same time that other authors emphasize the necessarily speculative, unprovable character of psychoanalytic theory. If we accept the inevitability of figuration, however, there is less reason to be dissatisfied with Freud's procedures. Freud's *Interpretation of Dreams* is consequently more a book about interpretation than it is about dreams. According to his theories, repression and the concomitant disguise necessitate interpretations that return to the hidden form of the distorted dream contents.

The interpreter of Freud's text can hardly extract fixed theses: as the dream work is essential to the dream, rhetorical devices are essential to the dream book. *The Interpretation of Dreams* tells elaborate stories toward an autobiography of its author, in which the demands of scientist and novelist contend. Beyond conscious control, rhetoric governs the psyche and its textual presentation.[62] The operations of the distorting dream work are analogous to figures of speech. What lies beyond, in the textual unconscious? In a footnote, Freud cites James Sully's image of the dream as a palimpsest that *"discloses beneath its worthless surface-characters traces of an old and precious communication"* (*Td* 152n/*ID* 169n; quoted in English and italicized by Freud). Freud's own writings on dreams are palimpsests over ancient sources.

---

62. See Freud's comparison of memory and writing in his "Note on the 'Mystic Writing Pad' " (*SA* 3, 365–69/*GPT* 207–12).

2

JOSEPH AND DANIEL: DISGUISES AND INTERPRETIVE POWER

The figures of Joseph and Daniel influenced Freud negatively, because contrary demands led him to renounce these biblical dream interpreters. Although this was a more or less obligatory scientific gesture, Freud exaggerated his repudiation and narrowed his own theories when he turned away from the future and focused on the past a dream expresses. Nevertheless, psychoanalytic treatment required a future orientation, and Freud moved in circles that brought him closer to his prophetic precursors than he cared to admit.

Ancient and modern dream interpretation have more in common than is often assumed. While Freud relied on a philological model based on the correspondence between dreams and their meanings, he also employed a more radical, displacement model of associative interpretation. Both interpretive directions have biblical precedents: Joseph and Daniel follow the clues provided by symbols and metaphors; in addition, by aiming toward future events, they anticipate the modes of displacement that Freud recognized in the dream work. Never fully reconciled with his powers of suggestion, however, Freud minimized his identification with biblical interpreters.

As Freud refined and revised his techniques of dream analysis, he curtailed the element of displacement by concentrating on recurring symbols. He conceived the patient's associations, increasingly linked to the past, as predetermined expressions of prior causes. Had Freud allowed real freedom to the free associations, he might have been obliged to acknowledge the continuing relevance of biblical dream interpretation. Instead,

Freud views the dream as a disguise that conceals deeper meanings, not future prospects.

Dreams and disguises are central to the stories of Joseph and Daniel, which also refer to signs, tokens, and interpretations. Unlike their easily duped contemporaries, these biblical protagonists see through external appearances to actual and virtual truths. The dream interpreter recognizes the meaning of obscure images and words, whereas most other characters are so deceived that they hardly even recognize their own kin.

Joseph and Daniel mediate between sleeping and waking visions, between night dreams and day fictions, and rise to power as interpreters. They discern potential realities beyond vague intimations, and rather than trace a dream back to past thoughts, they weigh its significance to future events. The dreams Joseph and Daniel interpret are not wish fulfillments, except in the sense that they allow interpreters to fulfill their own ambitions. The biblical meaning of dreams lies in the future, to be awaited or sought, in the dreamer's prophesied fortunes and the future of the interpreter as empowered prophet. The books of Genesis and Daniel present no theory of dreams, but demonstrate the active power of dreams over life.

Questions of authority confront every interpreter. Dream interpretation is associated with power struggles, since the successful interpreter appears to control others through his awareness of the future. With adept modesty, Joseph and Daniel attribute all interpretations to God, at the same time that they presume to divine God's meanings. The biblical narratives do not simply validate their claims. Joseph never receives such explicit reassurance as do the earlier patriarchs who experience theophanies; God does not openly intervene in his life.[1] While the story is not entirely secular, it does recount Israel's fate from an essentially human perspective.[2] In the Book of Daniel, God's presence to the prophet is evident, yet the nature of Daniel's authority as dream interpreter remains unclear.

---

1. On the absence of theophanies in the story of Joseph, see Benno Jacob, *Das erste Buch der Tora: Genesis* (Berlin: Schocken, 1934), p. 698. In English, see the abridged edition, *The First Book of the Bible: Genesis,* ed. Ernest I. Jacob and Walter Jacob (New York: Ktav, 1974), p. 250. See also Nahum M. Sarna, *Understanding Genesis* (New York: Shocken, 1970), p. 211.

2. E. A. Speiser discusses the narrative perspective in his *Genesis* (New York: Doubleday, 1964): "The theme is essentially personal and secular. Other aspects, to be sure, are in evidence here and there, yet they are never allowed to distract attention from the central human drama. In retrospect, of course, the story of Joseph was seen as a link in the divinely ordained course of human history. But while the writing is by no means oblivious to this approach, the theological component has been kept discreetly in the background" (p. 292).

"Will You Rule Over Us?"

The narrative of Joseph and his brothers opens with a conflict and sides with Joseph from the outset. "These are the generations of Jacob," the story begins, and turns immediately to Joseph, bypassing the sons of Leah (Gen. 37:2).[3] Jacob favors Joseph, and the narrative reflects this preference; as the central protagonist, Joseph dominates every scene in which he appears.

Joseph's predominance exists, then, on several planes. Most obviously, he is his father's favorite. Having himself wrested the birthright from Esau (Gen. 27), Jacob apparently has no compunctions about preferring the first son of his second marriage. Jacob makes Joseph a special robe (*k'tonet passim*) which indicates his elite status and privilege to a life without strenuous labor (Gen. 37:3). This is the first in a series of garments that will differentiate between those who can and cannot see beyond mundane appearances. Joseph is Israel's favorite, where "Israel" names both Jacob and the nation that will continue his seed. Moreover, Joseph is favored by God, as the hero of a narrative that allows him to assure the continuance of God's people. Human choice and divine will interact: Jacob creates Joseph's fate, if it is not predetermined, by setting him above his brothers.

The preferential treatment of Joseph has explicit consequences for the family romance: "When his brothers saw that their father loved him more than all his brothers, they hated him, and could not speak peaceably to him" (Gen. 37:4). Jacob has been thwarted in his passionate preferences before, agreeing to serve Laban seven years to marry the younger daughter, only to receive Leah instead (Gen. 29:18–25). Like Judah in a later chapter, Jacob is tricked into sleeping with a woman without knowing her true identity. By favoring Rachel's eldest son, Jacob recalls his love of Rachel and effectively provokes the rivalry of Leah's sons, Joseph's half-brothers. Hence the sons of Leah act as a counterprogressive force in the plot, true to their origins in the postponement of Jacob's marriage to Rachel by Laban's deceit.

Dreams quickly take on significance in this plot: "And Joseph dreamed a dream and told it to his brothers, and they continued (*va-yosifu*) to hate him more" (Gen. 37:5). When he tells his dreams, the chosen son intensifies his brothers' rivalry. Even the verb describing their continued hatred resonates with Joseph's name; in this way, too, Joseph continued

---

3. All biblical and Talmudic translations in this and the following chapter are based on the original Hebrew and Aramaic sources. Transliterations employ these approximate equivalents: Alef = '; Vet = v; Vav = v,w; Chet = ch; Tet = t; Kaf = k; Khaf = kh; Ayin = '; Tsadi = ts; Quf = q; Sheva *mobile* = '; Tav = t.

(*va-yosif*) the tradition of his father's sibling rivalry.[4] Presumably Joseph cannot be blamed for having dreamed; but his ingenuous reaction is to tell his brothers: "Hear this dream which I have dreamed: behold, we were binding sheaves in the field, and my sheaf stood up and remained upright; and behold, your sheaves gathered around and bowed down to my sheaf" (Gen. 37:6–7). Joseph relates his dream text to those it concerns,[5] establishing it as a point of reference for subsequent events.

The brothers' response combines apprehension and irony. Joseph begins his career as a dreamer; his brothers interpret for him: "Will you reign over us? Will you rule over us? (Gen. 37:8). Their recognition of meaning is qualified by its rhetorical form. Joseph's brothers take the interpretation for granted, but phrase it as a question, wondering whether the dream is fantasy or prophecy.[6] They hate him more "for his dreams and for his words" (Gen. 37:8), either because they perceive his ambition or because they fear his legitimate claims to power. Joseph's manner of telling his brothers, as if he were naively warning them of what will happen, is especially disconcerting.

The dreams of Genesis 37–41 come in pairs. Joseph's second dream intensifies the first by shifting from an agricultural scene to an astrological event: "Behold, the sun, the moon, and eleven stars bowed down to me" (Gen. 37:9). Albeit in the form of a question, his father interprets this dream as bearing on the lives of those who hear it: "Will I, your mother, and your brothers come and bow down to the ground before you?" (Gen. 37:1). Like the brothers' earlier remark, this rhetorical question leaves open the possibility of an affirmative response. In consequence, the brothers envy Joseph, but Jacob takes the dream more seriously and "heeded the thing (*shamar et ha-davar*)." The status of words and signs is at issue: the brothers previously hated Joseph because of his words (*d'varav*); now Jacob specially attends to the matter (*ha-davar*).[7] This key word echoes narrative

---

4. Genesis 30:22–24 alludes to the multiple meanings associated with Joseph's name.

5. Compare Sandor Ferenczi, "Wem erzählt man seine Träume?" in *Bausteine zur Psychoanalyse*, 2d ed. (Bern: Hans Huber, 1964), vol. 3, p. 47.

6. In his *Genesis: A Commentary*, rev. ed. (Philadelphia: Westminster Press, 1972), Gerhard von Rad refers to a "lack of theological directness" in the dream accounts. One may "understand them in two ways, either as real prophecies or as the notions of a vainglorious heart" (p. 351). Von Rad's original discussion is contained in *Das erste Buch Mose: Genesis Kapitel 25, 19—50, 26* (Göttingen: Vandenhoeck & Ruprecht, 1953), p. 308.

7. Central problems of dream interpretation revolve around the opposition between words and images, already implicit in the multifaceted Hebrew word *davar*. Com-

developments when Jacob sends Joseph on a mission to find out the well-being of his brothers and their flock, and asks that Joseph send word (*davar*). Only Jacob respects the signs of Joseph's divine mission.

Joseph's brothers continue to oppose him by their words. They plot against him, seeking to prevent the domination his dreams predict: "Here comes that dreamer (*ba῾al ha-chalomot*). Come now, let us kill him and throw him into one of the pits . . . and we shall see what will become of his dreams" (Gen. 37:19–20). The brothers' words combine disparate emotional attitudes. "We shall see" carries a strong ironic tone, implying: We shall show that his dreams were nonsense. But this bitter irony is unsettled by the brothers' nagging fear that they do indeed have reason to oppose Joseph's dreams. Like the rhetorical questions they posed earlier, their present words may be interpreted anew, and the reinterpretation will work against them, as "we shall see."

These characters in the story rise against the prescribed plot, trying to shake off a fate that they themselves foresee in their brother's dreams. Joseph's siblings express an ambivalence that may also characterize the reader's response: are Joseph's dreams true prophecies or wishful fictions that betray delusions of grandeur? In spurning Joseph, his brothers doubt the validity of dreams and, more broadly, question the existence of a God who has singled out Joseph.[8] Their skepticism is human, all too human perhaps, since they do not share Jacob's adulation of Joseph. Similar to any reader who questions what is narrated, the skeptical brothers are unwilling to accept the course of the narrative; but even their rebellion serves higher ends.

After they sell Joseph to the Midianites, the brothers dip his coat (*k'tonet passim*) in the blood of a kid and take it to their father. When Jacob recognizes the garment, he assumes that Joseph has been devoured by a wild animal. Similar to his blind father Isaac, Jacob misreads the external signs. His own sons are like wild animals, with the exception of Joseph, who will show his ability to decipher signs.

In a world that is permeated by deceit, only Joseph sees beyond ap-

---

pare Ernst Ludwig Erlich, *Der Traum im alten Testament, Beihefte zur Zeitschrift für die alttestamentliche Wissenschaft* 73 (1953), p. 7. In Gen. 37:8, when Joseph's brothers hate him both for his dreams and for his words, the narrative marks the difference between visions and their interpretation, while linking the words of an interpretation to the substance of its fulfillment.

8. Von Rad, in *Genesis: A Commentary,* writes of "a dark knowledge about the irrevocableness of such prophetic dreams. Only when it is expressed, only when it is told, does the prophecy contained in the dream become potent. . . . The brothers' hate is therefore a rebellion against the matter contained in the dreams, against the divine power itself" (p. 353). In German, see *Das erste Buch Mose: Genesis Kapitel 25, 19—50, 26,* pp. 308–9.

pearances. Two further scenes of disguise and false recognition occur in the subsequent chapters. Tamar, to attain the fertility she has been denied, disguises herself as a prostitute and sleeps with her father-in-law, Judah. As blind as his father Jacob and his father's father Isaac, Judah does not recognize the woman. In surety for payment, Judah leaves his seal, cord, and staff. Afterward, to reveal Judah's inequity at a crucial moment, Tamar presents these tokens and employs the same phrase that Joseph's brothers use in presenting Jacob with Joseph's bloody garment: "Pray recognize (*haker-na*)."[9] This theme continues when Joseph's clothing again causes him difficulties as a slave in Egypt. Potiphar's wife, failing in her efforts at seduction (in contrast to Tamar, who does seduce Judah), uses Joseph's garment to incriminate him falsely. Potiphar is unable to perceive Joseph's innocence beneath his superficial appearance of guilt; he incorrectly construes the signs. These mistakes enhance the drama of Joseph's convincing recognitions as an interpreter of dreams.

The Joseph narrative illustrates the tensions between divine providence and human will. Although the narrative ultimately seems to confirm Joseph's divine mission, the perspective is worldly. After Jacob learns of Joseph's disappearance, the narrative shifts to the story of Judah and Tamar. A disruption in the life of Joseph corresponds to a disruption in the narrative progress; the continuity of Jacob's line through Joseph has been threatened by the "breach" enacted by his brothers.[10] The clearest statements of Joseph's support from God precede and follow the story of Potiphar's wife: "YHWH was with Joseph, and he was a successful man" (Gen. 39:2; compare Gen. 39:21–23). The implied idea of God's presence in personal history assures that the worthy succeed, and Joseph's closeness to God benefits all of the household he oversees. Only here does the narrative assure us that the story is governed by God's will.[11] The intricate plot

---

9. Concerning this verbal echo, see Genesis Rabbah 84:19, 85:11. Compare Robert Alter, *The Art of Biblical Narrative* (New York: Basic Books, 1981), p. 11. In Egypt, at the conclusion of the plot development, the ability to recognize differentiates between Joseph and his deluded brothers.

10. Commentators dispute the place of Genesis 38 in the surrounding narrative. See, for example, Gerhard von Rad, *Genesis: A Commentary*, p. 356; Robert Alter, *The Art of Biblical Narrative*, p. 3–10; and James S. Ackerman, "Joseph, Judah, and Jacob," in *Literary Interpretations of Biblical Narratives*, vol. 2, ed. Kenneth R. R. Gros Louis and James S. Ackerman (Nashville: Abingdon, 1982), pp. 103–4. The outcome of this debate is not, however, crucial in the present context.

11. Josephus and several rabbinic commentators, unwilling to allow the biblical ambiguity, explicitly assert that Joseph's dreams are of divine origin. See Josephus, *Jewish Antiquities*, II.II.3;13–14, and Yalkut Shimᶜoni, chap. 141.

developments of Genesis 37–40 also intimate that a divine plan is at work. Joseph had to dream his dreams so that his brothers would hate him more; Jacob had to send Joseph after his brothers so that they could sell him to the Midianites; Potiphar's wife had to tempt Joseph so that he would resist and be imprisoned; the servants of Pharaoh had to be placed in prison with Joseph, so that he could interpret their dreams and rise to prominence as Pharaoh's interpreter. Dreams and the recognition of their disguised meanings are critically linked to power and future possibilities.

"Do Not Interpretations Belong to God? Tell Me"

Pharaoh's cupbearer and baker "both dreamed a dream on a certain night, each man dreamed his dream according to its interpretation" (Gen. 40:5). This description of dreams accompanied by interpretations prepares us to believe that Joseph will correctly guess their (predetermined) meanings.[12] This reading of the biblical account conforms to Freud's favored model of correspondence. In the past, Joseph has been known as a dreamer; now he becomes an interpreter.

Joseph is strikingly self-confident at this crucial point. Hearing that his fellow prisoners have dreamed, he responds: "Do not interpretations belong to God? Tell me" (Gen. 40:8). By answering in this way, Joseph modestly denies any special powers, while simultaneously diminishing his own responsibility for what he will say. With unaccountable assurance, he suggests that he acts as a mouthpiece for God.[13] The exact phrasing of Joseph's reply is significant, for he does not assert that interpretations come from God, but rather asks, "Do not interpretations belong to God?" Rhetorical questions continue to provide meanings and raise issues that remain open to interpretation.

The manifest contents of the dreams recounted by Pharaoh's cupbearer and baker conform to the professions of these two men. The first tells of vines, grapes, and a cup placed in Pharaoh's hand; the second tells

---

12. Ernest Ludwig Erlich, in *Der Traum im alten Testament,* argues that "each man dreamed his dream" only clarifies a potential ambiguity, excluding the possibility that the two men dreamed the same dream. He adds, nonetheless, that "each according to its interpretation" may hint at the productive power of dream interpretations (p. 67).

13. Erlich writes that "the tendency which lies at the basis of the Joseph story with regard to dream interpretation is thus clearly circumscribed: dream interpretation is only successful when God inspires the interpretation, when it comes from Him." This contrasts the prevailing Egyptian view of dream interpretation as "a science, which one must have learned" (ibid., p. 68).

of baskets and foods. Both dreamers mention the number three, which Joseph interprets as signifying three days hence, the day of Pharaoh's birthday.[14]

The pair of dreams gives rise to distinct and opposite fulfillments (Gen. 40:12–19). Joseph plays on minuscule differences that indicate completely incommensurable fates. In the first case, Joseph tells the cupbearer that Pharaoh will "lift up your head" and restore him to his office. In the second case, Joseph tells the baker that Pharaoh will "lift your head from you" by hanging him on a tree. While both heads will be lifted, Joseph's interpretations anticipate utterly disparate results. The future is foretold in linguistic subtleties, for those who are able to perceive them.

Without confirming or denying Joseph's claim to divine aid as an interpreter, the narrative states that all occurs "as Joseph interpreted to them" (Gen. 40:22). Joseph's interpretations are prophetic, in each case corresponding to future events. The cupbearer returns to his office, while the baker is hanged. From a literary standpoint, these dreams are a necessary link in the narrative chain that leads from Joseph's initial dreams to those of Pharaoh. Everything that occurs in Genesis 39–40 is justified by its part in allowing Joseph an opportunity to act as Pharaoh's dream interpreter. The basis of Joseph's ability to interpret dreams remains obscure, although its importance to the narrative line is evident.

Symbolic interpretation is Joseph's implicit method: three branches or baskets signify three days; an act of placing a cup in Pharaoh's hand symbolizes a return to the position of cupbearer; the birds eating from baskets stand for birds that will devour the flesh of the doomed baker. Apart from his evident recourse to symbols, Joseph attempts to validate his interpretive claims by reference to divine inspiration. The narrative gives no alternative explanation of his success.

Joseph's approach to dream interpretation becomes clearer in relation to that of Sigmund Freud, whose *Interpretation of Dreams* refers to Joseph several times. Freud observes that in his own dreams, because of the biblical prototype, characters named Joseph often stand for Freud himself (*Td* 466n/*ID* 522n). According to Freud, Joseph performs typical symbolic dream interpretations: "Seven fat cows, after which come seven thin cows that consume the first; that is a symbolic substitute for the prophecy of seven years of famine in the land of Egypt, which consume all the abundance created by the seven fruitful years" (*Td* 117–18/*ID* 129). Freud disparages Joseph's methods, in spite of his own reliance on symbols: "It is,

---

14. As Benno Jacob observes, Joseph may recognize that pardons and punishments are likely to occur on Pharaoh's birthday. See Jacob, *Das erste Buch der Tora: Genesis*, pp. 737–38; in English, see *The First Book of the Bible: Genesis*, p. 271.

of course, not possible to give instructions concerning how one finds the way to such a symbolic interpretation" (*Td* 118/*ID* 129). Success in this kind of dream interpretation "remains a matter of sudden inspiration (*des witzigen Einfalls*), of unmediated intuition" (ibid.). Freud suspects the biblical dreams of being "artificial," like those created by authors to introduce symbolic meanings.

Pharaoh's dreams form a significant, symbolic pair.[15] The dream of cows precedes a corresponding dream of ears of corn, touching on the primary sources of food: livestock and agriculture. At this point, too, the mode of presentation shifts. Previously, each dream report was followed by an interpretation (Gen. 37:5–8, 37:9–10, 40:9–13, and 40:16–19). Now the dream is first presented by the narrative before Pharaoh recounts it in slightly different terms. The variations are potentially significant. For example, Pharaoh adds an emotional comment about the cows: "I have never seen their like for badness in all the land of Egypt" (Gen. 41:19); and he adds that, after the lean cows had devoured the fat cows, "it could not be known that they had eaten them, for they appeared as bad as before" (Gen. 41:21). These differences show sensitivity to the possible discrepancies between dreams and dream reports. They also suggest that the narrative, like Joseph, has knowledge of realities beyond what is manifestly expressed. The narrative voice is omniscient, although it does not explicitly speak for God.

We do not know how Joseph arrives at his symbolic interpretations of Pharaoh's dreams; his success is assured by the plot, which requires that he attain a position of power. Joseph ascribes his dream interpretations to divine agency (Gen. 40:8; Gen. 41:28,32), and even Pharaoh asserts that "God has made all this known to you" (Gen. 41:39). One potential message of the text is that God chooses Joseph for a definite mission, sends dreams to prophesy that mission, and influences the sequence of events leading to Joseph's successful interpretations of Pharaoh's dreams.

"As He Interpreted to Us, So It Was"

The Joseph narrative is subtler than a simplistically pious reading would suggest; Joseph's interpretations need not have been predetermined by God. Although Joseph refers to God's will, His messages leave considerable freedom for interpretation. The fulfillment of Joseph's prophecies does not prove their inherent correctness, and the narrative maintains diverse possibilities.

---

15. Compare Freud's further reference to Pharaoh's dreams and Joseph's interpretations in *Td* 330–31/*ID* 369.

A key phrase for alternative readings of the narrative occurs in the cupbearer's belated report of Joseph to Pharaoh. He recalls his experience when imprisoned together with the baker: "One night we dreamed a dream, I and he, we dreamed each of us according to the interpretation of his dream" (Gen. 41:11). As in Genesis 40:5, the convoluted syntax may suggest that each dream has a corresponding, fixed interpretation. But the cupbearer's subsequent account of Joseph's interpretive success is more complex: "We told him, and he interpreted our dreams for us; each man according to his dream he interpreted. And as he interpreted to us, so it was: he restored me to my post, and he hanged him" (Gen. 41:12–13). This more literal translation of the final phrase,[16] instead of the passive form— "I was restored to my post, and he was hanged"—emphasizes the significant ambiguity of the original. Pharaoh was, of course, the person empowered to perform these acts (compare Gen. 40:20–21). Yet some interpreters understand the verse as saying that through his interpretations, Joseph effects the ascent and demise of Pharaoh's two servants.[17] The cupbearer's words, "As he interpreted to us, so it was (ka'asher patar-lanu ken haya)," may imply that Joseph's interpretations produce the results he foretells. In this case, Joseph does not simply get it right by guessing a hidden meaning; rather, he makes his words good by somehow influencing their fulfillment.

Several rabbinic sources tell a relevant anecdote concerning the power of dream interpretation. Genesis Rabbah recounts the story precisely in the context of Genesis 41:13.

> A certain woman went to R. Eliezer and said to him: "I saw in my dream that the second [beam or story] of my house was split." He said to her: "You will conceive a male child"; she went away and so it was. A second time she dreamed thus and went to R. Eliezer, who told her: "You will give birth to a male child"; and so it was. A third time she dreamed thus and came to him again but did not find him. She said to his students: "I saw in my dream that the second [beam or story] of my house was split." They said to her: "You will bury your husband," and so it was. R. Eliezer heard a voice of wailing and said to them: "What is this?" They told him the story, and he said to

---

16. Following S. R. Driver, *The Book of Genesis,* 11th ed. (London: Methuen, 1920), p. 341. In the earlier part of Gen. 41:13, "so it was" resembles the original (*ken haya*) more closely than does the usual translation, "so it came to pass." Compare *In the Beginning: A New English Rendition of the Book of Genesis,* trans. Everett Fox (New York: Schocken, 1983), p. 168.

17. See Ibn Ezra's commentary to Gen. 41:13.

them: "You have killed a man, for is it not written, 'As he interpreted to us, so it was'?"

R. Jochanan said: "All dreams follow the mouth, except for wine."[18]

This story gives a sharp turn to the biblical verse, "as he interpreted to us, so it was." The consequences of dreams appear to derive from the way they are recalled, retold, and interpreted. This problem reemerges at the center of an extended Talmudic dispute.[19]

Another version of the R. Eliezer story, in the Palestinian Talmud, shows subtle awareness of the problematic relationship between interpretation and reality. The woman's dialogue with R. Eliezer's students occurs after her second experience of the dream: "His students said to her: 'He's not here.' They said to her: 'What do you seek from him?'" This time, confronted by the students, the woman is wary (or a writer wishes to avoid using the first-person form), and she begins to tell the dream in third person. A grammatical infelicity gives her away: "That woman saw in my dream the second [beam or story] of my house broken." The students respond to the equivocation caused by her anacoluthon: "You will give birth to a male child, and that woman's husband will die." The dream evokes two distinct interpretations, and the students ineptly offer both alternatives. R. Eliezer's irate reply echoes Genesis Rabbah: "You have killed a soul, because dreams only follow their interpretation" (Maʿaser Sheni 4,6). Rabbinic commentators suggest that the power of a dream does not reside in its ambiguous images, but depends upon the effect of interpretive words. The dream disguise, then, does not veil any preexisting reality, and rather points to diverse contours of meaning in different contexts. This view indicates that Joseph's dream interpretations may simultaneously conform to reality and cause reality to conform to them.

Pharaoh accepts Joseph's interpretations without hesitation. While Joseph presumably could not influence Pharaoh's earlier decisions regarding the cupbearer and baker, the later situation is not so clear. After interpreting Pharaoh's dreams as prophecies of fruit and famine, Joseph adds some helpful advice: "Now let Pharaoh find [see] a man clever and wise, and set

---

18. Genesis Rabbah 89:8. This translation is based on the second critical edition of Chanoch Albeck, *Bereschit Rabbah* (Jerusalem: Wahrman Books, 1965). A slightly different English translation is contained in *Midrash Rabbah*, 3d ed., ed. H. Freedman and Maurice Simon, trans. H. Freedman (London: Soncino, 1983), vol. 2, p. 825.

19. Berakhot 55b–56b. See chapter 3, below, section entitled "All Dreams Follow the Mouth."

him over the land of Egypt'' (Gen. 41:33). Joseph implicitly proposes, Take me! when he offers a detailed plan of action (Gen. 41:34–36). Persuaded that Joseph's plan is good, Pharaoh concludes that there is no one else "clever and wise as you are," and accepts his proposal (Gen. 41:39–40). At once Joseph is transformed from a dreamer into a shrewd businessman and politician.[20]

Pharaoh does not wait fourteen years to see whether the crops will flourish and fail as Joseph predicts, but immediately appoints him agricultural overseer. After this change of fortunes, Joseph has both the motive and the means to assure that his prophecy will be fulfilled. He governs the land astutely for seven years, gathering surplus, and after the cycle of prosperity runs its course, famine sets in. Pharaoh's dream is not a good one, but Joseph makes it good in terms of his own fate. By virtue of Pharaoh's reaction, the plot takes its necessary course.

The story concludes when, as a result of the famine, Joseph's brothers travel to Egypt for grain. In consequence of Pharaoh's dreams and Joseph's interpretations, Joseph's present position enables fulfillment of his childhood dreams. The Joseph narrative is both a tale of apt interpretation and a story of words and actions that direct events. The prophet's words are not merely predictive, but also causative. In conflict with his surroundings, the prophet successfully imposes his dream—or his interpretation of others' dreams.

As the circle closes, the problem of recognition returns. Confronted by his brothers, the narrative repeatedly asserts that Joseph recognizes them. Yet Joseph disguises his voice and they do not recognize him, despite their interpretation of his childhood dream, which foretold that they would bow down to him. Only Joseph the interpreter is not deceived by appearances.

"This Is Your Dream"

Disguises are less prominent in the Daniel story: whereas Genesis 37–42 narrates Joseph's ascent in a style of limited omniscience, from a human perspective, the Book of Daniel more insistently asserts the efficacy of God's will. The narrative ascribes Daniel's talents and successes to God, and represents prophecies and miracles that evidently transcend mundane reality. In other respects Daniel is similar to Joseph: both rise to power in a foreign realm by interpreting the king's dreams. Like the Joseph narrative,

---

20. Compare Philo's essay "De Iosepho,"also known as "The Life of the Statesman," which discusses the politician's ability to actualize his dreams of what ought to be (chaps. 22–24).

the stories of Daniel center around acts of interpretation, but the Book of Daniel is more concerned to show God's providence behind the scenes or between the lines. Although Daniel has little to do with disguises, he does repeatedly demask dreams, discerning meanings in delusive images. The ultimately potent image is God's hand: a ruling force that governs the apparently random events of human experience.

The opening verses in the Book of Daniel situate its story historically, while they subordinate historical events to a divine plan: "In the third year of the reign of King Jehoiakim of Judah, King Nebuchadnezzar of Babylon came to Jerusalem and besieged it" (Dan. 1:1). The fall of Jerusalem and destruction of the First Temple result in the Babylonian exile, which is the setting for Daniel's life. The narrative does not dwell on causes of Nebuchadnezzar's victory, and merely asserts that "the Lord gave King Jehoiakim of Judah into his hand" (Dan. 1:2). The battle also assumes theological significance, because Nebuchadnezzar plunders "vessels of the House of God, and he brought them to the house of his god." These vessels reappear at a climactic moment, when their disrespectful use presages the fall of Belshazzar (Dan. 5:3–4).

Nebuchadnezzar's spoils include noble children of Israel, chosen to serve in the royal palace by virtue of their extraordinary intelligence. Perhaps they are designated to become translators as well as advisers, for they are taught the writings or learning (*sefer*) and language (*leshon*) of the Chaldeans (Dan. 1:3–4).[21] Ultimately, Nebuchadnezzar's plunder from Jerusalem undermines his own kingdom: by teaching Daniel the Chaldean traditions, Nebuchadnezzar educates a competent prophet of their destruction. Daniel learns to translate between Hebrew and Aramaic, as he learns to translate dreams into prophetic, historical narratives.

Twice in the opening chapter, the narrative ascribes Daniel's success to God. His wish to abstain from the king's food is satisfied because "God granted Daniel grace and compassion before the chief officer" (Dan. 1:9). Moreover, God gives Daniel and his three companions "knowledge and skill in all writings [or learning] and wisdom, and Daniel had understanding of visions and dreams of all kinds" (Dan. 1:17). The book takes on the hyperbolic quality of a folk tale when, before the king, Daniel and his friends answer questions "ten times better than all the magicians and con-

---

21. As a story of exile, the Book of Daniel frequently refers to differences of language and custom. The figure of Daniel is especially esteemed by rabbinic traditions because he exemplifies the Jews' continuing capacity to retain contact with God even when governed by hostile nations. Dreams illustrate Daniel's unwavering devotion to God, whose dream messages challenge human claims to independent power.

jurers in all his realm" (Dan. 1:20). Desite the odds against Daniel, the reader knows that with God's assistance he will prevail over Nebuchadnez-zar.

At this point in the story, although the exact chronology is unclear, "Nebuchadnezzar dreamed dreams, his spirit was troubled (*titpaᶜem ru-cho*), and his sleep left him" (Dan. 2:1). This description echoes Genesis 41:8: "And in the morning his spirit was troubled (*tipaᶜem rucho*)."[22] Like Pharaoh, Nebuchadnezzar first calls together his wise men and asks them to interpret his dream. But unlike Pharaoh, Nebuchadnezzar implies that he has forgotten his dreams and asks to be told both the dream and its inter-pretation. This demand baffles the king's wise men and gives Daniel his chance. Daniel's prophecies will not be easy to test, so that his royal sanc-tion initially depends on his ability to tell the king what he has dreamed.

Since the story takes place in a foreign land, it is perhaps fitting that the language now shifts.[23] The background narrative of chapter 1 and the opening verses of chapter 2 are in Hebrew, but as the scene becomes con-crete, the Chaldeans and Nebuchadnezzar speak Aramaic. During this comic exchange, Nebuchadnezzar three times asks to be told the dream and its meaning, while the Chaldeans tenaciously request that Nebuchadnezzar first tell them the dream (Dan. 2:3–9). Nebuchadnezzar doubts the honesty of his dream interpreters and demands that they relate the dream, for then "I will know that you can tell its interpretation" (Dan. 2:9).

The Chaldeans' final response infuriates Nebuchadnezzar, who does not wish to acknowledge the limits of his power. They inform him that "there is no man on earth who can tell the king's matter (*milat malka*)" (Dan. 2:10), and as a last resort the magicians taunt Nebuchadnezzar by insisting with some irony that only "the gods whose dwelling is not with [mortal] flesh" can satisfy his demand (Dan. 2:11). They unwittingly play into the hands of Daniel, who will confidently resort to God's assistance.

---

22. Some early commentaries suggest that Nebuchadnezzar's *trouble* is spelled with an additional *Tav* in order to imply an enhancement or exaggeration of Pha-raoh's condition. See Mizrachi and Gur Aryeh to Gen. 41; and compare Genesis Rabbah 89:5.

23. This view supplements the familiar redaction theories. Concerning the two lan-guages of Daniel, viewed from a less literary and more historical perspective, see James A. Montgomery, *A Critical and Exegetical Commentary on the Book of Daniel* (New York: Charles Scribner's Sons, 1927), pp. 90–92; *The Book of Daniel,* ed. R. H. Charles (Edinburgh: T. C. and E. C. Jack, 1913), pp. xiv–xxiv; and André Lacocque's two books: *Le livre de Daniel* (Paris: Delachaux et Niestle, 1976), pp. 23, 34, 42, and *Daniel et son temps* (Geneva: Labor and Fides, 1983).

The magicians' ironic evasion prepares for the success of Daniel's pious revelations.

In contrast to the wise men, Daniel confidently asks for time so that he can tell the interpretation to the king. He does not yet know what he will say, but prays for God's mercy and awaits divine aid. Whereas Genesis does not explain how Joseph arrives at his interpretations, we learn that "the secret was revealed to Daniel in a night vision" (Dan. 2:19). Daniel's initial manner of proceeding replaces a dream for a dream: he does not begin by substituting an interpretation for Nebuchadnezzar's dream, but by experiencing a vision of his own that solves the mystery.

Nebuchadnezzar repeats his question to Daniel, who at first seems to allude to Genesis 41:16 and Daniel 2:10–12: "The secret about which the king inquires, no wise men, conjurers, magicians, or diviners can tell the king" (Dan. 2:27). By agreeing with their own protests that for them the request is impossible, Daniel sets himself apart from his competitors. He also recasts Joseph's words to Pharaoh's servants: "Do not interpretations belong to God?" (Gen. 40:8). Rather than claim credit for his ability to interpret, Daniel tells Nebuchadnezzar that "there is a God in heaven who reveals secrets and has made known to Nebuchadnezzar what shall be in later days" (Dan. 2:28). Renouncing the idols worshiped in Babylonia, Daniel insists on the presence of a singular "God in heaven."[24] At the same time, Daniel tells the king that God has revealed the dream in order that Nebuchadnezzar may "know the thoughts" of his heart (Dan. 2:30). This passage becomes important for the psychologically oriented traditions in rabbinic dream theory.

Daniel next relates the dream, which consists of an image and its destruction:

> You, O King, did watch, and behold, a great image. This image, which was mighty and of surpassing brightness, stood before you, and its form was awesome. The head of the image was of fine gold, its breast and arms of silver, its belly and thighs of bronze, its legs of iron, and its feet part iron and part clay. As you watched, a stone was hewn out, not by hands, and struck the image on its feet of iron and clay and crushed them. Then the iron, clay, bronze, silver and gold were crushed, and became like chaff of the summer threshing floors; and the wind carried them away, so that no trace of them could be found. And the stone that struck the image became a great mountain and filled the whole earth. (Dan. 2:31–35)

---

24. Compare Montgomery, *A Critical and Exegetical Commentary on the Book of Daniel,* p. 162.

The dream Daniel relates is itself iconoclastic, in the original sense of the word: image-breaking. The "image" is evidently a statue, but Daniel's vague word, *tselem,* may also mean "shadow" or "picture." Finally it is no more than a dream image, an image of an image, and Daniel will pierce behind this illusion to arrive at a statement of its worldly significance.[25] Like Joseph and Freud, Daniel indicates that the dream imagery conceals a higher or deeper reality.

"This is the dream," Daniel continues, "and we will tell its interpretation before the king" (Dan. 2:36). The first-person plural form suggests that the interpretation cannot be accomplished by Daniel alone, but exclusively with God's help. Daniel addresses the king in an ambiguous way, accentuating the theological import of the story: "You, O king, king of kings, to whom the God of heaven has given kingdom, power, might, and glory" (Dan. 2:37). Another, somewhat less flattering, translation of these words is also possible: "You, O king—to whom the King of kings, God of heaven, has given kingdom, power, might, and glory." Yet Nebuchadnezzar is not willing to acknowledge any king higher than himself, and wishes to hear only that into Nebuchadnezzar's hands God has given man, wild beasts, and fowl of the skies (Dan. 2:38). Nebuchadnezzar's hands again symbolize his power, which is annulled within the dream itself, beyond the mundane realm over which Nebuchadnezzar exerts his influence; the stone that crushes his statue is hewn "not by hands" but by divine decree.

Daniel's interpretation grants Nebuchadnezzar a limited power in order to prophesy its revocation; his flattering address introduces a devastating historical narrative. God has given Nebuchadnezzar power over all things of the earth, and "you are the head of gold" (Dan. 3:38). Man cannot live by head and hands alone, however, and in the dream Nebuchadnezzar's lower parts initiate his destruction. Interpreting from the dreamer's standpoint, Daniel conceives the dream image as a representation of Nebuchadnezzar himself. He also places the dream in a larger historical process: "After you another kingdom will arise, inferior to you; and another third kingdom of bronze, which will rule over the whole earth. And the fourth kingdom shall be strong as iron" (Dan. 2:39–40). Commentators have debated the identity of these prophesied kingdoms, and have neglected the remarkable fact that Nebuchadnezzar himself does not ask for details.

Like Pharaoh, who immediately accepts the validity of Joseph's prophecy (Gen. 41:37), Nebuchadnezzar immediately bows down to Daniel, although his prophetic interpretation remains untested (Dan. 2:46).

---

25. Daniel's interpretation may allude to ancient traditions concerning the ages of men. See, for example, Hesiod, *Works and Days,* lines 109–201; and compare Ovid, *Metamorphoses* I, 89–150.

Empirical verification is not at issue. Nebuchadnezzar acknowledges that Daniel's God "must be the God of gods and Lord of kings," while his practical reaction is to submit to Daniel's interpretation and grant him political power (Dan. 2:48; compare Gen. 41:40).

"Worship the Image of Gold"

Apparently in consequence of Daniel's account and interpretation of the dream, Nebuchadnezzar builds a similar statue and improves upon it. He chooses both to receive and ignore Daniel's message: remaining within the imagery of greatness, he defies the transcendent power of God's hand. Instead of responding to the prophecy, Nebuchadnezzar constructs a statue in which his improved image (*tselem*) is entirely of gold. Art imitates the dream, and alters it, possibly at odds with Daniel's interpretation. Whereas the dream image receives a single interpretation in terms of future events, the statue Nebuchadnezzar builds suggests several further meanings. Like Daniel, the reader of the story must interpret.

Nebuchadnezzar tries to force his subjects to bow down before his image—his realized dream or fantasy. On one level, the image stands for Nebuchadnezzar himself, since the head of gold now extends to the entire body. By representing himself in this way, he tries to forestall the message Daniel has given him; his golden image usurps the course of history. On another level, within biblical contexts, this statue alludes to the Tower of Babel, traditionally interpreted as a challenge to God.[26] The image may also represent a pagan deity before which Nebuchadnezzar demands that his subjects worship. A peculiar scene follows, in which the officials who are invited to the statue's dedication hear the proclamation: "To you it is commanded, O peoples, nations, and languages, that when you hear the sound of the horn, pipe, zither, lyre, psaltery, bagpipe, and all kinds of music, you shall fall down and worship the image that King Nebuchadnezzar has set up. Whoever does not fall down and worship shall be cast at once into a burning fiery furnace" (Dan. 3:4–6). Nebuchadnezzar opposes Daniel's prophecy, which observed the ephemeral character of Nebuchadnezzar's reign. The king tries to shift the mode of performative language, transposing a prophecy of decline into a decree that assures enduring greatness.

Nebuchadnezzar strives to actualize his dream image, and at this point the narrative takes on the quality of a dream. Nebuchadnezzar's innumerable officers bow down to a golden statue while a motley band plays a weird symphony. This eerily comic moment is also the most treacherous point in the story, for now human and divine power come into direct conflict. The

---

26. See Rashi and Ibn Ezra to Genesis 11.

Jews of Babylonia, symbolized by Daniel's companions, refuse to engage in what they perceive as an idolatrous ceremony, and so provoke the king's wrath. When Nebuchadnezzar becomes enraged at these men who believe in a power greater than his own, the theological problem appears as a contest of hands: "If you do not worship," Nebuchadnezzar tells the dissenting Jews, "you shall be cast at once into a burning fiery furnace." With a fine but misguided touch of irony, he adds, "and what god is there that can deliver you from my hand?" (Dan. 3:15). His rhetorical question obviously intends the response "None," but the Jews heroically rely on a hand greater than human hands: "Our God that we serve is able to deliver us from the burning fiery furnace, and He will deliver us from your hand" (Dan. 3:17). Once again, as in the Joseph story, a question acts as a focal point for the plot reversal.

The story's dreamy, fairy-tale quality intensifies and reaches its first climax. Previously Daniel and his companions were "ten times better" at answering questions than the other wise men of Nebuchadnezzar's realm; now Nebuchadnezzar commands that the furnace be heated to "seven times its usual heat" (Dan. 3:19). Nebuchadnezzar's urgent and excessive demand leads to a catastrophe: the executioners are themselves destroyed by flames, and the three dissenting Jews fall into the furnace (Dan. 3:21–23).

Until this moment, the narrative voice relates events and, occasionally, also the thoughts of Daniel and Nebuchadnezzar. Here the narrative assumes Nebuchadnezzar's point of view, in order to emphasize his sudden recognition of fallibility.[27] "Did we not throw three men, bound, onto the fire?" he asks (Dan. 3:24). The account describes Nebuchadnezzar's perceptions rather than what actually happens: "I see four men, unbound and unharmed, walking in the midst of the fire" (Dan. 3:25). Nebuchadnezzar himself explains that "the God of Shadrach, Meshach, and Abednego . . . sent His angel to deliver his servants" (Dan. 3:28). The earlier order required that all Nebuchadnezzar's subjects bow down to his statue; at present Nebuchadnezzar decrees the greatness of the Jewish God (Dan. 3:29).

In accordance with the earlier shift to Nebuchadnezzar's perception of the miracle, the narrative takes on a first-person form, as if incorporating a letter from the Babylonian king into the text. Nebuchadnezzar relates an idealized, spiritual autobiography that bears obvious resemblance to the preceding story, although the exemplary dream differs. The king is frightened by a dream, finds that his wise men cannot interpret it, and finally learns its meaning from Daniel. In this instance, Nebuchadnezzar himself recounts

---

27. Compare Otto Zockler, *The Book of the Prophet Daniel*, trans. James Strong (New York: Scribner and Armstrong, 1876), p. 104.

the dream, which may be considered either as completely new or as a second version of the first dream: "I did watch, and behold, a tree in the midst of the earth, and its height was great. The tree grew, and became strong, and its top reached the heavens, and it was visible to the ends of the earth. Its leaves were fair, and its fruit abundant; there was food for all on it" (Dan. 4:7–9). Where the first dream presents the artistic grandeur of a statue, the second dream consists of a natural image.

Nebuchadnezzar's second dream also includes a scene of destruction, but the ostensible agent is a voice rather than a stone: "I saw . . . a holy watcher coming down from heaven. He cried aloud and said, 'Hew down the tree and cut off its branches' " (Dan. 4:13–14). This voice seems to speak for Nebuchadnezzar's conscience, to the extent that he recognizes his own failings, at the same time that it comes to him as an external decree (*g'zerah*). The commenting voice refers directly to Nebuchadnezzar: "Let him be wet with the dew of heaven, and let his portion be with the beasts in the grass of the earth. Let his heart be changed from that of a man, and let the heart of a beast be given to him" (Dan. 4:12–13). As patients of Freudians have Freudian dreams and patients of Jungians have Jungian dreams, Nebuchadnezzar has learned Daniel's prophetic style.[28] Daniel confirms that the tree is a symbol of Nebuchadnezzar, who will be destroyed. He predicts the worst: "You will be driven away from men, and your dwelling will be with beasts of the field. You will be made to eat grass like cattle, and shall be wet with the dew of heaven" (Dan. 4:22). The tree is a thinly veiled figure that represents Nebuchadnezzar's downfall.

Through the interpretative voice of another, then, Nebuchadnezzar's dreams are linked to madness. One moral of the story is that to defy God is madness, and Daniel is the mediator between God's presumed message and Nebuchadnezzar's subsequent decline. The narrative is out of Nebuchadnezzar's hands at the moment of his fall (Dan. 4:25–30). When he loses control of his reason, Nebuchadnezzar loses control of his self-presentation as well. The first-person narrative suddenly shifts to a third-person form. After the illness passes, Nebuchadnezzar resumes his account: "At the end of the days, I, Nebuchadnezzar, lifted up my eyes to heaven, and my understanding returned to me" (Dan. 4:31). A return to first-person narration signals a return to consciousness. By acknowledging God, Nebuchadnezzar regains self-control: "I blessed the Most High and . . . my reason returned

---

28. This particular dream is, in fact, congenial to C. G. Jung, who cites it in his "Allgemeine Gesichtspunkte zur Psychologie des Traumes," in *Über psychische Energetik und das Wesen der Träume*, 2d ed. (Zürich: Rascher, 1948), pp. 171–72. In English, see "General Aspects of Dream Psychology," in *Dreams*, trans. R. F. C. Hull (Princeton: Princeton University Press, 1974), p. 37.

to me" (Dan. 4:31–33). Nebuchadnezzar's humiliation renders his will to autonomy paradoxical, for only by recognizing a power outside himself does he come back to himself.

What is the status of Daniel's interpretations? Daniel does not perform attractive interpretations for Nebuchadnezzar, but the king's personal history makes them appear sound. Since the meaning of dreams is inseparable from their interpretation, one might infer that—within the fiction—Daniel's prophetic remarks undermine the king's sanity.

"Mene Mene Teqel Upharsin"

The events of Daniel 5–6 parallel those of Daniel 2–3, although in the later instance Daniel's interpretations are explicitly textual.[29] King Belshazzar, a son or more distant descendant of Nebuchadnezzar, continues the tradition of his forerunner's scorn for the Jewish God. Drunkenness and disrespect lead him to desecrate the vessels that Nebuchadnezzar took from the Temple in Jerusalem (Dan. 5:2; compare Dan. 1:2); his consorts engage in idolatrous praise of "the gods of gold and silver, brass, iron, wood, and stone" (Dan. 5:4). The list of idolatrous gods echoes the composition of Nebuchadnezzar's dream image (Dan. 2:31–33). This narrative once again assumes a dreamlike character: "In that hour, the fingers of a man's hand appeared and wrote over against the candlestick on the plaster of the wall of the king's palace; and the king saw the part of the hand that wrote" (Dan. 5:5). A mysterious hand challenges the hand of the king's mundane authority; like Nebuchadnezzar (Dan. 4:32), Belshazzar must recognize that God's power transcends his own. The supernatural event is presented from the standpoint of the king, who "saw (*chazeh*)," as Nebuchadnezzar "saw" in his dreams (Dan. 2:31). The verb of seeing is also employed by Nebuchadnezzar when he perceives the Jews' miraculous escape from the furnace (Dan. 3:25), and when he has visions in his bed (Dan. 4:6–7). This verb to some extent crosses the boundary between waking and sleeping "visions"; human beings are deluded, and only prophets can interpret the deceptive imagery. Visionary delusion can also become a pathway to higher truths.

---

29. Two seminal historical accounts concerning the Book of Daniel are Raymond Philip Dougherty's *Nabonides and Nebuchadnezzar: A Study of the Closing Events of the Neo-Babylonian Empire* (New Haven: Yale University Press, 1936), and Werner Dommerhausen's *Nabonid im Buche Daniel* (Mainz: Matthias Grunewald, 1964). See also Otto Zockler, *The Book of the Prophet Daniel*, pp. 20–41; *The Book of Daniel*, ed. Charles, pp. 48n–51n; and Joyce Baldwin, *Daniel: An Introduction and Commentary* (Ontario: InterVarsity Press, 1978), pp. 19–29.

Belshazzar's vision of a writing hand is not a dream, yet its interpretation proceeds like that of a dream.[30] Similar to a dream image, the writing on the wall requires an interpretation, but one that the king's magicians cannot accomplish. Taking on the role assumed by Pharaoh's cupbearer in Genesis 41, Belshazzar's queen informs the king that Daniel can interpret the alarming vision. As Nebuchadnezzar demanded that he relate both his dream and its interpretation, Belshazzar now demands that Daniel both "read the writing, and make known its interpretation" (Dan. 5:16). Like a dream that has been forgotten, the mystic writing is inaccessible to all, apparently including the king. His vision reveals and conceals its meaning, in textual form.

Before interpreting, Daniel recapitulates past events of Nebuchadnezzar's reign in order to explain the moral and theological significance of what has happened. One may wonder how Daniel can recount Nebuchadnezzar's fall and safely upbraid the present king; the narrative follows its own inner logic rather than any demands of realism. In order for Daniel's reading of the inscription to be fully convincing, the prophet first underlines its theological justification: "You lifted yourself up against the Lord of heaven" (Dan. 5:23).

Daniel then reads the writing on the wall: "mene mene teqel upharsin" (Dan. 5:25). This inscription remains the most enigmatic verse in the Book of Daniel. Numerous ancient and modern commentaries on these words have only multiplied the possible meanings. The riddle has remained, and some commentators even suggest that the author of the story misunderstands the traditional account that had been handed down.[31] The accepted understanding of the inscribed words was "numbered, numbered, weighed, and divided" until the publication of an article suggesting that these words name units of currency: "a mina [or, 'it was counted'], a mina, a shekel, and two half minas."[32] The older interpretation reads the inscrip-

---

30. On the association of dream interpretation with textual interpretation, see Lou H. Silberman, "Unriddling the Riddle: A Study in the Structure and Language of the Habakkuk Pesher," *Revue de Qumran* 3 (1961), 332. Silberman also discusses Daniel's manner of interpreting the writing on the wall by means of wordplay (p. 333).

31. See, for example, Emil G. Kraeling, "The Handwriting on the Wall," *Journal of Biblical Literature* 62 (1943), 11–18.

32. See Charles Clermont-Ganneau, "Mané, Thécel, Pharès, et le festin de Balthasar," *Journal Asiatique,* series 8, vol. 8 (1886), 36–67. Among the many other works that continue the lead of Clermont-Ganneau, see John Dyneley Prince, "*Mene Mene Tekel Upharsin:* An Historical Study of the Fifth Chapter of Daniel"

tion as a series of verbs, which Daniel then fits into a narrative of Belshazzar's demise. The more recent interpretation identifies the words as substantives, names for units of currency corresponding to the devaluation of successive kings or empires. But there is something comic about scholars' philological efforts to outdo Daniel and show the true meaning of the inscription, which serves literary purposes in the story. The real or actual meaning of "mene mene teqel upharsin," if such can be postulated, has no significance for the narrative. The same may be said of Pharaoh's and Nebuchadnezzar's dreams, which gain importance only as interpreted by Joseph and Daniel.

Daniel's interpretations evidently involve paronomasia, a play on words. Daniel successfully rewrites an ungrammatical sequence of signs to devise coherent statements, in which the initially inscribed words are modified slightly. *Mene* becomes *menah*: "God has *numbered* your kingdom and brought it to an end"; *teqel* becomes *teqiltah*: "You are *weighed* in the balance, and are found wanting"; *upharsin* first becomes *peres*, then *perisat* and *paras*: "Your kingdom is *divided*, and given to the Medes and the Persians" (Dan. 5:26–28). The essential matter is not what the inscription "in fact" means but what Daniel makes it mean. His approach to the writing on the wall may be conceived as an emblem of dream interpretation and of interpretation in general. Daniel's interpretation does not ncessarily arrive at the definitive meaning of the words he interprets—as scholars have abundantly shown. Nevertheless, his interpretation does convince those for whom it is intended, and within the fiction the results he predicts do occur.

After Daniel's second dream interpretation to Nebuchadnezzar, the king follows the course outlined by the prophecy and becomes mad; and after Daniel's prophecy to Belshazzar, "that very night Belshazzar, the king of the Chaldeans, was slain" (Dan. 5:30). This event may reflect the double meaning ascribed by rabbinic commentators to the verse, "as he interpreted to us, so it was" (Gen. 41:13). On the one hand, perhaps Daniel correctly predicts what will happen. Or, on the other hand, perhaps Daniel influences the events he prophesies, and helps to produce the effects he predicts. Even if Daniel does not take part in a conspiracy with Darius the Mede, he may foresee that a rebellion is imminent.

As a literary whole, the narrative in its present form claims to depict Daniel's rise to power through the hand of God. But if the writing of God's hand is open to such divergent interpretations, then His larger theological meanings are not necessarily secure. To follow Daniel's example would be

---

(Ph.D. diss., Johns Hopkins University, 1893); and Otto Eissfeldt, "Die Menetekel-Inschrift und ihre Deutung," *Zeitschrift für die alttestamentliche Wissenschaft* 63 (1951), 105–14. See also André Lacocque, *Le livre de Daniel*, pp. 84–86.

to recognize the multiple significations of dreams and texts, and to invent their meaning anew in conjunction with a prospective future. Although Joseph and Daniel seem to pierce through disguises, their commentaries may also be marked by further deceptions and distortions, rather than by sheer revelations of naked truth.

"Your God . . . Will Deliver You"

Daniel's subsequent encounter with the lions recasts the episode in which his three companions miraculously escape from Nebuchadnezzar's furnace.[33] Meanwhile, the story gradually shifts from questions of dream visions to problems associated with writing. Thus when Darius, like Nebuchadnezzar (Dan. 3:4–6), requires a ritual obeisance from his subjects, he does not simply proclaim this command, but is persuaded to write it. Darius's officers wish to trap Daniel by placing him at variance with an irrevocable decree.

Daniel is caught between Jewish practice and a Babylonian decree against petitions other than those made to the king; he shows his faith by unswervingly obeying what he understands to be God's command. Darius appears content to make an exception for his favored minister, yet when the king's other officers discover Daniel praying to the Jewish God, they remind Darius, employing the familiar form of rhetorical questioning: "Have you not signed a decree that every man who shall address a petition to any God or man besides you, O king, during the next thirty days, shall be thrown into a lions' den?" (Dan. 6:13). Again divine and human power, or the decrees of divine and human hands, come into conflict. The narrative repeatedly depicts kings' threats to Jewish practices. In this case, Darius "set his heart on Daniel to deliver him," only to discover that his hands are tied by the decree he has signed.

Whereas Nebuchadnezzar has said to Daniel's companions, "What God is there that can deliver you from my hand?" (Dan. 3:15), Darius says with some trepidation but without irony to Daniel, before throwing him to the lions, "Your God, whom you serve continually, will deliver you" (Dan. 6:17). He doubts his own words until Daniel has survived his overnight stay in the lions' den. In a letter to the peoples of the earth (Dan. 6:25–27), analogous to Nebuchadnezzar's letter (Dan. 3:31–4:34), Darius acknowledges the Jewish God. Finally accepting a hand or power that is beyond

---

33. There is also a distant echo of the early moment in the precursor story, when Joseph's brothers throw him into a pit. The Joseph-Daniel pair thus comes full circle when the dream interpreter is rescued from the malicious hands of those who envy him.

human force, the king refers to "the living God . . . who delivers and saves, and performs signs and wonders in heaven and on earth" (Dan. 6:26–27). As evidence, Darius writes that Daniel's God saved him "from the hand of the lions" (Dan. 6:28).

The *hand* is a key word and figure in this narrative.[34] In Babylonia, foreign kings repeatedly exert their power over the Jews, who resist when a secular hand interferes with the invisible hand of God. The hand that wields power is also the hand that can sign unalterable decrees, but the Book of Daniel shows that no royal hand can imprint the final word on a man's life.[35] On the contrary, God can annul what a king's hand commands, and can even produce a miraculous writing hand that condemns a sacrilegious king. An underlying premise, which the narrative strives to confirm, is that human hands are bound unless they act in accordance with what God's hand requires. Daniel's authority as prophet rests on his interpretive ability to read the writing on the wall and to foretell the fate that is signified by a dream vision. Daniel's activity as dream interpreter suggests a deterministic view, not of individual character, but of God's propitious influence. Acts of interpretation indicate a divinely favored destiny and refer equally to dreams and texts.[36]

The use of the word "hand" (*yad*) in contexts suggesting "power" is an anthropomorphizing figure of speech. Prophets also depend on figuration when they reveal higher realities and deeper truths. There can be no ultimately literal representation of divine sense, for language intrinsically relies on rhetoric and disguise.

Rabbinic traditions, then, revise the meaning of prophetic dream interpretation. "As he interpreted to us, so it was," applied to Joseph and Daniel, comes to mean that the prophet exerts power over the events he predicts. In connection with textual interpretation, this view may provoke doubts over the determinate meaning of a biblical verse such as "mene mene teqel upharsin." We need not conclude that interpretation is arbitrary and open to infinite variation, although the writing on the wall is still enig-

---

34. For discussions of key words and *Leitwörter* in biblical narrative, see: Robert Alter, *The Art of Biblical Narrative*, pp. 92–97, 179–80; Martin Buber and Franz Rosenzweig, *Die Schrift und ihre Verdeutschung* (Berlin: Schocken, 1936), pp. 211–38 and 262–75; and Martin Buber, *Werke* (Munich: Kösel, 1964), vol. 2, pp. 1095–1182.

35. Compare the Book of Esther, and an article by Ludwig A. Rosenthal illustrating the parallels: "Die Josephsgeschichte, mit den Büchern Ester und Daniel verglichen," *Zeitschrift fur die alttestamentliche Wissenschaft* 15 (1895), 278–84.

36. See Asher Finkel, "The Pesher of Dreams and Scriptures," *Revue de Qumran* 4 (1963), 357–70.

matic. Interpretation is not simply a cognitive process of discovery, but a performative act of invention. Daniel, a reader of cryptic words, invents fate by reinscribing the inscription into a new narrative. The interpreter's narrative gives direction to the life of the dreamer, as rabbinic commentators knew—and occasionally feared.

Daniel's activity as reader of a divine inscription parallels rabbinic interpreters' conception of oral Torah as a reading of written Torah. This association is not surprising, since dreams were conceived as texts to be interpreted. Talmudic and later rabbinic discussions of dream interpretation extend the notion that an interpreter may play an active role in the fulfillment of prophecy.

Repudiating Joseph and Daniel, Freud claimed to place responsibility on the dreamer, whose retelling and associations provide clues to the dream thoughts. Freud based his research on the past and situated dreams in the context of prior mental processes, disregarding what biblical interpreters took for granted: that every dreamer is most concerned with the implications of a dream. Although Freud conceived free associations as leading back to the dream thoughts, his method also encouraged a forward glance; he tacitly aimed his theories of dream interpretation toward the future, which is integral to every curative practice. Biblical dream interpretation thus supports an aspect of Freudian psychoanalysis that Freud was reluctant to acknowledge. Uneasy with the model of displacement, Freud shied away from the fullest consequences of his novel method.

Whereas Daniel read the writing on the wall, in an ambitious fantasy Freud imagined an inscription on the wall of his house, a marble plaque that would recall his accomplishment to future generations: "Here, on 24 July 1895, the secret of dreams was revealed to Dr. Sigm. Freud" (*AP/OP*, letter 137). The inscription Daniel reads points toward the future; Freud's engraving invents a future that preserves the past.

3

BAR HEDIA AND R. ISHMAEL:
BATTLES OF INTERPRETATION

Freud was understandably ambivalent toward Talmudic and Midrashic traditions of dream interpretation, for these sources both affirm and dispute the interpreter's power.[1] They provoke reevaluation of the task of the dream interpreter by suggesting that interpretations, rather than dreams themselves, can prophesy or alter future events. Rabbinic sources do not in general conceive the meaning of a dream as a divine message or plan; the meaning of a dream lies beyond it, and may be modified by an interpretation. Dream texts receive their meaning retrospectively, from the dreamer and from every interpreter called upon for assistance.

---

1. In a footnote of 1914 (*Td* 32n/*ID* 38n), Freud cites two recent works on Judaic dream interpretation: Adolf Löwinger, *Der Traum in der jüdischen Literatur* (Leipzig: M. W. Kaufmann, 1908), and Chaim Lauer, "Das Wesen des Traumes in der Beurteilung der talmudischen und rabbinischen Literatur," *Internationale Zeitschrift für Psychoanalyse und "Imago"* 1 (1913), 459–69. Later, Freud would also have read B. Cohen's "Über Traumdeutung in der jüdischen Tradition," *Imago* 18 (1932), 117–21, and Immanuel Velikovsky, "Psychoanalytische Ahnungen in der Traumdeutungskunst der alten Hebräer nach dem Traktat Brachoth," *Psychoanalytische Bewegung* 5 (1933), 66–69. Yoram Bilu mentions these essays in his "Sigmund Freud and Rabbi Yehudah: On a Jewish Mystical Tradition of 'Psychoanalytic' Dream Interpretation," *Journal of Psychological Anthropology* 2 (1979), 443–63. Despite Freud's awareness of the relevant passages, however, he neither wrote seriously about rabbinic views nor repudiated them as he rejected the methods of Joseph.

The discussion of dreams in the Babylonian Talmud, tractate Berakhot, raises central questions of interpretive method and validity. This extensive compilation of rabbinic views combines theories and narratives, legal assertions *(halakhot)* and legendary stories *(aggadot)*. Twentieth-century psychologists, philosophers, and intellectual historians have only scratched the surface of the chapter on dreams.[2] Sigmund (Solomon) Freud, when he learned of the last chapter of Berakhot and the parallel passage in Lamentations Rabbah, had reason to suppress the narratives they contain. Freud could not have dismissed the rabbinic discussions of dream interpretation as readily as he did their biblical precedents; the Talmud and Midrash cast two dream interpreters in the role of villain, when dream analyses expose a dreamer, his family, and the interpreter to mortal danger. In response to the challenge of the Talmud, Freudian theory would have to reconsider the quasi-prophetic effects achieved by suggestion.

Rabbinic voices in the Talmud and Midrash anticipate several aspects of Freud's work on dreams. First, in their underlying assumptions: rabbinic traditions emphasize the importance and complexity of interpretation. Second, in their skepticism: rabbis occasionally express disbelief and antagonism toward dream interpreters who claim to make prophetic pronouncements. Third, in their techniques: rabbinic commentators frequently arrive at their results by resorting to puns and verbal associations. Finally, in their content: some rabbis insinuate the sexual significance of dreams. Such resonances do not, however, imply a direct influence on Freud, who labored incessantly to avoid coming to terms with his precursors.

---

2. See Erich Fromm, *The Forgotten Language* (New York: Holt, Rinehart and Winston, 1951), pp. 127–30; David Bakan, *Sigmund Freud and the Jewish Mystical Tradition* (Boston: Beacon, 1958), pp. 257–63; Sandor Lorand, "Dream Interpretation in the Talmud," in *The New World of Dreams*, ed. Ralph L. Woods and Herbert B. Greenhouse (New York: Macmillan, 1974), pp. 150–58; and Susan A. Handelman, *The Slayers of Moses: The Emergence of Rabbinic Interpretation in Modern Literary Theory* (Albany: State University of New York Press, 1982), p. 129. The closest readings of Berakhot 55a–57a to date are contained in Gérard Haddad's *L'enfant illégitime: Sources talmudiques de la psychanalyse* (Paris: Hachette, 1981), pp. 207–21, and Emmanuel Levinas's "Quelques vues talmudiques sur le rêve," in *La psychanalyse est-elle une histoire juive?* ed. Adélie and Jean-Jacques Rassial (Paris: Editions du Seuil, 1981), pp. 114–28. The Talmudic discussion of dreams has not been included in popular anthologies. See, for example, *A Rabbinic Anthology*, ed. C. G. Montefiore and H. Loewe (London: Macmillan, 1938), and *Everyman's Talmud*, ed. Abraham Cohen (New York: E. P. Dutton, 1949). The major exception is Alexander Kristianpoller's *Traum und Traumdeutung*, in *Monumenta Talmudica*, vol. 4, pt. 2 (Vienna: Harz, 1923).

Berakhot contains theoretical statements on dreams, legends about notable interpretations, and explanations of common symbols. The relevant passage raises controversial problems of dream interpretation; to the extent that textual interpretation resembles dream interpretation, the Talmud uncovers risks inherent in all commentary. In this problematic situation, Midrashic texts attempt to differentiate sharply between rabbinic interpreters and their rivals.

"A Dream That Is Not Interpreted . . . "

The discussion of dreams in Berakhot opens by attributing several sayings to R. Chisda. One simile compares dreams to texts: "A dream that is not interpreted is like a letter that is not read."[3] This figurative equation poses problems that set the tone of the passage. R. Chisda suggests that a dream awaits interpretation, as a letter demands reading. A Freudian might comment that dreams contain censored messages from the unconscious, which require special techniques in order to be read. R. Chisda perhaps indicates that dreams can be interpreted because they are like letters.[4] He also points out that if we do not interpret our dreams, this is like ignoring a message we have received. Yet R. Chisda's words resist translation into a proposition, and his saying does not specify the ethical implications of the analogy; this statement may hint that it is better not to open some dream letters. Following the Midrashic commentary on Genesis 41:13, Rashi translates the elusive simile into more concrete and evaluative terms: "Such a dream is neither good nor bad, because all dreams follow their interpretation." Rashi alludes to the belief that only interpretation bestows positive or negative meaning on a dream. Sometimes the emotional response to a dream already acts as a kind of interpretation, however, so that we may not be as free in dealing with dreams as we are in deciding whether to read a letter.

The source of the dream, if it is analogous to the sender of a letter, remains obscure. Berakhot 55b subsequently cites the conflicting views that dreams may be granted by angels *(malakhim)* or aroused by evil spirits

---

3. Berakhot 55a. Translations are based on the original text of tractate Berakhot, chap. 9, henceforth cited as "Ber." with references to the traditional page numbers. In English, see *The Babylonian Talmud, Seder Zeraᶜim*, vol. 1, ed. I. Epstein and trans. Maurice Simon (London: Soncino, 1948), and *The Talmud: Berakhoth*, ed. A. Zvi Ehrman, vol. 4 (Jerusalem: El-ᶜAm, 1982).

4. R. Chisda's statement is not, however, necessarily equivalent to a positive assertion. "A dream that is not interpreted is like a letter that is not read" need not imply that an interpreted dream is like a read letter.

(shedim).[5] According to another opinion, in contrast, a dream is shown to a man only from "the thoughts of his heart" (Ber. 55b).[6] Transcendent and immanent explanations of dream origins appear to compete. The transcendent theory conceives dreams as minor prophecies, like letters sent from God; the immanent conception suggests that dreams derive from subjective thought processes. Yet the sharp distinction between these two poles ultimately breaks down, since both views recognize language—at once a subjective and an impersonal phenomenon—as the origin of dreams and the locus of their meaning. The opposition between transcendence and immanence reappears as two modes of language, centered around scriptural allusions and personal associations.

R. Chisda neither advises nor discourages the opening of dream letters, for the consequences are unpredictable. This leads to a skeptical view of dream prophecy, when R. Chisda adds that "the sadness of a bad dream is sufficient to it, and the joy of a good dream is sufficient to it" (Ber. 55a). No further consequences need be anticipated; awakening from a bad dream brings relief, whereas awakening from a good dream may bring disappointment. Paradoxically, he also states that "a bad dream is preferable to a good dream" (ibid.).[7] R. Chisda's chain of assertions might then imply that bad news in a letter is better than good news, or that a dream from an evil spirit is better than a dream from an angel. The difficulties are too easily reconciled by Rashi's gloss: "For it [the bad dream] brings a man to

---

5. Compare Chagigah 5b: "Although I [God] have hidden my face from him [the prophet], yet I will speak with him in a dream." The biblical source is Numbers 12:6, in which God tells Moses, Aaron, and Miriam that "if there is a prophet among you, I make myself known to him in a vision, and speak to him in a dream." Berakhot never resolves the dualistic tensions that may result from attributing some dreams to demons.

6. In its reference to thoughts of the heart, the Talmud alludes to Daniel 2:30. There are several other points of contact between Berakhot and the early chapters of Daniel. When King Nebuchadnezzar requests a dream interpretation, he asks to be told both the dream and its meaning (Dan. 2:26). Later, King Belshazzar asks that Daniel "read this writing, and make known its meaning" (Dan. 5:16). These passages perhaps influence the Talmudic notions that a dream is like a letter, and that interpretation revises the dream text.

7. Earlier in the Gemara (Ber. 55a), we learn of three things that require divine mercy: a good king, a good year, and a good dream. The commentator proves the latter by means of wordplay, quoting Isaiah 38:16, "And you will restore me and make me live." In this phrase, "restore me" *(v'tachalimeni)* contains the root of the verb "to dream" *(ch-l-m)*, which creates an undercurrent of meaning: make me have a dream, and I will live.

repentance.'' In accordance with this conception, R. Huna comments that "a good man is not shown a good dream, and a bad man is not shown a bad dream" (Ber. 55b). The impression arises that the response to a dream is even more decisive than the dream itself; Berakhot gradually refutes the assumption that dreams are intrinsically good or bad. The simile that likens dreams and letters also challenges our ordinary ideas of reading, because the message of a dream is not fixed, and depends on the interpretation it receives. If interpretation influences the significance of a dream, then there appear to be no univocally good or bad dreams; the dreamer is most endangered by negative interpretation. As a result, R. Chisda intimates, it may be best to avoid dwelling on the meaning of dreams, potentially causing misfortune.

Berakhot 55b explains how to cancel the effects of disturbing dreams: "One who sees a dream and whose soul is grieved will go and have it interpreted before three [men].''[8] More precisely, one should not interpret the bad dream, thereby strengthening its message, but merely improve it. The dreamer who feels grieved has, in a sense, already performed an interpretation. Such a person should go to three others and say, "I have seen a good dream,'' to which they must respond, "Good it is and good may it be.'' To cancel negative consequences, the three others must repeat biblical verses that refer to three turns, three redemptions, and three assurances of peace. To make a bad dream good is to displace it by returning to repentance, redemption, and peace—in scriptural contexts. This and the following procedure have entered the traditional ritual known as "improvement of a dream *(hatavat chalom)*,'' just as another prayer has been incorporated into the priestly blessing for the benefit of those who have dreamed but do not remember their dreams. Such rituals are attributed with the power to reverse negative effects.[9] Similarly, one of the Amoraim made a practice of annulling negative dreams and enhancing positive dreams. When he had a bad dream, Samuel cited Zechariah 10:2, saying, "And the dreams speak falsehood.'' When he had a good dream, he modified this phrase, saying, "Do the dreams speak falsehood?'' Then he added a verse from Numbers 12:6, recalling that "I [God] will speak with him in a dream" (Ber. 55b).

---

8. The number three suggests a legal court *(bet din)*, illustrating the close connection between the legend *(aggadah)* and law *(halakhah)* related to dreams.

9. Compare Nedarim 8a: If a man dreams that he has been excommunicated, a *minyan* of ten must release him from the dream. In this case, the dream and its fulfillment are treated as if they were identical; the dream performs its meaning. According to Shabbat 11a, fasting can also serve to cancel bad dreams. For further halakhic references, see the article on *hatavat chalom* in the *Entsiqlopedia Talmudit*, ed. S. J. Zevin (Jerusalem: Talmudic Encyclopedia, 1980), vol. 7, pp. 753–58.

As in the ritual of *hatavat chalom*, Samuel employed scriptural intertexts to assure either a positive outcome or the elimination of negative effects.

"All Dreams Follow the Mouth"

Prophetic dreams are commonly misunderstood as visual images of future events, albeit in disguised or distorted forms. Talmudic stories show that the actual locus of dream prophecy is neither the dream nor even the reported dream text. In the narrowest sense, a prophecy must state what will occur in the future; since dreams seldom provide such direct statements, their prophetic content depends on interpretation. A prophetic dream interpretation must, on the basis of a dream report, conclude that some future reality is imminent. Such a prophecy is fulfilled when the dreamer accepts it, perceiving a correspondence between the prediction and later events. This is not the only sense in which prophecy is attributed to biblical prophets; Hebrew and Aramaic sources refer to the prophet *(navi)* more broadly, as one who can speak God's words.

Certain voices in the Talmud propose that dreams may be God-given and prophetic although they do not literally represent what will happen. Dream distortions are inescapable, for "just as there is no wheat without straw, so there is no dream without worthless things" (Ber. 55a). Because even prophetic dreams are not literal representations, interpretation is necessary. The freedom of interpretation leads rabbinic authorities to fear that dream interpreters may retrospectively rewrite the dream message, and cause whatever they predict.

According to a long line of Tannaim, when R. Bana³ah went to twenty-four interpreters with a single dream, "each interpreted differently, and all of their interpretations were fulfilled." This story culminates in a metaphorically complex phrase: "All dreams follow the mouth *(Kol ha-chalomot holkhim achar ha-peh)*."[10] The Gemara asks whether this phrase is scriptural, as is implied by the introductory word, *she-ne³emar*, "as it is said." This is not a biblical verse, although it purportedly derives from Genesis 41:13, when Pharaoh's chief baker explains that "as he interpreted to us, so it was." If "the mouth" is a synecdoche for the interpreter, and if "dreams" stand for prophetic consequences, then this assertion indicates

---

10. Ber. 55b. Kristianpoller discusses the Midrashic versions of this formulation in his *Traum und Traumdeutung*, in *Monumenta Talmudica*, vol. 4, pt. 2, pp. 37n and 52n. Löwinger, in *Der Traum in der jüdischen Literatur*, pp. 25–27, oversimplifies this metaphorical assertion by viewing *peh* as a scribal error for an abbreviated spelling of *pitron*. But Löwinger also cites traditions, contained in the *En Ya³akov*, which take this "mouth" literally: "After an opulent meal at night, one has many and confused dreams; thus all dreams follow the mouth that takes in food."

that a prophetic dream will be fulfilled in accordance with its interpretation. Nevertheless, there are other senses in which "all dreams follow the mouth." After an emperor is told what he will see in his dream, he thinks about it all day and sees it at night (Ber. 56a). It is not clear whose mouth has the power to influence dreams or their consequences. In the case of the emperor, the words he hears during the day are the "residues" (Freudian *Tagesreste)* that return in his dream. But the words that are spoken after a dream, by the dreamer and the interpreter who retell and evaluate it, may also dominate or create meaning. At stake is the relationship between dreams and speech, as between Scripture and commentary, the written and the oral Torah.

The Talmud does not support an unquestioning belief in dream prophecy. A dream may be a minor prophecy (Ber. 55b; compare Genesis Rabbah 17:5), and yet "there is no dream without worthless things."[11] The manifest content of a dream always contains trivial elements; even a prophetic dream requires interpretation. When R. Bana'ah tells his dream to twenty-four interpreters, their interpretations are all fulfilled, but there is no way to determine whether the prophecies inhere in the dream or generate the effects that follow. Modern psychology cannot easily disregard the suspicion that, as "all dreams follow the mouth," dream interpreters perform self-fulfilling prophecies. In order for this to happen, the dreamer need only perceive or create conditions that reflect the interpretation. When interpretation is combined with powers of suggestion, as facilitated by the transference relationship between analyst and patient, the dreamer is indeed likely to enact whatever the interpreter proposes. As the Midrash on Genesis 41:13 comments that "all follows the interpretation," Talmudic sources are eminently aware of the pitfalls of dream interpretation. Dreams are like written messages, the meaning of which appears to be altered by acts of reading.

A lively tale of Bar Hedia illustrates the dangers of dream interpretation and at the same time modifies all previous theoretical assertions. The Gemara never definitively establishes whether the interpreter is a mercenary quack, a man capable of providing dreams' prophetic content, or both. In any event, the text unmistakably shows antagonism between the rabbi (Raba) and the dream interpreter (Bar Hedia). This story opens with a blunt statement of the economics of dream interpretation: "Bar Hedia was an interpreter of dreams. To one who gave him money, he interpreted for good, and to one who did not give him money, he interpreted for evil" (Ber. 56a). Bar Hedia's example suggests that dreams are in themselves

---

11. Skeptical voices in the Talmud frequently repeat that "things of a dream are worthless." See, for example, Sanhedrin 30a, Baraita. Deep, unspoken tensions characterize the relationship between dreams and Scripture.

neither good nor bad, and that the interpreter may impose a positive or a negative meaning. His story begins in a humorous vein and becomes increasingly tragic. At first, dream interpretation is simply a business, for which Bar Hedia is obliged to accept money. Serious matters are at stake, however, because his prophecies are fulfilled.

Abaye and Raba are famous rivals who disagree about many issues including the nature of dream interpretation, and who test Bar Hedia's interpretive powers by bringing him identical dreams. Abaye bets on Bar Hedia's talents, while Raba doubts them; consequently Abaye pays the usual fee, while Raba does not. In this context, then, Abaye represents the view that dream interpretation may be prophetic. Raba either believes that dream interpretation has no prophetic power, or that the power of dreams is contained in them, apart from interpretation. As a student and son-in-law of R. Chisda, Raba should know better, for R. Chisda's ideas about dreams include the comparison of an uninterpreted dream to an unread letter. He might have guessed that reading a dream letter could have drastic consequences. Raba and his family suffer as a result of his skepticism concerning Bar Hedia's prophetic interpretations.

In accordance with his business practices, Bar Hedia interprets identical dream reports positively to Abaye and negatively to Raba. While Abaye and Raba say that they have dreamed identically, at first they refer only to scriptural verses that appear in their dreams. This makes Bar Hedia's dream interpretations virtually equivalent to textual interpretations. Implicitly, then, Abaye and Raba disagree over methods of understanding the Bible and over Bar Hedia's claims to read Scripture as prophesying an individual's future. Previously, scriptural passages assisted the evaluation and amelioration of dreams. At this point, Scripture constitutes the dreams, underscoring the parallel between dream interpreters and rabbinic commentators.

To Abaye, Bar Hedia interprets: "Your business will prosper. . . . You will have numerous sons and daughters"; to Raba, he interprets: "Your business will fail. . . . Your wife will die" (Ber. 56a). Raba returns to Bar Hedia alone and recounts additional dreams without offering payment. Bar Hedia interprets: "Your sons and daughters will die. . . . You will receive two blows." A light moment intervenes, signaling that Raba has begun to acknowledge Bar Hedia's powers. After he hears Bar Hedia's most recent prophecies, Raba finds two blind men quarreling in the House of Study. He tries to separate them, and they strike him twice, fulfilling Bar Hedia's prophecy. They are about to hit him again, but he objects with a mixture of humor and resignation: "Enough! [In my dream, as interpreted] I saw only two!" (ibid.).

Some time later, probably after the death of his wife and children, Raba cedes to Bar Hedia's monetary demands. Finally Bar Hedia interprets

Raba's most recent dreams positively: "You will acquire wealth without limit. . . . Abaye will die and his school will go to you. . . . Your learning will be spread throughout the world. . . . Miracles will happen to you" (Ber. 56a). This final prophecy is a connecting link to the next story.[12] Bar Hedia has shown himself to be a merciless businessman, resolved to prophesy the worst for those who do not pay him.[13] Yet not until their next encounter does Raba believe he understands what Bar Hedia has done.

The dream interpreter and Raba are traveling in a boat when Bar Hedia recalls his previous prophecy and asks himself: "Why should I travel with a man to whom miracles will happen?" He perhaps imagines that the boat will sink and that only Raba will be miraculously saved. Bar Hedia's thought implies confidence in his own prophecy combined with the hope that it can be delayed or deflected. Bar Hedia attempts a quick escape, but "as he was disembarking, a book fell from him. Raba found it, and saw *(chazah)* written in it: All dreams follow the mouth" (Ber. 56a). A text within the text—perhaps an early dream manual—reveals one of Bar Hedia's interpretive principles. Either Raba was not previously aware of this maxim, or he did not realize that it played a part in Bar Hedia's interpretations. Raba instantly assumes that "all dreams follow the mouth" indicates the interpreter's power to influence events. When this theoretical proposition, already mentioned in the Talmudic discussion, becomes an active force in the story, Raba exclaims: "You wicked man! It was all fulfilled through your hand, and gave me all this great pain." In his angry response, Raba conceives the metaphoric dictum to mean that dreams' consequences follow the interpreter's mouth; Raba finally admits the power of dream interpretation. Raba also wields power, and now curses Bar Hedia: "May it be God's will that this man be given over into the hands of a kingdom that has no pity on him." Curses, like dream prophecies, may predetermine events; dream prophecies may also work essentially as curses, as in the stories of R. Ishmael and his students.

Bar Hedia's desperate reaction helps to fulfill the curse. Convinced that "a wise man's curse, even if undeserved, comes to pass," Bar Hedia sees no escape from punishment. He believes that he has been justly blamed, for he understands that interpretation may produce prophetic ef-

---

12. This prophecy also recalls the Mishna that opens Berakhot, chapter 9, which prescribes a benediction for "one who sees a place where miracles were performed for Israel" (Ber. 54a). These words of the Mishna allude to the crossing of the Red Sea, and contextualize the present references to the *Hallel* and to miracles.

13. Bar Hedia's demands may appear in a new light if, as Freud argues in connection with his fees, the payment is an essential part of the interpretive process without which he cannot perform.

fects such as the death of Raba's wife. Like Raba, who insists on receiving only two blows because the interpretation of his dream predicted only two, through his actions Bar Hedia effectively fulfills a curse. He flees in order to atone for his sin by exiling himself among the Romans, and Bar Hedia's story repeats itself. While he sits at the doorway of the emperor's wardrobe, the overseer recounts dreams. Bar Hedia's mercenary practices have not changed, and he refuses to offer interpretations without payment. After some time has passed, he nonetheless proclaims the meaning of what the overseer has dreamed: "Worms have been eating all the silks." The emperor prepares to punish the overseer for his negligence, but the man shrewdly displaces the guilt: "Why me? Bring the man who knew and did not tell!" All assume that the dream interpreter knew what was happening to the silks from the outset. Bar Hedia meets a terrible end, symbolically suited to his manner of giving equivocal interpretations: he is strapped to two cedars that are tied together, and when the rope is released, he is torn apart.

No clear lines separate the experience, recollection, transcription, translation, and evaluation of a dream; similarly, there is no firm distinction between fictive and prophetic contents. According to one reading, the saying "all dreams follow the mouth" means that the interpreter is a kind of sorcerer whose prophecies are invariably fulfilled. Another reading suggests that the interpreter may be a powerful personality whose suggestions influence the dreamer's future actions. The prophesied future is not intrinsic to the dream; it is actualized by an interpreter. The narrative of Bar Hedia, Raba, and Abaye does not merely illustrate this abstract statement, but proposes several possible interpretations and revisions. One conclusion is self-evident: dream interpreters can be dangerous both to others and to themselves. The meaning of dreams lies beyond them, and their interpretation may alter actions and events.

The story of Bar Hedia thus revises the meaning first given to the adage it contains. "All dreams follow the mouth" comes to mean, in part, that dream interpreters may create prophetic results by imposing their interpretations. This justifies Raba's initial skepticism, and yet the story narrates Raba's realization that dream interpretations do have prophetic potential. Thus he cannot forgive Bar Hedia's prediction about his wife, which anticipates her death. The assertion that "all dreams follow the mouth" hints at the linguistic structures that precondition dreams and the power of language to modify reality.

"Your Father Has Left You Money in Cappadocia"

Following the story of Bar Hedia's execution, the Talmudic discussion takes a new turn. The statement that "all dreams follow the mouth" does not receive a definitive commentary, and the relationship between interpretation and prophetic consequences remains inconclusive. In any event, since "mouth" is a figure for the interpreter or his interpretation, the significance of dreams appears to depend on language. This idea conforms to both Talmudic and Freudian practices of dream interpretation. The dream work and linguistic reformulation of a dream turn out to be essential to dream interpretation, and in practice they constitute the primary dream reality; this is a further sense in which "all dreams follow the mouth." As in its usual exegetical procedures, the Gemara places special emphasis on the linguistic component in dream interpretation. Whereas Freudian psychology bases its interpretations on personal associations of the dreamer, however, Talmudic interpreters most frequently associate dreams with scriptural language. In their milieu, Scripture provided familiar associations for a wide range of dreamers.

The Talmud offers numerous examples of dream interpretation on the basis of wordplay. According to one story, Bar Kappara tells Rabbi of a dream in which his nose *(af)* falls off. Because Hebrew and Aramaic employ the word for "nose" in expressions describing anger, Rabbi interprets: "Seething anger *(charon af)* has been removed from you." Similarly, Bar Kappara dreams that others tell him: "You will die in the month of Adar and not see Nisan." Rabbi converts these Hebrew names of months into signifiers, and interprets: "You will die in all honor *(adruta),* and not come into temptation *(nissayon)*" (Ber. 56b).[14] Wordplay of this kind is prominent in rabbinic commentary; the commentators would have maintained that to recognize the interactions of Hebrew signs is to receive God's meanings, not to impose or project one's own.[15] The rabbis assume that the essential structure of signification is divine, and for this reason dreams must be in-

---

14. The Palestinian Talmud, Maʿaser Sheni 4:6, ascribes this positive interpretation to R. Akiba. See also the parallel account in Lamentations Rabbah 1:1:16, in which R. Jochanan performs the interpretations. These are evidently stock tales without clear historical basis.

15. For a general discussion of wordplay in rabbinic interpretation, see Isaac Heineman, *Darkhei ha-aggadah* (Jerusalem: The Magnes Press, 1970), pp. 103–30. Saul Lieberman's section on "Rabbinic Interpretation of Scripture," in *Hellenism in Jewish Palestine* (New York: Jewish Theological Seminary, 1950), demonstrates the broader context of dream interpretation based on linguistic operations (pp. 47–82). See Ronald N. Brown, *The Enjoyment of Midrash: The Use of the Pun in Genesis Rabbah* (Ph.D. diss., Brown University, 1980), for countless examples. In connection with the role of words and wordplay in dream interpretation, see also Baba Kama 55a, Berakhot 57a, and the Palestinian Talmud, Maʿaser Sheni 4:6. Kristianpoller collects and comments on these passages in his *Traum und Traumdeutung,* in *Monumenta Talmudica,* vol. 4, pt. 2, pp. 46–49.

terpreted in accordance with scriptural language. But even an appropriate allusion to Scripture requires interpretation, and does not simply convey the literal meaning of a dream.

While Freud finds meaning through free associations of the individual, Talmudic dream interpretations, like rabbinic commentaries, center on quotations from Scripture. Textual tradition is the basis for a shared symbolic code. For instance: "One who sees a reed *(qaneh)* in a dream may hope for wisdom, as it is said, 'Acquire *(q'neh)* wisdom' [Proverbs 4:5]." If one sees several reeds *(qanim)*, one may expect understanding, "because it is written, 'And with all your acquisitions *(qinyanekha)*, get *(q'ne)* understanding' [Proverbs 4:7]." According to Baba Kama 55a, the letter *Tet* is a good sign in a dream, because this letter first appears in the Torah when God creates light and sees that it is good *(tov)*. Later passages in Berakhot 56b–57a explain diverse dream images by reference to Scripture. This practice supports the belief that dreams are sent by God, at least in the sense that God's Torah is the key to meaning and truth. Rabbinic sources actively prescribe recourse to Scripture; to assure good outcomes of dreams it is essential to place their imagery in a favorable scriptural context. If one sees a river, one should say, "I will extend peace to her like a river" (Is. 66:12), in order to avoid the negative consequences of thinking, "for distress will come in like a river" (Is. 59:19). If one sees a bird, one should say, "as birds hovering, so [the Lord of hosts] will protect" (Is. 31:5), in order to forestall the association, "as a bird that wanders from its nest" (Prov. 27:8). The Talmud gives numerous examples of this kind.

One hardly knows what one has seen in a dream until it is placed in a scriptural context. Some sexually charged dreams lose their unsettling manifest content by being related to linguistic associations: "One who has intercourse with his mother *(imo)* in a dream may hope for understanding, for it is said, 'Yes, if *(im)* you call for understanding' [Prov. 2:3]." Or again, "One who has intercourse with a betrothed girl *(m'orasa)* may hope for Torah, for it is written, 'Moses commanded a Torah, an inheritance *(morasha)* of the congregation of Jacob' [Deut. 33:4]. Do not read *morasha*, but *m'orasa*" (Ber. 57a). In Freudian terms, the rabbis appear to deny sexual wishes by resorting to puns. From the Talmudic standpoint, however, such wordplays are not only possible, but necessary.[16]

In another case, local usage rather than Scripture provides the proof text: "One who sees a cat in a dream, in a place where it is called *shunara*—for him a beautiful song *(shira na'ah)* is made; in a place where it is called *shinara*, a change for the worse *(shinui ra^c)* will occur to him" (Ber. 56b). Such verbal plays on dialect variants begin to detract from Scripture as the exclusive place of signification.

---

16. Compare Haddad, *L'enfant illégitime*, pp. 216–18.

The dreams of an unnamed *min* (sectarian or heretic) illustrate both the linguistic subtleties and sexual significance of dreams. This passage is especially significant, since it enacts a drama of interpretation relating to R. Ishmael—who is remembered for his thirteen rules of scriptural commentary. R. Ishmael has no qualms about interpreting negatively, in this case, possibly because he is dealing with a notoriously wicked person; or perhaps the dreamer is called a sectarian precisely because he dreams at a distance from the language of Scripture. Berakhot 56b places R. Ishmael in a position of power, confidently revealing the meaning of dreams. The interpreter seems to anticipate certain Freudian precepts, and many of the interpretations refer to sexual transgressions. First, the sectarian dreams of pouring oil on an olive tree, and this image of oil returning to its source leads R. Ishmael to pronounce, "He has had intercourse with his mother." A dream of one eye kissing the other suggests to R. Ishmael, "He has had intercourse with his sister." A dream of kissing the moon indicates that "he has had intercourse with the wife of an Israelite." A dream of ravens coming to his bed signifies, according to R. Ishmael, that "your wife has prostituted herself with many men." Unlike Joseph and Daniel, in this story R. Ishmael interprets dreams in relation to the dreamer's mundane past. The interpretations are not prophetic, but diagnostic or descriptive; as Freud argued in general, these dreams are like symptoms that form part of the mental life of the dreamer. This conforms to the saying attributed to R. Jonathan: "A man is shown [a dream] only from the thoughts of his heart" (Ber. 55b). R. Ishmael is evidently a skillful judge of dreams' meanings, but he does not prophesy events. A long sequence of incriminating interpretations leads the dreamer to confess his guilt and confirm R. Ishmael's powers.

In Berakhot, after hearing several unfavorable interpretations, the sectarian dreamer adds, "I dreamed they were telling me: Your father has left you money in Cappadocia" (Ber. 56b). R. Ishmael first confirms that the dreamer has no money in that city, and that his father never went there. He then treats *Kapadokia* as a bilingual signifier, and interprets on the basis of linguistic clues. *Kapa* means either "beam" in Aramaic or "twenty" in Greek. *Dokos* means "beam," and *deka* means "ten," both in Greek. R. Ishmael interprets: "*Kapa* means 'beam' and *deka* means 'ten.' Go and examine the beam *(kapa)* which is at the head of ten, for it is full of coins." Even Freud would have had reason to be pleased with this story, when the dreamer returns home and finds coins at the tenth beam. [17] From a Freudian standpoint, this dream demonstrates the effectiveness of unconscious pro-

---

17. Gen. Rab. 68:12, Lam. Rab. 1:1:17, Sanhedrin 30a, and the Palestinian Talmud, Maʿaser Sheni 4:6, contain versions of this popular Cappadocia story. Compare Marcus Jastrow, *A Dictionary of the Targumim, the Talmud Babli and*

cesses; the dream seems to have revealed a repressed awareness. Yet money could also have been located near the twentieth beam, or nowhere at all; the interpreter chooses a meaning that the subsequent narrative confirms. The Gemara does not explain how the interpretation works, and only reaffirms that language is the blueprint for the world. Nevertheless, the presence of Greek words in a dream is troublesome; a serious threat lurks on the horizon if certain dreams are structured and deciphered by associations outside the Hebrew Scriptures.[18] The linguistic diaspora of the Jews threatens to displace the totalizing claims of Scripture when several languages signify infinitely and elusively, as does the holy tongue *(leshon ha-qadosh)*.

The rivalry between rabbis and other interpreters is most explicit in one parallel encounter between a later R. Ishmael and a Samaritan.[19] The variations in the two stories attest to the considerable anxieties and polemics associated with such meetings. In Berakhot 56b, the rabbi acts as dream interpreter, ruthlessly bringing to light the sectarian's sins. In Lamentations Rabbah, however, a Samaritan sets himself up as a dream interpreter, and R. Ishmael ben R. Yose comes to disparage him. Whereas Bar Hedia infamously gives opposite interpretations for a single dream, the Samaritan gives the same interpretation to many dreams, and R. Ishmael corrects his vague, empty prophecies:

> A Samaritan *(kuti)* made himself out to be an interpreter of dreams. R. Ishmael ben R. Yose heard this and said, "Shall I not go and see this foolish-hearted Samaritan who tricks people?" He went and sat by him. A person came and said, "In my dream I saw an olive tree feeding oil." The Samaritan told him, "The olive denotes light and

---

Yerushalmi, and the Midrashic Literature (1903; repr. New York: The Judaica Press, 1971), pp. 288, 1398. Because of the references to Greek in this example, Quf has been transliterated by "k."

18. Saul Lieberman's *Greek in Jewish Palestine* (New York: Jewish Theological Seminary, 1942) shows the extent to which Greek language permeated rabbinic thought, but de-emphasizes the associated threat to Hebrew and Aramaic which arose—as the linguistic concomitant of assimilation—in Hellenized Jewish culture. If the significance of dreams can derive from all the languages of the nations, for example, then prophecy threatens to exceed the boundaries of *leshon ha-qadosh*. Cf. Max Weinreich, *History of the Yiddish Language*, trans. Shlomo Noble and Joshua A. Fishman (Chicago: University of Chicago, 1980), pp. 59–65. Weinreich concludes that, despite the famous words of R. Judah concerning study of Greek wisdom, "in Greek there lurked danger for Jewishness" (p. 64).

19. The author wishes to express his debt to Bruce Birdsey, David Blumenthal, and Michael Swartz, who suggested several insights concerning this Midrashic variant.

oil denotes light; you will see light in much light." R. Ishmael said to the interpreter: "May that man's spirit faint! [The dream signifies that] he had intercourse with his mother." Another person came and said, "I dreamt that one of my eyes swallowed the other." He told him, "You will see light in much light." R. Ishmael ben R. Yose said to the interpreter, "May that man's spirit faint! That man has two children and one of them had intercourse with the other." Another came to him and said, "I dreamt that I swallowed a star." He told him, "You will see much light. The star denotes light and you are light, so it is light added to light." R. Ishmael said to the interpreter, "May that man's spirit faint! He has killed a Jew." Whence did R. Ishmael know this? From the verse, 'Look now toward heaven and count the stars' [Gen 15:5].[20]

In each instance, after the Samaritan offers a favorable, prophetic interpretation, R. Ishmael ben R. Yose curses him (in the third-person form) and asserts a more immediate and incriminating meaning. Only in the final interpretation cited here does R. Ishmael interpret in relation to Scripture. Concluding that a star symbolizes a Jew, as God suggests to Abraham in Genesis 15:5, R. Ishmael imposes a scriptural meaning on the dream of one who has already turned away from rabbinic views of Scripture. This explicit scene of rivalry over interpretation is absent from the story in Berakhot.

The subsequent dénouement recalls Bar Hedia's demise, but here R. Ishmael ben R. Yose self-righteously wields power. The rabbi exposes a dreamer to financial ruin, as if to punish him for his misguided faith in the Samaritan interpreter:

Another came and said, "I dreamt that everybody pointed their fingers at me." He [the Samaritan] told him, "You will rise to greatness and all will point their fingers at you." R. Ishmael said to the man, "Give me a fee and I will interpret for you"; but he replied, "It is already interpreted." The same man came again and said to the interpreter, "I dreamt that all the people were puffing at me with their cheeks and praising me with their fingers." He told him, "You will rise to greatness, and everybody will praise you with his cheeks." R. Ishmael said to him [the interpreter], "May that man's spirit faint! He has a store of wheat; and when he dreamt that people pointed their fingers at him, it denotes that the drippings [of the rain] had fallen

---

20. Lam. Rab. 1:1:14. Translations from Lamentations Rabbah are modified from *Midrash Rabbah*, 3d ed., ed. H. Freedman and Maurice Simon, trans. A. Cohen (London: Soncino, 1983), vol. 7, pp. 80–82.

upon it; and when he dreamt that people were puffing at him with their cheeks, it denotes that the wheat had become swollen; and when he dreamt that the people praised him with their fingers, it denotes that the wheat had sprouted so that he would get nothing from it." (Lam. Rab. 1:1:14)

The dreamer sustains a loss as a result of his lack of confidence in R. Ishmael, whose timely interpretation could have saved his store of wheat. Whereas Bar Hedia is executed for withholding his presumed knowledge of worms spoiling the Emperor's wardrobe, by showing his skill R. Ishmael triumphantly defeats a false interpreter.

The Midrash to Lamentations next describes the Samaritan's efforts to avenge himself on R. Ishmael ben R. Yose. He says, "I will go and see a certain old Jew who jeers at everybody" (Lam. Rab. 1:1:15). In an attempt to reverse the roles, he comes to the rabbi with a dream: "I dreamt of four cedars, four sycamores, a hide stuffed with straw, and an ox riding upon them." R. Ishmael ruthlessly foretells the Samaritan's death:

R. Ishmael said to him, "May that man's spirit faint! The four cedars are the four bedposts, the four sycamores are the four legs of the bed, the hide stuffed with straw indicates its cords, and the ox riding upon them is the leather mattress upon which you sleep. You will rise up [into bed] but not come down." And so it happened to him. (Ibid.)

The narrative shows its concern with punishing interpreters who oppose rabbinic interpretations.

This version of the story has special contextual significance. In connection with the Book of Lamentations, which mourns the fall of Jerusalem, Lamentations Rabbah contains a sequence of stories about the relationship between Jerusalemites and Athenians. Every Athenian who comes to Jerusalem is outwitted. These stories play on the anxious condition of Hellenized Jews, for whom Greek language and culture—and alternative forms of dream interpretation—potentially threatened the primacy of Scripture. This threat was obvious to R. Ishmael ben R. Yose, who reportedly sought to discredit a Samaritan interpreter.

Because Talmudic sources conceive Scripture as divine language, they suggest that dreams are most genuinely meaningful by juxtaposition with Scripture. Dreams do not intrinsically contain their prophetic power, but rather await fulfillment through a process of textual substitutions and displacements. While a scriptural passage is not the literal meaning of a dream, it can function as an intertext that makes interpretation possible. Ideally, a dream is associated with a biblical story that contains a favorable outcome. The rabbinic practices of interpretation struggle to ensure that

Jewish life will be defined by Scripture; an opposing view has, however, tacitly intervened: all linguistic associations are meaningful.

"Because of Your Mouth . . . "

Sefer Chasidim, a medieval work by German pietists, returns to and extends the Talmudic discussion of dreams. One lengthy analysis in this text focuses attention on the enigmatic ways in which "all dreams follow the mouth."[21] As in Lamentations Rabbah, highly charged interpretations take place during meetings between Jews and non-Jews.

A first example illustrates the possibly hazardous effects of dream interpretation: "One of the priests told a Jew one of his dreams. He interpreted it that they [the Christians] would give him [the priest] several matters of idol worship, and that he would approve them and teach the people to imitate the [pagan] nations" (par. 440). The implicit assumption is that Christians are not necessarily idolatrous, but that they are in danger of becoming so. A friend of the dream interpreter complains: "Since dreams follow the mouth, because of your mouth *(al piekha)* he [the dreamer] will perform idol worship." In more general terms, the paragraph comments that "whoever interprets to a Jew that he will sin, it is as if he caused him to sin." A moralistic conclusion completes the passage: "Although the interpreter may be a sage and know that even if he does not interpret, it will happen thus, even so he should not interpret that the man will fall into the hands of sin" (par. 440). The figures of "mouth" and "hand" interact, signaling the dangerous relationship between language and power. As a result of their linguistic force, negative dream interpretations play into the hands of evil.

The consequences of dream interpretation may follow the mouth of the interpreter, but *Sefer Chasidim* indicates that not all dreams derive from human thoughts. The problem is to distinguish between those dreams that come "at the hands of" angels, and those that come from demons. The pietists propose a simple criterion to determine which dreams do not come from angels: if while dreaming "a man thinks of a picture that he has seen and if he has [previously] thought the thought [which he dreams], this is not a dream at the hands of an angel" (par. 441/382). Dream images that derive from waking experiences—the Freudian "day's residues"—indicate non-

---

21. I refer to the editions based on Bologna and Parma manuscripts, respectively, indicating paragraph numbers separated by a slash: *Sefer Chasidim,* ed. Reuben Margulies (Jerusalem: Mosad ha–Rav Kook, 1957); and *Das Buch der Frommen,* 2d ed. by Jehuda Wistinetzki and J. Freimann (Frankfurt am Main: M. A. Wahrmann, 1924). The first passage cited is, however, extant only in the former edition.

angelic origins. A simile likens the process of dreaming to the situation when someone "throws something round and it rolls by itself to a place which the thrower did not aim at." Such dreams appear to evolve beyond the dreamer's intention, but they are no more significant than is the random course of a thrown object. Following an associative path backward we may discover day's residues, as does Freud, but these are insignificant and "neither the thought nor the dream will be fulfilled" (par. 441/382).[22] Truly significant dreams are given by angels, whose divine intervention assures meaning. And yet even these dreams require an interpretive agency, in turn provided by God's assistance.

Sefer Chasidim explicitly links problems of dream interpretation to those of scriptural interpretation, in an extended discussion of the Talmudic views:

> Why does a dream follow the mouth? It is because if dreams did not follow the mouth, we would have to say that dreams are not from God. For behold, the Torah is from Him and follows the mouth and the heart for the interpretation. Now [if you were to say that] one cannot know a dream—and everything that is from the Holy One, blessed be He, is given a heart to know and a mouth to interpret—[then the dream would not be from God]. If not, what is a dream for except to tell us that it is from God, to make known that He knows all the future and makes known to the people what will be in the future, so that one will do repentance, pray to Him, and not sin? (Par. 441/382)

If the written Torah constitutes the collective dream of the Jews, the oral Torah provides interpretations that give meaning and practical force to these dreams. One modern scholar explains, in connection with *Sefer Chasidim:* "The written Torah which is God-given can only be understood through the oral Torah. . . . Just as the written Torah's meaning is determined by the oral Torah *(she-be^cal peh)*, just as the oral Torah is in an ultimate sense God-given, so is the dream interpretation [i.e., following after the mouth, oral] also God-given in an ultimate sense; for it is God who has given the interpreter a heart to understand and a mouth to interpret."[23] Thus the belated oral traditions claim a unique authority based on God's support of their interpretive activities. Dreams and Scripture follow the mouth of the interpreter; "the dream is a kind of divinely written Torah that needs an

---

22. While agreeing with this devaluation of the day's residues, Freud might add that they also lead to deeper complexes that will be fulfilled by lived repetitions.

23. Monford Harris, "Dreams in the *Sefer Ḥasidim," Proceedings of the American Academy for Jewish Research* 31 (1963), 63. Brackets in the original.

oral Torah *(she-be'al peh)* to interpret it'' (ibid.). The rabbinic commentators appear to justify their own activity of interpretation in relation to the concurrent practices of dream interpreters.

Sefer Chasidim repeats the Talmudic story of twenty-four dream interpreters in Jerusalem, whose interpretations of a single dream are all fulfilled. This does not necessarily reflect badly on the interpreters, as *Sefer Chasidim* explains by reference to an assertion in the Babylonian Talmud, Sanhedrin 34b: ''A single scriptural verse gives rise to several interpretations *(ta'amim)*'' (par. 444/1522). But the pietists add the proviso that ''the interpretation should be of the same genre *(me'ein)* and like *(domeh)* the dream'' (ibid.). Similarly, ''the interpretation of a scriptural verse is like its meaning [as it sounds, *domeh le-mashma'uto*].'' In other words, the meaning of Scripture is inseparable from its oral performance, or from its meanings as interpreted by the oral Torah.[24]

The Talmudic discussion and narration of dreams comments on its own operative methods. The dream is like a story or material from the *aggadah*, and thus dream interpretation is analogous to the interpretation of a legend. A dream containing its own interpretation is likely to be fulfilled (Ber. 55b); similarly, the story of Bar Hedia incorporates its thesis: ''All dreams follow the mouth.'' As becomes apparent, however, no interpreter can entirely master the consequences of this metaphorical assertion, and the statement cannot control the narrative frame that surrounds it. To understand Talmudic narratives, then, we need to apply methods of interpretation similar to those employed in the interpretation of dreams. We can no longer maintain the opposition between transcendent and immanent views of dream prophecy, because this dichotomy has been translated into a distinction between two literary and linguistic forms that may blur into each other: the scriptural source and the personal association.

The Babylonian Talmud orients the interpretation of dreams—and of *aggadah*—toward Scripture, although life in the diaspora presupposes an alienation from sacred language: written Torah and spoken Hebrew are dis-

---

24. Solomon Almoli's sixteenth-century *Pitron Chalomot* rejects the associated view of dream interpretation on the grounds that it would make all interpretation as arbitrary as it is binding. In his *Jewish Magic and Superstition* (New York: Behrman, 1939), p. 236, Joshua Trachtenberg comments that Almoli has professional reasons for disputing the Talmudic view. And yet differences of opinion are already present in the Talmud. Apart from the complications suggested by Berakhot, other passages in Yoma 83b, Gittin 52a, and Horayot 13b question the supposed prophetic character of dreams. The hazards of dream interpretation are only mitigated if God presides over the interpretive process, but Berakhot unsettles any confident belief that God or Scripture controls dream interpretation. Contrast Maimonides' *Guide for the Perplexed*, II, 36–38.

placed by oral Torah, Aramaic, and Greek. Despite its claim to complement the teachings from Sinai, the Gemara adds a multilingual dimension that brings with it all of the problems of translation. The tension between law and legend reappears, transformed into a competition between scriptural and vernacular languages. As the interweaving of *halakhah* and *aggadah* might have complicated legal conclusions, so the decentering of biblical Hebrew was an implicit danger. Can God's language be maintained and understood despite the dispersion of Jewish expression into all the languages of the nations?

Berakhot implicitly depicts a contest between conflicting schools of interpretation. At one extreme is the belief that dreams literally prophesy future events; at another extreme is the view that dreams do not bear meaning until interpreted. Thus when twenty-four dream interpreters offer R. Banaʾah different readings, all are fulfilled, because—as Torah has seventy faces—there are countless possible interpretations of a dream text, and all may contain or create truth. One cannot simply discover the meaning of a dream or text if finding meaning invents meaning. Every interpretation may be prophetic to the extent that it imposes itself as truth; the meaning of dreams cannot be severed from the interpretation of their meaning. Prophetic contents are not the underlying component of dream texts, but futures to be actualized.[25]

Caught in the tension between interpretive theories and dream narratives, or propositions and figures, the sources quoted in tractate Berakhot never definitively privilege either mode. Storytelling occurs within the discussion of essential questions, but it neither subordinates itself to nor refutes the accompanying statements. Bar Hedia's execution stands as an emblem for the dangers of prophetic dream interpretation, especially in exile, since every postexilic interpreter is prey to analogous disasters. By claiming a meaning outside the realm of Scripture, the interpreter may stand in opposition to this Great Original. Berakhot does not deny the efficacy of interpretation, although it does emphasize its risks. Ultimately, the text recognizes, we desire only to make our dreams good; but a positive interpretation is not always a good interpretation. A sectarian narrates dreams that reveal the extent of his wickedness, and yet his story ends when

---

25. Samuel Edels (Maharsha) attempts to resolve these difficulties by distinguishing three types of dreams: 1) dreams that come from demons and depend on interpretation for their meaning; 2) dreams that have some inner truth, but whose meaning may be influenced by interpretation; 3) dreams that come from God and are in themselves prophetic, even without interpretation. This system of classification strives to protect dream interpretation from the radical threat of arbitrariness, while acknowledging that in some cases the interpreter can impose his prophecy on the dreamer. Cf. Löwinger, *Der Traum in der jüdischen Literatur*, p. 8.

he finds treasure "at the tenth beam." Theories of good and bad dreams cannot master their actual consequences. Oral Torah strives to complete the written Torah; meaning unfolds in the revisionary processes of storytelling. The role of oral Torah becomes clearer if we read between the lines of dream interpretation: as an interpreter partially creates a dream, so interpretation of Torah recreates it. Thus the Midrash to Ecclesiastes 1:9 pronounces that "if you have heard Torah from the mouth of a scholar, let it be in your estimation as if your ears had heard it from Mount Sinai."[26]

Berakhot and Lamentations Rabbah describe three antagonistic pairs: Raba and Bar Hedia, R. Ishmael and a sectarian, and R. Ishmael ben R. Yose and a Samaritan. In all three cases, well-known rabbinic commentators oppose nonrabbinic dream interpreters. These passages discredit the rabbis' opponents and implicitly warn against consultations with dream interpreters. The Talmudic and Midrashic narratives strive to secure the rabbis' position as the authoritative interpreters of Scripture and dreams.

Some interpretations may transgress the bounds of acceptable reading, even if they cannot be replaced by a single, definitive statement. Dreams are neither legal assertions nor moral judgments, and can only be imaginatively translated by juxtaposition with scriptural or personal contexts. Rabbinic interpretation seeks the meaning of a dream or Midrashic text in the Great Original, in order that human existence may continue to fulfill itself as a retelling of God's Torah. After Babel, however, and following exile from a world structured primarily by Hebrew, interpretation is endangered by meaninglessness amid the infinite possibilities for translation. Chaos threatens if Scripture is merely one text among many. "All dreams follow the mouth," together with the accompanying stories, comes perilously close to hinting that every interpretation alters reality.

---

26. In *Midrash Rabbah*, 3d ed., ed. Freedman and Simon, vol. 8, p. 34. Mixing metaphors synesthetically, the original in Ecclesiastes Rabbah reads: "If you have heard Torah from the mouth of a scholar *(talmid chakham)*, let it be in your eyes as if your ears had heard it from Mount Sinai."

4

FREUD: DEMYSTIFICATION AND DENIAL

Freud's dream book and essays reveal his discomfort with regard to prophetic views of dreams. Freud separates himself as much as possible from biblical and rabbinic practices of dream interpretation, at the same time repressing the Hebrew he learned as a child. Nevertheless, the repressed returns in dreams and interpretations that raise "the Jewish question"— despite Freud's conscious and unconscious efforts to displace this question by other concerns.[1]

At the start of *The Interpretation of Dreams,* Freud dissociates himself from ancient traditions of dream interpretation as divination *(Mantik).* Classical authors held that "dreams stood in relation to the world of superhuman beings in which they believed, and brought revelations from gods and daemons."[2] According to Freud, whereas the ancients commonly assumed that dreams were divinely inspired, Aristotle reconceived them as products of the dreaming psyche. Freud observes that these are "the two opposing streams which we will discern at every period in the evaluation of dream life" *(Td* 31/*ID* 37).

Freud overstates his preference for the tradition begun by Aristotle, and disregards the messages of ancient Judaic dream interpretation. Exag-

---

1. In 1914, Freud belatedly adds two footnotes to *The Interpretation of Dreams* that associate his work with Judaic traditions. He cites Isaiah 29:8 and a Jewish proverb *(Td* 143n, 150n/*SE* 158n, 165n), acknowledging that they anticipate his solution to the riddle of dreams as wish fulfillments.

2. *Td* 30/*ID* 36. Freud's fuller discussion of classical traditions dates from the 1914 edition.

gerating the opposition between transcendent and immanent conceptions, he apparently rejects interpretations based on anything beyond the mind of the dreamer. He cannot strictly uphold this orientation, however, because the unconscious transcends individual awareness; free association receives almost oracular communications from beyond mundane consciousness. In a different way, one rabbinic perspective exceeds the boundaries of psychology by framing the meaning of dreams within the words of Torah—since the Bible provides the materials of both divine references and psychological associations. Freud can only deny this joint significance in a society that no longer lives and dreams Scripture. The breakdown of religious life liberates consciousness from the rhetoric of revelation and threatens interpretive confidence.

Language itself, so central to dream texts and interpretations, both transcends individual consciousness and finds immanent expression. Freud conceives formal structures and puns as preconditions of mental events, much as rabbinic authors assume that scriptural sources predetermine meaning. Linguistic observations, gradually systematized into a chapter on symbols (*Td* 345–94/*ID* 385–439), inspire the new Freudian Bible. Unlike the first edition of *The Interpretation of Dreams,* later editions decode dozens of relatively unchanging dream contents, dispensing with the method of free association in dealing with familiar symbols. To the extent that such symbols are shared by many minds, regardless of cultural differences, C. G. Jung's theory of archetypes is a logical consequence. But despite his discussions of symbols and universal claims for the agency of the dream work, Freud is skeptical of meanings beyond those framed by an individual consciousness.

Freud's insistence on the immanence of mental phenomena is evident in his discussions of prophetic and telepathic dreams. He repeatedly argues that presumably prophetic dreams can be explained psychologically, and that telepathy may be understood more plausibly as thought transference. Freud plays his role of demystifier, arguing that mundane causes account for the illusion of prophetic effects. Freud's revelations serve to conceal his own steps in the direction of prophecy and his modified ideas of transference.

Although Freud distances himself from prophetic traditions, *The Interpretation of Dreams* contains hints of prophecy. To account for the ambition his dreams express, for example, Freud recalls a story he often heard as a child. At his birth, an old peasant woman prophesied that his mother had given the world a great man (*Td* 204/*ID* 225). This prophecy seems to have haunted Freud's imagination and influenced the course of his life. In a requisite gesture of modesty, Freud shrugs off the memory by observing that "such prophecies must occur very frequently" (ibid.). The old woman's anticipatory narrative has nevertheless penetrated Freud's self-interpretation, counterbalanced by harsh words of his father. Freud recalls that in chastising him, his father once proclaimed, "Nothing will come of the boy" (*Td* 225/*ID* 250). Like the peasant woman's pronouncement, these words insinuate themselves into Freud's imagination, for "references to this scene always recur in my dreams and are regularly connected with an enumeration of my achievements and successes, as if I wished to say: You see, I *have* come to something" (ibid.). Through his ambition, Freud responded to contradictory predictions about his future.

Freud's autobiographical examples suggest an altered meaning of prophecy, in the light of psychoanalysis: a narrative proves to be prophetic if it guides the course of further narratives. Freud, for instance, retells his life story in relation to opposing narratives of greatness and insignificance. From a skeptical standpoint, prophetic utterances appear to contain no intrinsic truth, yet as narratives they may impose themselves and become self-fulfilling.[3] Scientists attempt to explain such self-fulfilling prophecies in terms of suggestion; after a prophetic narrative is fulfilled, however, there is no way to differentiate between the appearance of prediction and the effects of suggestion.

Dreams and their interpretations may also enter a cycle of self-fulfilling prophecy. In Freud's terminology, this is linked to the problems of psychoanalytic transference and suggestion. Freudian dream interpretation cannot entirely renounce the prophetic mode, which may include provocative utterances that influence future events. No dream in itself, but only an interpretation that has consequences for the dreamer's future, is prophetic.

Dreams of Prophecy and Telepathy

There are several major and minor essays by Freud on dreams, telepathy, and the occult.[4] He confronts "the occult significance of dreams" repeat-

---

3. On the importance of narrative in Freud's treatment, see Georges Politzer, *Critique des fondements de la psychologie*, 3d ed. (Paris: Presses Universitaires de France, 1968). Politzer observes that Freud "replaces introspection by narrative" (p. 81). See also Roy Schafer, *A New Language for Psychoanalysis* (New Haven: Yale University Press, 1976), and "Narration in the Psychoanalytic Dialogue," *Critical Inquiry* 7 (1981), 29–53; Paul Ricoeur, "Image and Language in Psychoanalysis," trans. David Pellauer, in *Psychoanalysis and Language*, in *Psychiatry and the Humanities*, vol. 3, ed. Joseph H. Smith (New Haven: Yale University Press, 1978), 297–98; and Donald P. Spence, *Narrative Truth and Historical Truth: Meaning and Interpretation in Psychoanalysis* (New York: W. W. Norton, 1982). Jean Laplanche and J.-B. Pontalis discuss related questions of fantasy in "Fantasme originaire, fantasmes des origines, origine du fantasme," *Les Temps Modernes* 19 (1964), 1833–68; translated as "Fantasy and the Origins of Sexuality," *International Journal of Psycho-Analysis* 49 (1968), 1–18.

4. English translations of six of these texts are collected in *Psychoanalysis and the Occult*, ed. George Devereux (New York: International Universities Press, 1953), pp. 49–109. Jule Eisenbud analyzes ambivalences toward parapsychology in "Te-

edly, during a period of over twenty-five years; his sporadic publications on this subject indicate his interest and his ambivalence.[5] Rather than paraphrase Freud's arguments, which reinterpret parapsychological reports, the present discussion delineates textual strategies by which Freud undermines the supposed prophetic significance of dreams. In order to deny that dreams can function prophetically, Freud strives to show that psychology can explain their supposedly prophetic contents.[6] Granting that dreams have meaning, Freud limits this meaning to the psyche of the dreamer.

Prophetic and telepathic dreams pose a special threat to Freud, because their existence would oppose the claim that dreams are a determinate result of psychological processes, like symptoms. Parapsychological dreams point beyond the chain of an individual's mental acts. Whereas Freud's own writings hint that impersonal powers influence psychology, he conceives the dream work as an independent mental activity that operates in the mind of each dreamer.[7] In a sense that Freud does not fully accept, the dream work suggests a force that transcends the mental life of the dreamer.

Freud recounts the dream of a father whose child has died. The body

---

lepathy and Problems of Psychoanalysis,'' in *Psychoanalysis and the Occult*, ed. Devereux, pp. 229, 236. For a general discussion, see Ernest Jones, *The Life and Work of Sigmund Freud* (New York: Basic Books, 1957), vol. 3, chapter 14.

5. On the publication history, see *SE* 18, 175–76, and Jones, *The Life and Work of Sigmund Freud*, vol. 3 p. 392. Compare Jacques Derrida's essay "Télépathie," in *Psyché: Inventions de l'autre* (Paris: Galilée, 1987), especially pp. 251–52. One impetus for Freud's work on the occult and dreams may have been Wilhelm Stekel's *Der telepathische Traum* (Berlin: Johannes Baum, 1920); see the reference to Stekel's book in *UTT* 93n/*SP* 66n. Freud's essay also alludes to the work of A. Adler, C. G. Jung, and H. Silberer. Another impetus for Freud's work on parapsychology was the fact of his being invited to act as coeditor of three periodicals on occultism (see Jones, *The Life and Work of Sigmund Freud*, vol. 3, p. 401). Jones perhaps exaggerates Freud's sympathies toward "occultism," but cites from a surprising letter to Max Eitingon: "Conversion to telepathy is my private affair like my Jewishness" (ibid., vol. 3, pp. 395–96). Freud explicitly links occult phenomena to his repressed background.

6. A skeptical forerunner of Freud is F. W. Hildebrandt, in his *Der Traum und seine Verwertung für's Leben*, 2d ed. (Leipzig: Reinboth, 1881), pp. 30–34. Aristotle is the distant precursor.

7. Compare the linguistic traditions that view language as a "deposit" or mental competence in the mind of every speaker. See, for example, Ferdinand de Saussure, *Cours de linguistique générale*, ed. Charles Bally and Albert Sechehaye (1916), newly ed. Tullio de Mauro (Paris: Payot, 1972), pp. 21, 30, 30n. In English, see Ferdinand de Saussure, *Course in General Linguistics*, trans. Wade Baskin (New

of the child is being watched by an old man in an adjoining room when the father dreams that his child approaches him and says, "Father, don't you see that I am burning?" (*Td* 488/*ID* 547–48). On awakening from this dream, the father notices an actual glare and discovers that the old man has fallen asleep and that a candle has in fact ignited the dead child's clothing. Freud readily accepts the rational explanation that this dream was aroused in the sleeping man by his perception of bright light.

At first, the dream of the burning child does not seem to require interpretation (*Td* 489/*ID* 549). Like some dreams provoked by bodily stimuli, this dream appears to represent the actual situation literally. But Freud observes that this dream transforms reality; fulfilling the father's wish, it brings the child back to life imaginatively and does not literally depict the fire. Though the material source of a dream is clear, its processes of transformation remain complex. By focusing attention on this complexity, Freud disarms any efforts to evaluate the dream's possible telepathic significance.

In "A Fulfilled Dream Premonition," dated 1899 yet published posthumously, Freud's dismissal of prophetic claims requires a more involved strategy.[8] The dream is simple enough: a "Mrs. B." dreams of meeting "Dr. K." on a certain street in Vienna. The next morning she does in fact meet the doctor there. Freud contradicts any parapsychological interpretation of this dream by showing its relationship to a determinate sequence of mental events.

Freud casts doubt on whether the dream actually occurred, and reverses the sequence that his patient has narrated to him. He postulates that on encountering the doctor one morning, prior wishes evoke in Mrs. B. a kind of déjà vu experience. Freud's hypothesis allows him to turn to repressed wishes that might have caused the retrospective fantasy of a dream. This unpublished manuscript narrates the woman's life history, including details that Freud omitted in the discussion he later published.[9]

There are two Dr. K.s in Mrs. B.'s past: the helpful house doctor and a passionate lawyer who "for the first and only time set passion aflame in her" (*UTT* 7/*ID* 662). But "scruples of her education and way of thinking

---

York: McGraw Hill, 1966), pp. 6, 13. The students' notes on which this edition is based are less emphatic in tracing language to psychology; Charles Bally's work shows particular interest in this direction, as does the subsequent psycholinguistic literature.

8. "Eine erfüllte Traumahnung," in *UTT* 7–9; an English translation entitled "A Premonitory Dream Fulfilled" is contained in *ID* 661–64.

9. See *Zur Psychopathologie des Alltagslebens (The Psychopathology of Everyday Life)*, chapter 12, section D (*GW* 4, 291/*SE* 6, 262).

spoiled the surrender for the woman *(Bedenken ihrer Erziehung und Den-kungsart verdarben der Frau . . . die Hingebung)."* On one occasion, as she knelt in longing for her friend, the passionate Dr. K. arrived unexpect-edly to visit her. Freud views the event as a relatively commonplace coin-cidence, and interprets the imagined dream as a repetition of this wish-fulfilling experience. An earlier meeting is the "authentic content" of a later fantasy *(UTT 8/ID 663)*.

Freud's story has an odd tonality and is punctuated by surprising ob-servations. He writes, for example, that the woman's happiness was ruined by moral scruples, and notes that the dynamics of the love relation subse-quently shift: the lawyer "is not so pressing as he once was." Freud sup-poses that the woman achieves an imaginative substitute by indirectly dreaming of their earlier rendezvous. This dream is, then, "a part of the belated punishment which falls to the woman in consequence of her cruelty in youthful years" (ibid.) The wish-fulfilling function is combined with a self-chastisement. As a result of supposedly frequent dreams of this kind, the encounter with another Dr. K. awakens a sense of having dreamed the meeting. The dream has not acted prophetically, Freud concludes; in a mechanism of self-punishment, it has been retrospectively invented by as-sociation with the real encounter. Freud reverses the causal sequence, gen-eralizing that only "retrospective dream creation establishes the illusion of prophetic dreams" *(UTT 9/ID 664)*. What might have been viewed as evi-dence of a supernatural bond between dreams and worldly events, Freud explains as the product of an individual's emotional history.

"Psychoanalysis and Telepathy," written in 1921, was not published during Freud's lifetime. Freud admits his anxieties in dealing with his topic, saying that he discusses it "under the greatest resistance" *(GW 17, 41/SE 18, 190)*; his cautious relationship to occultism screens his deep am-bivalence toward Jewish mystical traditions. The essay opens with a defen-sive gesture, in which Freud dissociates psychoanalysis from occult studies. Embattled, Freud compares the precarious position of psychoanalysis to the situation of war refugees who were caught between two opposing nations and treated as enemies by both *(GW 17, 31/SE 18, 180)*. Freud perceives psychoanalysis as standing in danger of being rejected by both the scientific and the superstitious. After noting superficial resemblances between psy-choanalysis and occultism, then, Freud attacks occultists by observing their lack of true "desire for knowledge *(Wissbegierde)."* He writes that they are already convinced of what they should impartially examine, and merely seek to confirm their beliefs. Studies of the occult consequently signify a "danger *(eine Gefahr)"* to psychoanalysis. This danger from the occultists reflects the age-old hostility between science and religion: "The faith, which they themselves first manifest and then wish to impose on others, is the old religious faith, which in the course of human development was repelled by science, or another, which stands even nearer to the obsolete convictions of primitive peoples" (*GW* 17, 29/ *SE* 18, 178). Freud's critique of occultism conforms to his explicit rejection of all religious faiths.[10] Under cover of this general opposition to belief, Freud keeps his distance from biblical and Talmudic precursors.

Freud separates the spheres of analytic and occult research, as he later dissociates prophecy and telepathy from dreams. He insists that the psychoanalyst must concentrate on "the unconscious element of mental life" (ibid.); turning attention to occult phenomena, Freud writes, is likely to confirm their existence. In each of his confrontations with purportedly occult occurrences, Freud tries to show that psychoanalysis can explain these events by using its own terminology. Throughout, Freud admits, "my personal attitude toward this material remains unwilling, ambivalent" (*GW* 17, 31/*SE* 18, 181). Freud's affective condition is in some ways more significant than his theoretical observations, and partially accounts for the fact that he never published this essay.

Freud recasts the occult in psychoanalytic vocabulary and reinterprets its meaning. He refers to telepathy as "thought transference," which recalls psychoanalytic transference, and he discusses prophecy in relation to wishes. In some cases, Freud grants the possibility that thoughts may be "transferred" between individuals "by an unfamiliar path, excluding the means of communication that are familiar to us" (*GW* 17, 35/*SE* 18, 184). He further associates prophecy with wishes, remarking in one instance that "the content of the prophecy coincides with a wish fulfillment" (*GW* 17, 35/*SE* 18, 185); the "wonder worker" reveals a person's future by revealing an "intimate wish" (*GW* 17, 42/*SE* 18, 192). In this case, Freud nevertheless admits that interpretation may have been influential, and may even have "created the occult fact" (*GW* 17, 40/*SE* 17, 189). He approaches the recognition that interpretations, not dreams in themselves or even dream reports, have powers sometimes viewed as prophetic. Analysis of a dream may generate the subsequent illusion of prophetic effects.

In the midst of this essay, Freud alludes to a passage in his *Jokes and Their Relation to the Unconscious*. Laconically citing the Yiddish-German phrase, "look [or view] of the Rebbe *(Kück des Rebben),*" in which *Kück* is Yiddish and *Rebbe* refers to a Chassidic leader, Freud recalls a joke at the expense of the Chassidim. He earlier attacks the religious thoughts that are concealed behind occult research; this later reference significantly alludes to

---

10. Compare Freud's comments in the *New Introductory Lectures,* where he suspects "that the occult interest is really a religious one, that one of the secret motives of the occult movement is to come to the assistance of religion, which is threatened by the progress of scientific thought" (*SA* 1, 475/*NIL* 31).

Jewish superstitions in Eastern Europe. Freud's *Jokes and Their Relation to the Unconscious* tells the joke after apologizing for its language, "which I cannot fully divest of the jargon [Yiddish] *(die ich des Jargons nicht völlig entkleiden mag).*"[11] Freud translates from an unspecified written or oral Yiddish source, which he has largely but not entirely divested of its original language:

> In the Cracow synagogue sits the great Rabbi N. and prays with his students. Suddenly he utters a cry, and—questioned by the concerned students—says: "Just now the great Rabbi L. in Lemberg has died." The congregation mourns the deceased. In the course of the subsequent days, those arriving from Lemberg are asked how the Rabbi died, what was wrong with him; but they know nothing of it, they left him in the best state of health. It finally becomes entirely certain that Rabbi L. in Lemberg did not die during the hour in which Rabbi N. telepathically sensed his death, because he is still alive. A foreigner takes the opportunity to tease a student of the Rabbi of Cracow with this situation: "It really was a great disgrace for your Rabbi, when he saw Rabbi L. in Lemberg die. The man is still alive." "It doesn't matter," the student answers, "the view [*Kück*] from Cracow to Lemberg was great, anyhow." (*SA* 4, 62/*SE* 8, 63)

In the book on jokes, Freud categorizes this story as an example of humor based on illogic, involving "deviations from normal thinking" (*SA* 4, 59/*SE* 8, 60). The joke satirizes Chassidic followers whose admiration for their Rebbe leads them to suspend the rules of sound judgment. This accounts for Freud's reference to the story in his essay on "Psychoanalysis and Telepathy," in which he himself plays the role of the outsider who remarks on a superstitious error; Freud dismisses his contemporary occultists with as much animosity as does the mocker of a Chassidic Rebbe. His passing allusion in this posthumously published essay provides a clue to Freud's distaste for occult research: it savors of Eastern Europe and recalls the Yiddish world of the Chassidim.

"Dreams and Telepathy," which Freud wrote in 1922, is both his most detailed discussion of parapsychology in dreams and a veiled polemic.

---

11. *SA* 4, 62/*SE* 8, 63. Compare Karl Abraham's observation in a letter to Freud of 11 May 1908: "The Talmudic way of thinking cannot have suddenly disappeared from us. A few days ago I was captivated in a peculiar way by a short paragraph in *Jokes*. As I considered it more closely, I found that—in the technique of setting in opposition and in its entire construction—it was thoroughly Talmudic." See Sigmund Freud and Karl Abraham, *Briefe 1907–1926*, ed. Hilda C. Abraham and Ernst L. Freud (Frankfurt am Main: S. Fischer, 1965), pp. 48–9.

The connection between telepathy and dreams can be neither proved nor disproved, he observes: individual examples cannot prove a telepathic component, nor can counterexamples disprove it. Freud turns attention away from the question of whether dreams and telepathy are linked; rather than consider this question on its own terms, Freud introduces a psychoanalytic explanation. Although he claims to have no set views on the question, Freud is evidently suspicious of telepathic claims.

Freud immediately warns us that his title may awaken false expectations—like a false prophetic claim. He hastens to counter these expectations, as he will contradict superstitious notions of prophecy. Instead of discussing the connection between dreams and telepathy, Freud will show that "the two have little to do with each other" (*UTT* 91/*SP* 63). He denies ever having had a telepathic dream, and argues that even if telepathic dreams did occur, "there would be no need to alter anything in our conception of dreams" (ibid.). Two potentially telepathic experiences, in which Freud dreamt of the death of a son and of a sister-in-law, prove to be "purely subjective anticipations" (*UTT* 91–92/*SP* 64).

In disclaiming knowledge about telepathic dreams, Freud betrays a peculiar relationship to his topic. A recent, potentially prophetic dream provoked "a period of painful waiting" to hear whether his dream would be fulfilled. His uncomfortable experience occurred, Freud believes, "immediately before I resolved to compose this small communication" (*UTT* 92/*SP* 64). Freud's ill ease at the prospect of having a telepathic dream influences his decision to write an essay about the nonexistence of such dreams. Although Freud expresses his lack of experience with telepathic dreams, his text conceals a fear that he may have them. He would rather acknowledge indiscreet wishes in himself and others than grant the possibility of supernatural dreams that are not determined by unconscious forces.

Since Freud denies having encountered telepathic dreams in his own experience or in that of his patients, he bases his analysis on the reports of two correspondents. Freud consequently dispenses with broader case histories and relies on the evidence contained in their brief texts. His work is analogous to that of a literary critic, and one of his informants appropriately offers his sample to Freud in case he should wish to "make literary use of it" (*UTT* 93/*SP* 66).

In the first purportedly telepathic dream, a correspondent writes, "my wife has given birth to twins" (*UTT* 93–94/*SP* 66). Freud points out that this event does not literally come true; the same night, the dreamer's daughter gives birth to twins, one month before her anticipated delivery. Freud diverts attention from the question of whether the dream is telepathic by asking the dreamer for associations and related information. The response disappoints Freud, who fears that his audience, like the dreamer, will be primarily interested in the possible occult implications.

Freud maneuvers for a stronger position on the issue of telepathy in dreams. He tests several postures before choosing the one he considers most effective: "I will not take the standpoint that I am nothing but a psychoanalyst, and that the questions of occultism do not concern me; you would only judge that to be an evasion of the problem" (*UTT* 97/*SP* 70–71). Freud anticipates the reactions of his audience, as he does when his lectures pause to acknowledge possible objections. Aware of critical voices, he writes: "I maintain that it would be a great pleasure to me, if through faultless observations I could convince myself and others of the existence of telepathic occurrences" (ibid.). But data are lacking, and Freud doubts whether adequate proof can ever be secured. A "disturbing occult interest" obstructs any clear-headed inquiry. Freud expresses his dissatisfaction over the ways in which neurotics deceive him by omissions, suppressions, displacements; he trusts that his audience will understand him, "if under the present conditions, I refuse to judge whether the dream that has been communicated to us corresponds to a telepathic fact or an accidental coincidence" (*UTT* 98/*SP* 71–72). The background material provided by the dreamer is insufficient.[12]

Like an astute literary critic, Freud finds one point in the dreamer's account that rewards close scrutiny. The dreamer's warm relationship to his daughter and an inadvertent insult against her husband convince Freud that an unconscious wish stands behind the dream: the dreamer would like his daughter to be his second wife. The dream work masks the repressed wish, so that in the dream his wife rather than his daughter gives birth.

Two conceptions of the dream stand side by side: "According to the first the dream is the reaction to a telepathic message: Your daughter is now bringing twins into the world. According to the second, the dream is based on an unconscious process of thought" (*UTT* 99/*SP* 73). The latter possibility accounts for the dream through a combination of preconscious dream thoughts and unconscious wishes. A blind spot in Freud's analysis arises from his assumption that dream prophecy must inhere in the dream itself, since the power of dreams may in fact result from the interpretation they receive. Freud subsequently asserts that telepathy has nothing to do with dreams. Instead, "the essence of the dream consists in the peculiar process of the dream work, which transports preconscious thoughts (day's residues), with the help of an unconscious wish stimulus, to the manifest dream content" (*UTT* 100/*SP* 74). Once again, Freud dispels presumed prophetic contents by turning to the unconscious processes that give rise to dreams. If

---

12. Freud interprets this purportedly telepathic dream again in *VEP* 478–79/*NIL* 33–35.

he were seriously concerned to explore prophetic meanings, he would have to look forward to future consequences; yet as Freud interprets dreams, they are characterized by the mechanisms of the dream work.

Freud essentially excludes prophecy from the realm of dreams by positing that "a dream without condensation, distortion, dramatization, above all without wish fulfillment, does not deserve this name" (*UTT* 101/*SP* 75). In other writings Freud refers to infantile dreams as undisguised wish fulfillments, but here he insists that distortion characterizes all dream phenomena. As expressions of the dream work, Freud writes, dreams come "from within" the dreamer; telepathic dreams would involve passive receptivity to something external (ibid.). The dream work and symbolism extend beyond the psyche of any individual, however, and in a sense they do represent external phenomena. Discounting such reflections, Freud conceives the dream work in relation to preconscious and unconscious thoughts, the psychological activity of an individual. Telepathy and prophecy threaten Freudian theory to the extent that they transcend the presupposed autonomy of mind. Moreover, recognition of the prophetic power of dream interpretation would challenge Freud to acknowledge that—through his own cultivation of the transference relationship—he achieves suggestive results that resemble fulfilled prophecies.

Freud's second example of a supposedly telepathic dream has little to do with prophecy. Freud apparently prefers not to confront his topic directly, and does not concern himself with the dreams afforded by publications of the English and American Societies for Psychical Research. He assures us that he is a member of these associations, and objects that they do not attempt to evaluate dreams psychoanalytically (*UTT* 93/*SP* 65–66). Although he denies having polemical intentions, Freud struggles to dispense with all reports of dream phenomena that might endanger his theories. The second dream suits him perfectly, because he can account for it in terms of sexual symbols and complexes (*UTT* 103–6/*SP* 78–82). Freud's model remains intact at the close of his essay: latent dream thoughts, together with an unconscious wish, produce the dream. Freud concludes that "if the telepathic phenomenon is only an accomplishment of the unconscious, then no new problem lies before us" (*UTT* 111/*SP* 88). Even if telepathic dreams existed, Freud indicates, they would have to follow the mechanisms of the dream work.

Whereas in "Dreams and Telepathy" Freud strives to appear unbiased, in "The Occult Significance of Dreams" (1925) he freely expresses his biases. He expects that eventually "the specter of prophetic dreams *(prophetische Wahrträume)* will resolve itself into a nothing" (*GW* 1, 570/ *TT* 228), betraying its illusory status. Despite Freud's gestures toward impartiality, then, "Dreams and Telepathy" conceals a hidden agenda; in

"The Occult Significance of Dreams" he is explicitly critical and nevertheless ascribes greater validity to telepathic claims. Freud does not recognize the connection between dreams and telepathy, but he does admit that a kind of thought transference *(Gedankenübertragung)* may account for certain kinds of prophetic dream interpretation: in one particular situation that he observes, "a strong wish of the questioner . . . made itself known to the fortune-teller through direct transference" *(GW* 1, 572/*TT* 230).[13]

Freud introduces a nontechnical version of "transference" *(Übertragung)*, which strictly speaking names emotional carryovers to the psychoanalyst. In more general terms, transference refers to the processes by which feelings toward and perceptions of one person are displaced onto another. According to the familiar Freudian explanation, this transfer is a mental process in the emotional life of an individual. In the context of Freud's examination of telepathic dreams, however, transference indicates an occurrence between two minds, a carryover of a wish to another's consciousness.[14] Furthermore, the word *Übertragung* suggests the process of translation that Freud associates with dream interpretation.

The two kinds of transference are not necessarily distinct, if the transferring psyche is not autonomous in expressing its wish. This extraordinary form of communication by thought transference may have serious implications for psychoanalysis, and specifically for dream interpretation. Unless the interpreter can "telepathically" guess a dreamer's concealed wishes, the most convincing interpretations are likely to proceed by transferential suggestion.[15]

The Prophetic Interpreter

Freud uneasily moves toward and yet evades the recognition that prophecy is not an issue for dreams in themselves, but only for dream interpretation. Prophetic dreams depend on an interpretation that gives sense to otherwise

---

13. Compare Martin N. Damstra, "Telepathic Mechanisms in Dreams," *Psychiatric Quarterly* 26 (1952), 115.

14. Freud also discusses thought transfer in the *New Introductory Lectures,* lecture 30. In a letter of 7 August 1901, he cites a relevant, critical remark which Fliess directed at his work *The Psychopathology of Everyday Life:* "The thought-reader reads into the other only his own thoughts" *(AP/OP* letter 145).

15. Jan Ehrenwald observes that, had Freud taken telepathic claims seriously, he would have had to extend his theoretical framework beyond the model of transference and countertransference. See "Presumptively Telepathic Incidents during Analysis," *Psychiatric Quarterly* 24 (1950), 742.

ambiguous images. When he rejects prophetic dreams, Freud shows far less tolerance than he does in connection with telepathic claims. Freud's own unconscious mechanism of denial *(Verneinung)* is at work: by disputing that there are prophetic dreams, he admits to suspicions that certain kinds of prophecy do occur with respect to dreams. The hasty denial of connections between dreams and prophecy is symptomatic of an avoidance.

Freud for the most part chooses to overlook his own prophetic powers, otherwise known as the powers of "suggestion."[16] Disavowing one dimension of psychoanalytic technique, he declines to take full responsibility for the influence of his interpretations on patients' lives. With the neurotic transference securely redirected toward cure, Freud neglects its role in the handling of dreams and ascribes an almost exclusively cognitive function to dream interpretation. Nevertheless, Freud cannot entirely subordinate his interpretations to the goal of increasing a patient's recognition of repressed material: analyses of symbols and associations often imply evaluations and anticipations of future prospects.

Freud briefly confronts the hazards of influence and suggestion in his "Remarks on the Theory and Practice of Dream Interpretation." He notes that "the analyst will perhaps be frightened at first, when he is warned of this possibility," and he counters that the influencing of a patient's dreams is no worse than "guiding his conscious thoughts" (*SA* Supp. 263/*TT* 210). Freud's readiness to accept responsibility for such direct guidance is itself somewhat surprising. He observes that daily experiences including the psychoanalytic encounter are incorporated into the latent dream thoughts, while "one never gains influence over the mechanism of the dream formation, over the authentic dream work" (*SA* Supp. 264/*TT* 211). Here as elsewhere, Freud limits his consideration of suggestion to the role played by the analyst in the production of dreams (compare *VEP* 239–40/*ILP* 237–38).

---

16. Some authors have revised the Freudian notions of interpretation by emphasizing the necessity of an active procedure that results in practical advice. See, for instance, Ernst Konrad Specht, "Der wissenschaftstheoretische Status der Psychoanalyse. Das Problem der Traumdeutung," *Psyche* 35 (September 1981), 761–87. Specht proposes that we "conceive dream interpretations as recommendative interpretations and not as descriptive propositions. With the interpretation of a dream the interpreter would thus not establish any provable hypothesis, but rather make a suggestion to the dreamer" (p. 783). In summary, Specht writes that "the method of interpreting dreams developed by Freud does not fit into the framework of explanation and prediction which theorists of science have derived from the example of the natural sciences. The method is not arbitrary, however. Its criterion of validity is internal, namely in the structure of dream narration. Like literary fiction, the dream product goes beyond the conscious intentions of the author. The optimal interpretation therefore refers to the *potential* meaning of the text" (p. 785).

The unexpressed risk is also a therapeutic requirement: that dream interpretation shall influence the life of the dreamer. Freud's concern with the theory of the dream work distracts attention from the pragmatic consequences of interpretation.

Familiar problems of psychoanalytic suggestion arise in connection with transference, for the employment of transference in treatment superficially resembles hypnotic suggestion (*VEP* 429/*ILP* 446). Freud anticipates the objection: "Are you not able to force what you wish and what seems correct to you on the patient?" To some critics, psychoanalysis appears like hypnosis, in which a doctor suggests, "Nothing is wrong with you, it's just nerves, so I can sweep away your complaints with a few words and in a few minutes" (*VEP* 433/*ILP* 450). In connection with his most central insights, Freud strives to effect the patient's recognition of complexes, instead of directly seeking to influence symptoms or general behavior. Dream interpretation does not necessarily afford insight into the past, however, and knowledge of the past cannot always be distinguished from influence over the present and future.[17]

Freud concludes his late discussion of psychical topography with the provocative and prophetic slogan: "Where It [id, *Es*] was, I [ego, *Ich*] shall be" (*VEP* 516/*NIL* 71).[18] Freud's dynamic figuration likens the psychoanalytic cure to a territorial conquest, a reclaiming of unusable land, comparable to a "cultural work, like the drying up of the Zuider Zee" (ibid.). An inaccessible, murky realm shall become inhabitable; blocked libido will again stand at the disposition of the ego (compare *VEP* 439/*ILP* 457).

Freud's motto takes on new meanings in connection with dream interpretation, for example: Where the primitive language of dreams was, there the rational language of analysis shall be. Dream interpretation reclaims a dark code through a kind of translation into the familiar modes of expression. But analysis works from the dreamer's report, never directly from dream experience; the rational translation amounts to the analyst's interpretation. Freud's motto thus intimates a further transformation: Where the patient's dream text was, there the analyst's dream interpretation shall be. Associations and symbols allow Freud to displace the dream text by his own revision.

---

17. Compare Jacques Derrida, *La carte postale de Socrate à Freud et au-délà* (Paris: Flammarion, 1980), which refers to the "failure of a purely interpretive psychoanalysis" (p. 360). As a result of the transference, with its therapeutic effects, interpretation can never merely further the patient's intellectual awareness.

18. *"Wo Es war, soll Ich werden."* Compare Jacques Lacan, *Ecrits* (Paris: Editions du Seuil, 1966), especially pp. 416–17, 426, 801, 864–65, and *Le Séminaire*, ed. Jacques-Alain Miller (Paris: Editions du Seuil, 1975), vol. 1, p. 257.

Psychoanalysis claims to work in the service of greater awareness and more thorough knowledge of the mind. Freud's image suggests that this is a cultural task like the recovery of bad land. Do dreams indeed constitute a primitive realm of expression that must be dried out and given a useful function? Freud excludes alternative forms of interpretation of the dream language on its own terms.

In one of his more elaborate interpretations, Freud considers a woman's dream that she is at a theater with her husband. A series of associations leads Freud to translate the latent dream thought: "It was really *nonsense* on my part, that I hurried so much to be married!" (*VEP* 137/*ILP* 124). Freud assumes that this dream thought stands behind the dream as its meaning; it may also follow and modify the dream. In any case, the interpretation will influence the patient's future behavior, and perhaps confirm itself accordingly.[19] The woman may oppose Freud's revelation, but to the extent that the psychoanalytic transference guides her thoughts, his statement may challenge or undermine the woman's marriage. Freud cannot so readily isolate future actions and events from the meaning he finds in dreams.

Languages of Dreams

Freud frequently compares the dream work, which governs the relationship between latent and manifest contents, to a process of translation. Both the dream work and the analytic work resemble translation, and are characterized by the multivalent word *Übertragung*. Dream images are like primitive hieroglyphics that ambiguously translate dream thoughts; the work of interpretation attempts to return from the pictorial language of dreams to ordinary waking expressions. This indicates that everyday language is the more genuine, while the dream language has been distorted by the dream work.

Freud's vacillation between interpretation by correspondence and displacement reappears in his conception of the dream work and its deciphering as analogous to translation. This analogy combines aspects of the correspondence theory (when a word appears to have an equivalent in another language) with the association or displacement theory (when a word appears to play approximately the same role as a word in a different linguistic network).[20] Freud often refers to the central metaphor, without dis-

---

19. On dreams that appear to be prophetic by becoming self-fulfilling prophecies, see George Devereux, "The Technique of Analyzing 'Occult' Occurrences in Analysis," in *Psychoanalysis and the Occult*, p. 394.

20. See chapter 1, above, section on "Interpretation by Correspondence and Displacement."

tinguishing between different practices of translation: "Dream thoughts and dream content stand before us like two representations of the same content in two different languages; or, better stated, the dream content appears to us as a translation of the dream thoughts into another mode of expression" (*Td* 280/*ID* 311–12). At first, Freud suggests a simplistic model of agreement between "two representations of the same content." His modified formulation points to a translation in which the outcome is "another mode of expression." The meaning and the expression are not necessarily identical. In theory, Freud's methods of dream interpretation claim scientific rigor on the basis of a presumed correspondence, yet his practices acknowledge that displacements instead of one-to-one relationships characterize dreams and interpretations. Rather than conceive dream images merely as corresponding to repressed wishes, Freud observes a difference between expressive modes: like a picture puzzle, the dream employs a pictographic script to express dream thoughts.[21]

The model of translation does not necessarily imply that the meaning of a dream is simply contained in the dream thoughts that have produced it. While secondary revision may radically distance the dream report from its hypothetical source, the process of distortion is itself significant. The ways in which a dream is reported are also as decisive to its meaning as is the dream work. The dreamer becomes a narrator in the act of recalling a dream; the method of free association requires that the patient generate waking narratives. Dream interpretation begins when the patient relates a dream text followed by a series of associated memories and thoughts. Relying on his bipartite model, Freud searches for dream thoughts beyond the manifest content, although the secondary revision and the associations challenge the implicit dual conception.

---

21. Compare "Das Interesse an der Psychoanalyse," in *GW* 8, 403–5/*SE* 13, 176–78. See also Lacan, "L'instance de la lettre dans l'inconscient ou la raison depuis Freud," in *Ecrits*, pp. 493–528, and Jacques Derrida, "Freud et la scène de l'écriture," in *L'écriture et la différence* (Paris: Editions du Seuil, 1967), pp. 293–340. In English, see Jacques Lacan, *Ecrits: A Selection*, trans. Alan Sheridan (New York: W. W. Norton, 1977), pp. 146–78, and Jacques Derrida, *Writing and Difference*, trans. Alan Bass (Chicago: University of Chicago Press, 1978), pp. 196–231. Sarah Kofman, in *L'enfance de l'art: Une interprétation de l'esthétique freudienne* (Paris: Payot, 1970), comments that "art and dream have their own procedures of expression" and that "both are untranslatable into the language of reason. . . . The unconscious thoughts are neither translated nor transcribed into a language of dream or language of art. . . . The text of the latent content is nothing but a collection of traces which are discovered in the details of the manifest text. . . . The deformation of the text does not imply the presence of an originary, transformed text, but the absense of originary sense" (p. 59).

In Freud's alternative model of interpretive translation, then, tensions persist between correspondence and association (or displacement) theories of meaning. The essential structure is not that of a text as projection of a psychological act; one text is a clue to another. In *The Interpretation of Dreams*, Freud conceives the dream content as "a pictographic script, the signs of which are to be individually translated into the language of the dream thoughts" (*Td* 280/*ID* 312).[22] This analogy points toward a hermeneutics of radical textualism: the text does not stand for a thought behind it, but displaces the assumed original and undergoes renewed displacements at every turn, in every new context.

A quarter of a century after writing *The Interpretation of Dreams*, in "Remarks on the Theory and Practice of Dream Interpretation," Freud returns to the figure of translation. He attempts to bypass the difficulties contained in the metaphor of translation by dividing dream interpretation into "two phases, the translation and the evaluation or utilization of the same" (*SA* Supp. 261/*TT* 208). Freud provides the example of reading Livy: "First one wants to know what Livy narrates in this chapter, and only then does the discussion begin as to whether what one has read is an historical account, a legend, or a digression by the author" (*SA* Supp. 262/*TT* 208). The analogy is not entirely convincing. Freud ignores any incommensurabilities that may obstruct efforts to translate Livy from Latin into German; a literal translation seems to him possible without the slightest difficulty. Only critical evaluation of the translated text poses serious problems, which in the case of dreams Freud resolves by referring to childhood etiology. Freud shies away from accepting the consequences of his metaphor when he makes translation appear unproblematic, in order to reassure us that dream interpretation is also straightforward. Yet the "evaluation" of the translation cannot be so unequivocally separated from the procedures of translation. Freud does not fully acknowledge that the model of translation introduces an inescapable element of displacement along with that of correspondence.

In his *Introductory Lectures on Psychoanalysis*, Freud also speaks of dream interpretation as a process of translation, and—perhaps for rhetorical reasons—shows greater readiness to acknowledge its obstacles. He anticipates uncertainties over the possibility of a "secure translation of the manifest dream into the latent dream thoughts" (*VEP* 231/*ILP* 228). To

---

22. On the Freudian metaphor of translation, see Dalia Judovitz, "Freud: Translation and/or Interpretation," *Sub-Stance* 22 (1979), 29–38. Compare Johannes Volkelt's *Die Traum-Phantasie* (Stuttgart: Meyer and Zeller, 1875): "The language of concepts is lacking in the dream fantasy; what it *(die Traumphantasie)* wishes to say, it must depict graphically" (p. 31).

overcome these doubts, Freud recalls that the dream work itself enacts a kind of "translation of the dream thoughts into a primitive mode of expression analogous to pictographic writing" (*VEP* 232/*ILP* 229). This accounts for the ambiguities in the dream language and nonetheless encourages hopes that translation in the opposite direction may succeed. In addition to the topological model, Freud suggests a linguistic, structural relationship between dreams and their meanings. He explains that unlike even the most ambiguous language, dreams are not a vehicle of communication, but aim precisely not to be understood (*VEP* 234/*ILP* 231). Freud conceives the dream report as a kind of monologue that can only be overhead, and that is not intended as a communication.[23] Subsequent analysts have, however, recognized the strategic significance of dream texts in a psychoanalytic context, and in the efforts of consciousness to come to terms with inaccessible contents.[24]

Freud was aware of possible objections to his claims to make dream interpretation into a scientific method, and expressed the problems of dream interpretation as the question of "whether one can give, for every product of the dream life, a complete and assured translation into the mode of expression of waking life" (*GW* 1, 561/*TT* 219). This forms part of a larger issue in efforts to know the unconscious: "We know it, of course, only as something conscious, after it has undergone a transformation *(Umsetzung)* or translation *(Übersetzung)* into something conscious" (*SA* 3, 125/*GPT* 116). In turn, the translation from the dream language into waking language parallels the transference *(Übertragung)* of psychical energies from one investment *(Besetzung)* to another. Because these transfers combine metaphoric substitution and metonymic association, however, there is no direct homology between the two components.

At variance with his more confident assertions, at times Freud complains that the dream work does not follow the predictable patterns of translation: "It is remarkable and incomprehensible that in this translation, a carryover as if into another script or language, the methods of merging and combination find their application" (*VEP* 180/*ILP* 172). Ordinarily, Freud admits, a translation is more concerned to preserve distinctions; but the dream work mixes everything up, multiplies ambiguities, and is, in short, an eminently unreliable translator. The model of translation takes a turn that

---

23. In this respect, Freud stands in a tradition that likens dream language to the monologues of children. See L. Strumpell, *Die Natur und Entstehung der Träume* (Leipzig: Veit, 1874), pp. 57–8, and Volkelt, *Die Traum-Phantasie,* p. 20.

24. See, for example, Mark Kanzer, "The Communicative Function of the Dream," *International Journal of Psycho-Analysis* 36 (1955), 260–66.

unsettles the notion that a dream's meaning corresponds to a clear dream thought.[25]

Given that dreams—like "primitive languages"—are characteristically ambiguous, how can the interpreter claim to discern and specify meanings? Just as authorities on hieroglyphics will produce relatively similar translations of sample writings, Freud claims, "correctly schooled analysts" will arrive at similar interpretations (*VEP* 235/*ILP* 232). The "correct" school was, of course, Freud's own, a conclusion that avoided the problems of divergent methods of translation.

The theory of dream symbolism is one aspect of dream interpretation that Freud modifies and radically expands in later editions of *The Interpretation of Dreams*. During his years as a psychoanalyst, he becomes familiar with recurring symbolism common to dreams, popular tales, and literature. To the extent that Freud relies on dream symbols as fixed elements that have uniform equivalents, he dispenses with the patient's associations and relies on simple correspondences between symbols and their meanings. In assuming the possibility of "fixed translations," he inclines toward a more traditional view, closer to that of the ancient dream books (*VEP* 160/*ILP* 150). Whereas Freud initially searches for the meaning of a dream in the interaction between a dream report and the dreamer's associations, he later perceives recurrent patterns of signification in the dream language and reduces the role of successive displacements for certain symbols. In a footnote of 1925, Freud indicates the possibility of interpreting some dreams by translating them independently of associations (*Td* 247n/*ID* 274n).

According to Freud's first edition of *The Interpretation of Dreams*, the dreamer's associations are necessary for interpretation of all but the most transparent, infantile dreams. In later editions and in his *Introductory Lectures on Psychoanalysis*, Freud attributes to symbols an increasingly constant signifying function. Rather than base his theories on a practice that resists all stability, Freud alters his prior model. Thus evolve the maligned "phallic symbols" among other commonplaces of anti-Freudian discourse. Freud's own writings illustrate the interaction between interpretive

---

25. In one context, Freud remarks that "a dream is, as a rule, not translatable into other languages" (*Td* 120n/*ID* 132n). Compare Derrida, "Freud et la scène de l'écriture," in *L'écriture et la différence:* "The possibility of translation, if it is far from being annulled—because between the points of identity or of adherence of the signifier to the signifier, experience never stops spreading out distances—appears principally and definitively limited. . . . There is no translation, or system of translation, except if a permanent code allows one to substitute or transform the signifiers in preserving the same signified" (p. 311). In English, see Derrida, "Freud and the Scene of Writing," in *Writing and Difference*, pp. 209–10.

correspondences and displacements. His revisions consistently diminish the role of metonymic disruptions, as if these were repressed, unacceptable thoughts or ancient precursors.

The competing models of interpretation by correspondence and association are in some ways analogous to the basic mechanisms of the dream work: condensation *(Verdichtung)* and displacement *(Verschiebung)*. Condensation parallels a general correspondence view in which latent dream thoughts are translated into equivalents; displacement evokes a movement of association or allusiveness, in which manifest contents transpose loosely connected correlates. The interpreter tries to reverse these processes, guessing at the original contents behind distorting translations and transpositions. The overdetermination of dream contents does not disqualify such efforts, although multiple correspondence complicates the model. When the dreamer provides associations to components of a dream, texts pile up on texts and vie for dominion. Continuous displacements prevent the interpreter from arriving at a definitive reading, although certain interpretations are more compelling or more therapeutically effective than others.

The analyst finds himself in the situation of translating a translation, without any firm assurance that he can restore the hypothetical original. The dreamer endlessly distorts anew, and the interpreter can never produce a completely whole text, without gaps. The analytical situation hence becomes an interweaving of narratives in which Freud tries to secure a recognition of the past. As life continues, the narratives cannot pause, and the dreamer struggles to guide certain fantasies into the future.

Freud protests too much when he insists that his dream interpretations have no bearing on future events and only reconstruct dream thoughts that are represented in the dream. The analyst need not be overly disturbed by the suspicion that dreams are influenced by suggestion (*SA* Supp. 263/ *TT* 210). While Freud grants that the manifest content of dreams will be influenced by the analyst, he denies all influence on the latent dream thoughts or on the mechanism of the dream work (*SA* Supp. 264/*TT* 211; cf. *VEP* 240/*ILP* 238).

Freud discounts the claims of interpretive suggestion, then, by describing two distinct phases of dream interpretation: translation and evaluation (*SA* Supp. 261/*TT* 208). While the dream work transforms the latent dream thoughts into manifest content, the dream interpretation moves in the opposite direction, translating from manifest to latent content. Subsequently Freud evaluates the personal meaning of the latent content, implying that this content is not altered by interpretation. At the same time, there are hints that the elusive processes of translation from one language to the other are themselves an essential feature of the dream.

Freud links his comments on dream interpretation as translation, moving from manifest to latent dream contents, to a genetic history of linguistic development. The manifest dream expression is like a primitive language that employs pictorial signs and concrete metaphors; waking thought, like modern languages, favors abstraction. The abstract is directly linked to the concrete by a genealogical model: "most abstract words are faded concrete ones" (*VEP* 183/*ILP* 175). The dream work revives dead metaphors, returning to the primitive forms that are rich in imagery.[26]

Freud's dream theory aims to show that dreams express the past that has determined them. Strictly speaking, Freud maintains, nothing new can arise in a dream. Whereas image sequences may be explained as elaborations of previous thoughts and wishes, then, novel thought processes in dreams threaten to disturb the Freudian model of the distorting dream work. Thus Freud occasionally reduces speech in dreams to being a repetition of the day's residues and minimizes its creative role in psychological development; he insists that dialogue in dreams derives from actual exchanges during waking experience. Certain unacknowledged demands compel Freud to deny that the language of dreams has a creative aspect.[27]

The agency of the dream work is beyond the conscious control of the subject, and represents a sense in which language speaks.[28] Freud tends to limit the dream work by writing as if mental activities governed the linguistic distortions in dreams. Ultimately, Freud wishes to trace the dream work to particular modes of censorship that operate in each dreamer. The mechanisms of the dream work are similar to rhetorical figures, however, and it may be incorrect to assume that consciousness controls them. On the contrary, consciousness itself may be dominated by turns of rhetoric. Everything is determined in mental life, Freud asserts, and he conceives this determination as a chain of relationships in the psyche. But if language is the determinant, then dreams cannot simply be interpreted as the product of

---

26. One extensive discussion of language in dream interpretation is Marshall Edelson's *Language and Interpretation in Psychoanalysis* (New Haven: Yale University Press, 1975).

27. See Robert Bossard, *Psychologie des Traumbewusstseins* (Zürich: Rascher, 1951), p. 181.

28. Several nineteenth-century authors anticipate this Heideggerian formulation; dream theorists note that dreams give expression to forces beyond reason. See, for example, Hildebrandt, *Der Traum und seine Verwertung für's Leben*, p. 56: "The dream warns . . . from within"; a sense of passivity leads the *Sprachgenius* to say, "this or that came to me in a dream *(mir hat dies oder das geträumt)*" (p. 17). In *Die Traum-Phantasie*, Volkelt links the unconscious forces to Socrates' *daimonion*, which he interprets as a power of conscience that is attributed with a divine origin (p. 160). What is given by the unconscious, Volkelt paraphrases Eduard von Hartmann, has something mystical and daemonic about it (p. 167).

an individual's past. Freud himself breaks the boundaries of personal history when he notes shared symbols, linguistic devices, and predictable mechanisms of the dream work.

The dream work is like the work of rhetoric, and its characteristic turns are analogous to figures of speech. This partially explains Freud's image of the dream as an architectural facade, an ornamentation that stands for or in front of the substantial edifice. Freud ambiguously ascribes to the dream image the functions of both concealment and revelation. At times Freud acts as if he must tear away the surfaces that mask a more "authentic" content, the repressed infantile wishes. Yet he also recognizes that the real interest in dreams derives neither from their shared sexual origins nor from the materials of latent thoughts, but from their multifarious means of disguise.

Dreams employ figures that simultaneously present and distort, represent and misrepresent. In accordance with his philological assumptions, Freud has recourse to mental contents that are the "authentic" meanings beyond the "inauthentic" forms. At the same time, his practice of free association challenges the bipartite model of meaning, which is fundamental to Freud's entire interpretive program. Moreover, the figurative activity of a dream need not stand for determinate literal contents. Freud implicitly relies on a hermeneutic model of translation by resemblance, although the overdetermination of linguistic expressions casts doubt on whether translation ever fully succeeds.

Freud grants importance to "every nuance of the linguistic expression, in which the dream lay before us" (*Td* 492/*ID* 552). Behind apparently "meaningless or inadequate" language, Freud discerns a significant distortion of an underlying draft, and hence he respects "even this defect in the expression" (ibid.). His approach is reminiscent of certain interpretive practices in religious contexts. For Freud, the dream is analogous to Scripture; both employ vivid, "primitive" expressions. Like ancient rabbis, the Freudian commentator is never justified in discarding a garbled passage or in assuming that the text is corrupt. "In short," Freud writes, "what according to the opinion of other authors is supposed to be an arbitrary improvisation, hurriedly brought together in the embarrassment of the moment, this we treated as a holy text" (*Td* 492–93/*ID* 552).

Dreams of Wordplay

Freud provides many examples of dreams that operate by linguistic play.[29] In a note of 1909, he observes that "oriental dream books" often take ver-

---

29. The growing literature on this subject renders unnecessary an extensive discussion here. See, for example, Didier Anzieu, *L'auto-analyse de Freud et la découverte de la psychanalyse,* 2d ed. (Paris: Presses Universitaires de France, 1975), and

bal echoes into consideration; this accounts for the incomprehensibility of popular translations of these works. Freud calls one of Artemidorus's reports "the most beautiful example of a dream interpretation, which has been handed down to us from antiquity." Based on Alexander's dream of a satyr (Greek *satyros*), Aristander interpreted: "Tyre is yours" *(Sa tyros)*. Alexander confirmed the interpretation by mounting an attack and conquering this city. Freud emphasizes the inner connections between dreams and language, citing Ferenczi's notion that "every language has its own dream language" *(Td* 120n/*ID* 132n). He also obliquely identifies with the ancient "dream books" when he adds that his own book on dreams may be similarly untranslatable.

Freud frequently employs linguistic resonances as clues to the meaning of dreams. A dreamer "*pulls out (zieht . . . hervor) a* (certain, familiar) *woman from behind a bed.*" This means, Freud states, that he "*prefers* this woman" ("gibt dieser Dame den *Vorzug*") *(VEP* 135/*ILP* 120–21; cf. *Td* 398/*ID* 444). The physical movement of *hervorziehen* signifies an emotional *Vorzug*. Freud interprets the dream without reference to the life of the dreamer, as if verbal echoes (like some symbols) were immutable components in dream interpretation. Ambiguity and overdetermination suggest, however, that no single verbal relation is definitive, but merely forms part of a more extensive chain of significations.

In its "considerations of representability," the dream work takes advantage of concealed figures in language. Freud explains that dreams employ words that "were originally intended pictorially, concretely, and that are at present used in a faded, abstract sense"; the dream work returns to their "earlier, full significance" *(Td* 396/*ID* 442). Some dreams enact a condensation by combining key words. Freud himself dreams of an "Autodidasker," which he interprets as a composite of "author" *(Autor)*, "autodidact" *(Autodidakt)*, and "Lasker," a proper name *(Td* 299–300/*ID* 334). The significance of the dream may be derived from particular associations related to this neologism. Other dreams are structured around verbal reversals *(VEP* 186/*ILP* 180).

Freud's most interesting sequence of dreams based on wordplay occurs at the close of his discussion of condensation in *The Interpretation of Dreams (Td* 297–304/*ID* 331–39). One example alludes to Yiddish. To begin with, Freud narrates the dream of a female patient, and analyzes its final, "meaningless word combination":

Alexander Grinstein, *On Sigmund Freud's Dreams* (Detroit: Wayne State University Press, 1968). Compare *The Psychopathology of Everyday Life*, chapter 5, on "Das Versprechen." A. A. Roback associates Freudian practices with rabbinic commentaries based on verbal association, in *Jewish Influence in Modern Thought* (Cambridge, Mass.: Sci-Art Publishers, 1929), pp. 162–65.

> She finds herself with her husband at a peasants' festivity *(Bauern-festlichkeit)* and then says, "This will end in a general 'Maistollmütz.' " In the dream [she had] the vague thought that this was a pudding made from corn, a sort of polenta. Analysis divides the word into corn *(Mais)*—mad *(toll)*—mad for men *(mannstoll)*—Olmütz [a place name], all of which were recognizable as remnants from a table conversation with her relatives. *(Td* 297–98/*ID* 331)

Freud may read his own concerns into the association from *Maistoll* to *mannstoll;* his brief account does not explain the patient's role in the dream analysis. Freud next probes deeper into the meaning of the first component, *Mais:*

> Apart from the allusion to the recently opened Jubilee Exhibition [of Emperor Franz Josef in 1898], behind *Mais* were concealed the words: *Meissen* (a Meissen [Dresden] porcelain figure representing a bird); *Miss* (her relatives' English governess had traveled to Olmütz); and *mies*=disgusting, unpleasant in the jokingly used Jewish jargon, and a long chain of thoughts and associations led away from every syllable of the word cluster. *(Td* 298/*ID* 331)

This allusion to Yiddish, which Freud calls the "Jewish jargon," has broader implications.[30] As an ancient sectarian appears to dream of Cappadocia in a mixture of Aramaic and Greek, this patient dreams of *Mais/mies* in a mixture of German and Yiddish. The repressed "primitive" language, for assimilated Austrian Jews, was Yiddish. Freud does not reflect on the significance of this linguistic conglomerate, nor does he convey his subsequent interpretation. This dream could perhaps have been interpreted in connection with a popular Judaic tradition of which this woman may have been consciously or unconsciously aware. Freud's own reference to Yiddish encourages juxtaposition of this *Maistoll* dream with a story purportedly told by R. Nachman of Bratslav:

> Once a king told his beloved, the viceroy: "I see in the stars that whoever eats any grain that grows this year will go mad. If so, what is your advice?" And he answered him: "Therefore let us prepare grain for them so that they will not have to eat from this year's harvest." And the king answered him, "If so, when only we are not mad, and all the world is mad, then it will appear the opposite, that

---

30. Compare Régine Robin, "Le yiddish, langue fantasmatique?" *L'écrit du temps* 5 (1984), 43–50.

we are the mad ones. (And to prepare grain for everyone is impossible.) Therefore, certainly we too must eat this year's grain. But we will make a sign on our foreheads, so that at least we will know that we are mad. For when I look at your forehead and you look at mine, we will know from this sign that we are mad."[31]

This story refers to themes that engrossed Freud: madness, prophecy, and consciousness. The legendary king, like Freud, aims at *recognition* of a mental condition. There is no way to determine whether Freud's patient knew this particular story, or only a smattering of Yiddish words. Freud does not reflect on the larger questions raised by dreams that contain bilingual expressions; he seems to assume that all languages may play a part in dream formation. In another instance, Freud interprets one of his dreams by reference to German, English, and Latin (*Td* 227/*ID* 333). At issue is the linguistic tradition or textual canon, presumably linked to the dreamer's associations, that permits dream interpretation.

An Absurd Decree

At the end of Freud's discussion on "absurd dreams," his dream of "My Son, the Myops" is like a palimpsest—in James Sully's words quoted by Freud—that *"discloses beneath its worthless surface–characters traces of an old and precious communication"* (*Td* 152n/*ID* 169n). Greek and Hebrew have been covered by layers of Aramaic, Yiddish, and Austrian-German slang. On the basis of his associations, Freud shows that this dream is not as absurd as first appears. He translates "nonsense" words by recognizing the foreign signifiers they conceal, in order to decipher their hidden message. Freud will conclude this analysis by affirming that "the dream is often deepest *(am tiefsinnigsten)* when it appears most mad" (*Td* 429/*ID* 480).

In the first part of Freud's dream, a man refers to *"my son, the Myops"* (*Td* 273/*ID* 303). According to Freud's interpretation, the father and son represent Freud and his eldest son. *Myops* is a condensation of *myopia* and *Cyclops*. The classical Greek reference is, however, overshadowed by Hebraic allusions; one aspect of Freud's myopic shortsightedness is his

---

31. Translation modified from *Rabbi Nachman's Stories*, trans. Aryeh Kaplan (New York: Breslov Research Institute, 1983), p. 481. My revisions are based on the Hebrew text contained in *Sippurim Niflaʾim*, ed. Samuel Horowitz, in *Kokhavei Or* (Jerusalem: Chassidei Braslav, 1961), p. 26. See also Arthur Green's *Tormented Master: A Life of Rabbi Nahman of Bratslav* (New York: Schocken Books, 1981), pp. 173–74.

one-sided neglect of ancient Judaic traditions. The references to Hebrew and Yiddish counter Freud's pretense that he knows little of these languages. Since Freud learned Hebrew as a child, it must have remained active in his unconscious processes; in any case, his associations lead him directly to "the Jewish question" and to Passover.[32]

The context of Freud's dream is Theodor Herzl's play *The New Ghetto*, which he saw in early January 1898.[33] Although Freud does not mention Herzl's name in his analysis, he acknowledges that the dream thoughts relate to "concern for the future of children, to whom one cannot give a fatherland; concern about educating them in such a way that they will be free-minded [or independent, *freizügig*]." Much to the point, Herzl's play deals with Jewish efforts to escape "the new ghetto" that remains within after Jews have freed themselves from the external barriers.[34] Freedom of movement and thought had been crucial issues for European Jews since the eighteenth century; Jewish emancipation culminated in the dual solutions of assimilation and Zionism. In a note, Freud further associates his dream—of evacuating his children from Rome—with a childhood envy of relatives who had been able to relocate in another land (*Td* 429n/*ID* 481n). Combining Roman and Hebraic elements, the dream reflects Freud's concern with questions of national identity:

---

32. While Freud's parents left behind most Jewish practices when they moved to Vienna, they did retain the Passover ritual. See Jones, *The Life and Work of Sigmund Freud*, vol. 3, p. 350, and Paul Roazen, *Freud and His Followers* (New York: Alfred A. Knopf, 1975), p. 26.

33. See Freud's letter of 4 January 1898, in *BWF/CL*. Compare Grinstein, *On Sigmund Freud's Dreams*, p. 326. Grinstein also provides a synopsis of Herzl's play. Peter Loewenberg explores deeper meanings in "A Hidden Zionist Theme in Freud's 'My Son, the Myops . . . ' Dream," *Journal of the History of Ideas* 31 (1970), 129–32. See also William J. McGrath, *Freud's Discovery of Psychoanalysis: The Politics of Hysteria* (Ithaca N.Y.: Cornell University Press, 1986), pp. 235–50; Avner Falk, "Freud and Herzl," *Contemporary Psychoanalysis* 14 (July 1978), 357–87; and Immanuel Velikovsky, "The Dreams Freud Dreamed," *Psychoanalytic Review* 28 (1941), 508–10. On the broader political context of Herzl's *The New Ghetto*, see Amos Elon, *Herzl* (New York: Holt, Rinehart and Winston, 1975), chapter 6, and Alex Bein, *Theodore Herzl: A Biography*, trans. Maurice Samuel (New York: Meridian Books, 1962), chapter 4. A controversial essay on this subject is Leo Goldhammer's "Theodor Herzl und Siegmund *[sic]* Freud: (Träume)," contained in *Theodor Herzl Jahrbuch* (Vienna: H. Glanz, 1937), pp. 266–68.

34. See Theodor Herzl, *Das neue Ghetto* (Vienna: "Welt," 1897) and, in English, *The New Ghetto*, trans. Heinz Norden (New York: The Theodor Herzl Foundation, 1955), act I, scene viii, act II, scenes i and v, act IV, scene viii.

As a result of certain events in the city of Rome, it is necessary to evacuate the children, which also takes place. The scene is then in front of a gateway, a double door in the ancient style (the Porta Romana in Siena, as I am already aware during the dream). I sit on the edge of a fountain and am very dejected, close to tears. A female person—an attendant or nun—brings the two boys out and delivers them to their father, who was not myself. The older of the two is clearly my eldest; I do not see the face of the other one. The woman who brought out the boy requests a kiss from him in parting. She is remarkable for having a red nose. The boy refuses her the kiss, but while reaching out his hand in parting says: *Auf Geseres,* and to both of us (or to one of us): *Auf Ungeseres.* I have the notion that the latter signifies a preference. (*Td* 426/*ID* 477–78)

The dream opens with a scene of crisis in a Roman context.[35] Freud's first interpretive act alludes to Psalm 137:1, "By the waters of Babylon we sat down and wept."[36] Although Freud does not discuss this biblical reference, its intimations of national misfortune are directly relevant to the dream. The psalm refers to a moment of oppression during the Babylonian exile:

By the waters of Babylon, we sat down and wept, when we thought of Zion. We hung up our harps upon the willows, in the midst thereof.

---

35. Freud does not specify the reason for the need to evacuate children from Rome. His later associations indicate that plague may have been the cause, and in particular a plague against the first-born (compare Exodus 11–12). This adds significance to the presence of Freud's first-born son in the dream, in direct confrontation with *Geseres*. Robert Paul has suggested to me that Rome, a place of Christian exile in this dream, may be a symbolic substitute for Egypt and Babylon. Concerning Freud's dreams of Rome, compare Grinstein, *On Sigmund Freud's Dreams,* chapter 3, and Carl E. Schorske, *Fin-de-Siècle Vienna: Politics and Culture* (New York: Alfred A. Knopf, 1980), pp. 189–93. In another context, Schorske states that Freud's "wish to be free himself from anti-Semitism reasserted itself in his dreams" (p. 188). On a picture postcard of the Arch of Titus addressed to Karl Abraham in 1913, Freud wrote: "*Der Jude übersteht's!* (the Jew endures or withstands it [the Roman exile?])." See Freud and Abraham, *Briefe 1907–1926,* p. 145.

36. It is unlikely that Freud is referring to Swinburne's *Super Flumina Babylonis,* as Grinstein suggests in *On Sigmund Freud's Dreams,* p. 322. Anzieu, in *L'auto-analyse de Freud et la découverte de la psychanalyse,* vol. 1, more plausibly notes that Freud quotes from Luther's Bible translation (p. 346n). Théo Pfrimmer agrees with Anzieu, in *Freud: Lecteur de la bible* (Paris: Presses Universitaires de France, 1982), p. 124.

For they themselves who held us captive bid us sing, and be joyful in our wailings . . . sing us a song of Zion.[37]

Freud's associations recall this exilic mourning for Zion. The psalm gives additional meaning to Freud's concern over his children's freedom. In connection with issues of exile and return, Freud performs a further interpretation with reference to the Israelites' flight from Egypt.

The key words in Freud's analysis are the coinages *Auf Geseres* and *Auf Ungeseres* in place of the expected parting, *Auf Wiedersehen*. After Freud follows a series of linguistic associations, the dream emerges as a reflection on Passover. Freud works from linguistic clues:

> According to information which I have received from rabbinic scholars *(Schriftgelehrten), Geseres* is a genuine Hebrew word, derived from a verb *goiser,* and is best conveyed by "imposed sufferings, doom." According to the use of the word in the jargon [Yiddish], one would think that it meant "weeping and wailing." (*Td* 427/*ID* 478)

From whom did Freud receive his philological information, which contradicts the leading scholarship available in the late nineteenth century? The nineteenth-century Christian scholar Gesenius calls *g'zerah* an Aramaism.[38] Freud's information is inaccurate; *Geseres* is not "a genuine Hebrew word," but is rather Yiddish, of Aramaic origin. The Hebrew root *g-z-r* means to cut or separate; in Aramaic and late Hebrew sources *gazar* and *g'zerah* refer to a decree.[39] It is unlikely that Freud deliberately contradicted the leading biblical philologist of his day, although this might also be explained in terms of the Jewish-Christian tensions that characterize the dream. Even Freud's transliteration is questionable, since it renders the

---

37. I translate Psalm 137:1–3 from *Die Bibel,* trans. Martin Luther, 13th ed. (Stuttgart: Bibel-Anstalt, 1851), p. 636.

38. See F. H. W. Gesenius, *Thesaurus philologicus criticus linguae hebraeae et chaldaeae Veteris Testamenti,* 2d ed. (Leipzig: F. C. G. Vogelii, 1829–53), vol. 1, p. 279.

39. Ibid. See also *A Hebrew and English Lexicon of the Old Testament,* William Gesenius et al. (Oxford: Clarendon Press, 1951), pp. 160, 1086. Pfrimmer also observes the inaccuracy of Freud's philological information in *Freud: Lecteur de la bible,* p. 122. The Aramaic word *g'zerah,* meaning "decree," occurs in the Book of Daniel 4:14 and 4:21, in the relevant context of Nebuchadnezzar's ominous dream and Daniel's interpretation. Of the many anti-Semitic decrees that preceded Freud's dream, one may recall the Vienna *g'zerah:* in 1421, after an accusation of ritual murder, the Jews were killed or expelled.

verb according to its Yiddish pronunciation.[40] Freud indeed seems to have consulted an Eastern European rabbi; or he himself may have provided the misinformation which he then attributed to another source. While Freud attempts to deny his own knowledge of Hebrew, his questionable philology indicates that he was responsible for the gloss on *Geseres*. In any event, the interpretation Freud gives to his dream depends on his partial knowledge of Yiddish.

Freud both insists on the relevance of a Hebrew association and denies knowledge of the Hebrew word. He tells us that he receives his information from rabbis,[41] thereby distancing himself from what his unconscious affirms. At the same time, Freud himself associates the Yiddish *gezeres* with "weeping and wailing." While *Geseire* has come to mean this in modern (especially Austrian) German,[42] *gezeres* more exactly refers to evil decrees or misfortunes.[43] Freud recalls a doctor's words, responding to a distressed mother: *"Was machen Sie für Geseres?"* (*Td* 428/*ID* 480). This implicitly refers to the Yiddish-German expression *machen ein Geseire,* meaning "to make an uproar" or "to make a fuss."[44] In connection with his dream of exile, Freud raises linguistic issues relating to Hebrew, Aramaic, and Yiddish—and evokes themes of misfortune and suffering. At the beginning of his dream, confronted by the exilic scene of Psalm 137, Freud himself had been near to tears. Having experienced some kind of evil de-

---

40. A German-Jewish scholar would have been more likely to transliterate this verb form *gauzer,* as David Blumenthal has pointed out to me.

41. The word *Schriftgelehrten* is incorrectly translated by James Strachey as "philologists"; it specifically refers to rabbinic scholars, as in Luther's Bible translation, and may carry a light ironic tone.

42. See *Deutsches Wörterbuch,* ed. Gerhard Wahrig (Berlin: Bertelsmann, 1977), p. 1528. Even more striking is the entry under "Geseier" in the *Deutsches Wörterbuch,* ed. Jacob and Wilhelm Grimm (Leipzig: S. Hirzel, 1897), vol. 4, pt. 2, p. 4023. Freud may have consulted this work, which derives the word from Hebrew. In any event, Freud did not concern himself with accurate philology, instead basing his interpretation on his own (Yiddish-influenced) associations. Indeed, *machen ein Geseires* was not an unusual expression in Austrian German, according to information I have received from the Grimm *Wörterbuch* and Maximilian Aue.

43. See Alexander Harkavy's *Yiddish-English-Hebrew Dictionary,* 2d ed. (New York: Hebrew Publishing Company, 1928), p. 144. In Chassidic circles, a decree (*g'zerah*) was also employed during ritual exorcisms.

44. Martin S. Bergmann writes that this sense of *Geseire* is "Jewish Viennese dialect," in his article "Moses and the Evolution of Freud's Jewish Identity," *Israel Annals of Psychiatry and Related Disciplines* 14 (March 1976), 13.

cree (Aramaic *g'zerah*), he makes a fuss (Yiddish-Austrian *Geseres*). The meaning of Freud's coinage, *Auf Geseres*, is lost and found in translation.

On another level, the word pair *Geseres* and *Ungeseres* reminds Freud of dough that is *gesäuert* and *ungesäuert*, leavened and unleavened. He explains that "during their hasty departure from *Egypt*, the children of Israel did not have time to let their dough rise, and to this day, in memory of this, eat unleavened bread at Easter-time." In his assimilated Viennese context, Freud does not employ the word *Passah* (or *Pesach*), but instead refers to Passover as *Osterzeit,* Easter time. This linguistic quirk aptly reflects Freud's cultural predicament. In any case, Freud gives meaning to his apparently meaningless verbal combination by recalling the Jewish practice of eating unleavened bread in memory of the Exodus. This is all the more reason for his concern that his children will become free-minded or independent, *freizügig*. Freud's relevant associations further include the office of a "Dr. Herodes" (*Td* 428/*ID* 479), whose name approximates that of Herod the Great, king of Judea, who captured Jerusalem in 37 B.C.E. with the help of the Romans. "Herod" is also the name of the later king who massacred the children of Judea.[45]

Freud's dream enacts a drama of conflicting cultures. The opening difficulties suggest persecution; the eldest son appears to choose between the female attendant, possibly a nun, and Freud.[46] The father experiences a measure of relief when the boy gives a sign of preference, the words *Auf Ungeseres* rather than *Auf Geseres*. The negative form of this Aramaic decree, misfortune, or Yiddish clamor, suggests a possible relief. But in light of Freud's associations to Passover, the word *Ungeseres* indicates a further preference for unleavened bread, following the Jewish tradition. By refusing to kiss the nun and associating her with evil decrees and leavened bread, Freud's eldest son chooses to remember the Jewish condition of exile; he affirms the bread of servitude.[47] The freedom of his relatives to emigrate is one of Freud's childhood memories, as it is also a collective memory of the Jews.

If *Auf Geseres* and *Auf Ungeseres* have significance, what do they mean? The speaker's movement, as he addresses himself to the attendant

---

45. Alexander Grinstein mentions the possible significance of Freud's association to either of the Herods. See *On Sigmund Freud's Dreams,* p. 329.

46. Freud's dreaming reference to the female attendant recalls the nanny who cared for him as a young child. Compare Paul C. Vitz, *Sigmund Freud's Christian Unconscious* (New York: Guilford, 1988).

47. Freud's sons were members of Zionist youth organizations, according to Jacob Meitlis's recollections. See Jacob Meitlis, "The Last Days of Sigmund Freud," *Jewish Frontier* 18 (September 1951), 21. See also Falk, "Freud and Herzl," 378.

and to Freud, may be interpreted as signifying personal pronouns; then we might supply the missing words in these garbled statements: "*Auf Ihnen—* Geseres (Upon you [nun]—evil decrees)" and "*Auf dir—*Ungeseres (Upon you [father]—revoked evil decrees)." Freud's eldest son commands or prophesies misfortune to the woman, and revokes misfortune with respect to Freud. *Auf Geseres* is both a word of parting to the ghetto of Jewish separatism and a reaffirmation of Yiddish resonances in German-Jewish speech.

Freud interprets his dream as expressing a fear of one-sidedness, and in particular as attempting to resolve his concern over a one-sided intellectual development (*Td* 428/*ID* 480). His own one-sided interpretation states that the dream "contradicts this concern" (ibid.). But his eldest son's dual gesture does not merely balance the emotional and intellectual realms; it counters a one-sidedness in Freud's preference for Greek and denial of Judaic traditions.[48] In the process of his interpretation, despite his associations to Yiddish and Aramaic, Freud avoids acknowledging further meanings of *Auf Geseres*.

Freud's denials take many forms. Most immediately, he excludes the two key words, "Herzl" and "Passover," from his discussion of the dream. Although he mentions *The New Ghetto*, he chooses to omit its author's name, which later became synonymous with Zionism. Furthermore, he avoids the words *Pesach* and *Passah*, instead referring to Passover as Easter time. On a deeper level, Freud evades the themes raised by Herzl's play. In brief, *The New Ghetto* acknowledges the superficial achievements of Jewish emancipation in order to assert that Jews have nevertheless failed to free themselves from a new, internal ghetto. At this point in his pre-Zionist thought (1894), Herzl viewed assimilation favorably, as a means to greater freedom. Freud's dream, in contrast, shows a preference for the Zionism that has been associated with Herzl's name since the First Zionist Congress of 1897.[49]

Freud calls this central dream "My Son, the Myops," privileging its allusion to the Greek Cyclops and diminishing the importance of the Ara-

---

48. Compare Falk, "Freud and Herzl," 383. In *Freud's Discovery of Psychoanalysis*, McGrath associates Freud's concern with vision to the biblical stories of Jacob and Joseph (p. 239). For an alternative interpretation of this dream, see Vitz, *Sigmund Freud's Christian Unconscious*, pp. 90–92. In particular, Vitz asserts that "Freud's rejection of *Geseres* or 'salted', and his preference for 'unsalted' or *Ungeseres*, suggested a preference for non-kosher food—that is, for the 'advantage' of the gentile world" (p. 91).

49. Compare Loewenberg's "A Hidden Zionist Theme in Freud's 'My Son, the Myops . . . ' Dream," 129–32.

maic *g'zerah*. If this Passover dream fulfills a wish, it does so by resolving a specific conflict concerning Jewish identity. Freud worries about the fate of his children and hints at a solution through a linguistic innovation. Although he himself speaks condescendingly of Yiddish as "the jargon," Freud's *Auf Geseres* dream decrees for his son the task of upholding it. In *The New Ghetto*, the mother of the protagonist explains that she educated herself in order not to shame her son, and "became accustomed to a better way of speaking than Jewish-German *(Judendeutsch)*" (act I, scene iv). Directly at variance with Herzl's earlier vision, Freud's dream returns to Yiddish and counteracts the assimilatory, pre-Zionist ideas. His dream-son recalls the flight from Egypt, and instead of employing an entirely assimilated Austrian German, brings together Hebrew, Aramaic, Yiddish, and German in a unique verbal compound. While he shows that his dream is not absurd, Freud declines to read its decree.

The Grand *Verneinung*

Freud's "talking cure" and methods of dream interpretation have occasionally been understood in the context of Jewish traditions, yet the nature of this association remains unclear. His essay "Negation" ("Die Verneinung") facilitates an understanding of his own relationship to Judaic dream interpretation.[50] Although Freud refers to a drama that unfolds during psychoanalysis, his discussion—like that of transference—has broader implications.

"Negation," perhaps better rendered by "denial" or "disavowal,"[51] names a mental and verbal strategy, in some ways analogous to distortions of the dream work, by which repressed thoughts find conscious expression. The repressed material is expressed at the same time that it is

---

50. The present analysis of Freud's seminal essay focuses on certain key moments. Wilfried Ver Eecke offers a detailed reading of "Negation" and a review of secondary literature in *Saying "No": Its Meaning in Child Development, Psychoanalysis, Linguistics, and Hegel* (Pittsburgh: Duquesne University Press, 1984), pp. 1–44. Perhaps the subtlest reading of Freud's essay in Jean Hyppolite's "Commentaire parlé sur la 'Verneinung' de Freud," contained in the original French edition of Lacan's *Ecrits* (Paris: Editions du Seuil, 1966), pp. 879–87.

51. Some authors attempt to establish a terminological distinction between *Verneinung* and *Verleugnung*. In their *Vocabulaire de la psychanalyse* (Paris: Presses Universitaires de France, 1967), Jean Laplanche and J.-B. Pontalis differentiate between logical or grammatical *négation (Verneinung)* and psychological *dénégation (Verleugnung)*. They acknowledge, however, that Freud's essay on "Die Verneinung" leaves ambiguity between these two possible senses (p. 113); it employs only the word *Verneinung*. See also Ver Eecke, *Saying "No,"* pp. 3–7, 20.

denied: "Negation is a means of taking cognizance of what is repressed; it is really a lifting *(Aufhebung)* of the repression, but indeed not an acceptance of what is repressed" *(SA* 3, 373/*GPT* 214). Freud observes the evident split that arises between the intellectual function and affective processes, when the intellect recognizes what has been repressed, while repudiating it under the influence of the emotional life. Freud subsequently alludes to his seminal essay on "Remembering, Repeating, and Working Through" *(SA* Supp. 207–15/*TT* 157–66). This earlier article presents the elaborate analytical procedure through which Freud aims at an overcoming *(Überwindung)* of repressed materials, after making them available to the intellectual and emotional faculties of a patient.[52]

Freud describes negation by providing examples and explaining their linguistic forms. He writes that "to deny something in one's judgment means, at bottom [to say]: 'That is something which I would most like to repress' " *(SA* 3, 374/*GPT* 214). Instead of simply repressing the materials, the intellect expresses them together with a denial, a "no." At this point Freud employs a suggestive metaphor, comparing this "no," which is "the hallmark *(Merkzeichen)* of repression" to a "stamp of origin *(Ursprungszertifikat)*, such as 'made in Germany' " (ibid.). Freud's figure implicitly represents the individual psyche as a European topography, divided by national boundaries. The politics of trade require that products bear an imprint stating their place of origin; the laws of repression, Freud suggests, require that repressed materials bear the negating stamp of "no." Foreign goods are stamped in the international language of trade, English; unconscious materials are marked by the function of judgment.[53] Consciousness may thereby boycott unconscious contents.

Like a consumer who must decide whether to buy or not to buy foreign goods, the psyche reflects: "I would like to eat that, or I would like to spit it out . . . I would like to bring this into me and exclude that" *(SA* 3,

---

52. Freud's concise essay "Negation" illustrates his strategic considerations. Freud employs the free associations and phenomena of negation to set a trap; the German language makes the connection between associations and traps particularly evident. "Negation" opens with a reflection on the manner in which patients provide associations *(Einfälle)*. The second paragraph subsequently sets a trap *(Falle)* for the patient by asking what the least likely association might be.

53. John Murray Cuddihy suggests that the "id" is analogous to the "yid," striving to enter consciousness as the Jew strives to enter European civilization. See *The Ordeal of Civility: Freud, Marx, Lévi-Strauss, and the Jewish Struggle with Modernity* (New York: Basic Books, 1974). From a linguistic standpoint, one might say that the id is like Yiddish, striving to become German in the mouths of assimilating German Jews.

374/*GPT* 215). Freud calls this the "language of the oldest, oral instinctual impulses," and it is a language against which the conscious "I" struggles. The boundaries of the psyche are comparable to political borders, separating national cultures and languages; boundaries divide both within the psyche and between the psyche and what is external to it. Reality testing performs the work of a border guard when it "controls" the distortions of perception (*SA* 3, 375/*GPT* 216).

Freudian *Verneinung* combines the emergence and disavowal of a repressed mental content. Conscious judgment corresponds to the workings of unconscious repression when it hinders free movement in the psyche by stamping foreign materials with a "no." Hence Freud concludes his essay by observing that this negative stamp indicates the presence of unconscious materials: "There is no stronger proof of the successful uncovering of the unconscious than when the patient reacts: 'I never thought that' " (*SA* 3, 377/*GPT* 217). According to Freud's analysis, these words are the trademark, assigned by the intellectual function of judgment, signifying (to caricature the Freudian psychoanalytic landscape) "Made in the Unconscious."

Later authors have applied the Freudian theory of denial to more general psychological and literary problems, although without always drawing attention to Freud's own denials. Anna Freud's *The Ego and the Mechanisms of Defense* (1936) analyzes the battles of the "I" with its affective life. Harold Bloom has extended the Freudian model, and has shown that the relationships between authors may be understood in terms of mechanisms of defense. According to Bloom's interpretations of Romantic poetry, the poetic ego struggles against prior authors, attempting to clear imaginative space for its own productions.[54] A kind of denial or "lie against time"

---

54. See Harold Bloom, *The Anxiety of Influence: A Theory of Poetry* (New York: Oxford University Press, 1973), and *A Map of Misreading* (New York: Oxford University Press, 1975). The "mechanisms of defense" are not identical with the more elusive "mechanisms of the dream work." Both represent individual (yet typical) ways in which reality is revised; they tend in opposite directions. Whereas the mechanisms of defense are components of rational control, close to the workings of intellectual judgment, mechanisms of the dream work are beyond the sphere of the I (or ego, *Ich*). Freud associates the dream work with censorship, although it does not correspond to any personal agency. Our life stories undergo narrative revision in our dreams, but the author of these revisions is not the same as the reasoning self of the dreamer. On the role of defense mechanisms in poetic creation, see Harold Bloom, "Freud's Concepts of Defense and the Poetic Will," in *Agon: Towards a Theory of Revisionism* (New York: Oxford University Press, 1982), pp. 119–44. One may begin to differentiate denial from defense by observing that denial involves an "undoing of the defense." See Ver Eecke, *Saying "No,"* p. 10.

enables strong poets to vie with their precursors.[55] Bloom's literary criticism arises, in part, from a strong reading (or "misreading," in his own term) of Freudian *Verneinung*. His central assumption may be paraphrased: Every major text represses, and employs a system of defenses against, prior texts. Hence a text "is not a gathering of signs on a page, but is a psychic battlefield upon which authentic forces struggle for the only victory worth winning, the divinating triumph over oblivion."[56] Bloom focuses attention on the poetic dramas in which battles for strength work themselves out.[57] This is one sense in which we may apply Freud's *Verneinung* to Freud himself, especially concerning the relationship between his methods of dream interpretation and ancient traditions.

Freud's discussion of denial applies to his own work, which both affirms and negates Judaic sources. The new science of dream interpretation acknowledges—and yet establishes itself at an overstated distance from— prior models. Freud's *Interpretation of Dreams* is subject to distortions like those of the dream work; his interpretation of dreams invented a dream of

---

55. Current literary theory has been divided over questions of psychology and textuality. Paul de Man's review of *The Anxiety of Influence* remains an incisive reading of the Freudian dimension in Harold Bloom's project. De Man criticizes Bloom's psychological approach, emphasizing the textual status of misreading: "Texts originate in contact with other texts rather than in contact with the events or the agents of life (unless, of course, these agents or events are themselves treated as texts). To say that literature is based on influence is to say that it is intratextual." See Paul de Man, "Review of Harold Bloom's *Anxiety of Influence*," in *Blindness and Insight: Essays in the Rhetoric of Contemporary Criticism*, 2d ed. (Minneapolis: University of Minnesota Press, 1983), p. 273. De Man questions the psychological basis of Bloom's analyses, arguing that beneath the psychological "drama" lies a "linguistic model that could be described in a very different tone and terminology" (ibid., p. 274). De Man, then, preferred to "set aside the trappings of psychology" in order to understand the relationship between texts.

56. Harold Bloom, *Poetry and Repression: Revisionism from Blake to Stevens* (New Haven: Yale University Press, 1976), p. 2. This assertion stands directly in a Nietzschean line.

57. Tensions between the psychology and the textuality of influence are evident in one exchange between Jacques Derrida and Harold Bloom. In his essay "Freud and the Scene of Writing," Derrida writes: "What is a text, and what must the psychical be in order to be represented by a text?" (See *L'écriture et la différence*, p. 297; in English, see *Writing and Difference*, p. 199.) He refers to the Freudian metaphor of the *Wunderblock*, a writing toy which shares certain characteristics with the mind (see *SA* 3, 365–69/*GPT* 207–12). Harold Bloom explicitly reverses Derrida's quotation, asking: "What is a psyche, and what must a text be if it can be represented by a psyche?" (See *Poetry and Repression*, p. 1.)

interpretation that separated its inventor from his precursors. The present work uncovers the Freudian tactics that allow him to clear space for his writings by disavowing their Judaic antecedents. This denial was virtually inevitable, since Freud could only have cast further doubt upon his views by linking them to biblical or Talmudic sources. While Freud insisted on the scientific status of psychoanalysis, he censored from all of his exports the imprimatur: Made in (Exile from) Jerusalem. This Jewish *goiser* or *g'zerah*, doom or decree, was a malaise that Freud always repressed and yet never renounced.

Freud carefully distinguishes his practices of dream interpretation from those of ancient times, replacing the divine apparatus by mechanisms of the dream work. Dreams thereby become expressions of individual wishes and lose their potentially prophetic significance. According to ancient beliefs, dreams are primarily concerned with the future, but Freud understands them as expressions of past desires: the dream represents an aspect of personal history. Freud's essays on "the occult significance of dreams" reject the notion that dreams can foretell the future and reconceive telepathy as thought transference.

In the final paragraph of *The Interpretation of Dreams*, Freud again raises questions about the relationship between dreams and the future. Although he dismisses the prophetic view of dreams, he grants a certain similarity between ancient beliefs and his own theories. His first gesture is entirely negative: "And the value of dreams for knowledge of the future? There is naturally no question of that *(Daran ist natürlich nicht zu denken)*" (Td 588/ID 659). Freud's denial literally asserts that a prophetic value of dreams is "naturally not to be thought." Freud did not wish to entertain such archaic thoughts; he raises the question of this possible content only to reject it vigorously. Rather, he repeats, dreams are of value "for knowledge of the past" (Td 588/ID 660). Here Freud's language is again significant. Where the standard translation reads, "it would be truer to say instead," a more accurate translation is, "one would prefer to [or, one might] substitute for this *(man möchte dafür einsetzen)*." Freud virtually acknowledges his own wish to replace the ancient future orientation in dream interpretation with an orientation toward the past.

Freud writes as if dreams rather than interpretations were at issue, and asserts that "dreams derive from the past in every sense." Claiming to have solved the riddle of dreams, Freud nevertheless does grant some merit to earlier views: "Indeed, the old belief that dreams show us the future is not entirely lacking in the import of truth." He alludes to the fact that a wish inherently aims toward the future; a dream that represents a repressed wish thus does reveal something about the future. Yet Freud is still concerned to contradict Joseph, and recasts the older views in his own terms: "By representing a wish as fulfilled, the dream by all means leads us into the future; but this future, taken by the dreamer to be present, is shaped by the indestructible wish into the image of its past" (*Td* 588/*ID* 660). The wish-fulfilling dream reveals a desired future that is, however, predetermined by the dreamer's past. A biblical echo is close to the surface of Freud's resonant concluding words. Having just admitted that the "old belief" contains some truth, Freud proceeds to appropriate an ancient tradition. In place of "God created man in his image" (Gen. 1:27), Freud asserts his humanistic dogma: the indestructible wish creates the future in the image of its past. Libido takes the place of God as the determinant of human destiny.

Freud revises Hebraic traditions, replacing religious belief by an interpretive discipline purporting to be a twentieth-century science. Where the Bible represents dreams as messages from God, Freud views them as messages from the unconscious; where Joseph and Daniel discover the meaning of dreams in the future, Freud shows how dreamers' wishes arise from the past.

Freud's dominant theme in *The Interpretation of Dreams* is not dreams, but interpretation. In an unspoken confrontation with Judaic traditions, Freud evades this point by avoiding rabbinic statements on dream interpretation, concentrating instead on renouncing the prophetic procedures of Joseph. The Talmud and Midrash anticipate his skepticism, including his recognition of mundane meanings behind what others wished to view as prophetic. Moreover, tractate Berakhot and Lamentations Rabbah might have forced Freud to recognize that no meaning inheres in a dream; all meaning depends on interpretation. Wishes are always present, and future-directed, guiding the hand of the interpreter.

A dream of interpretation leads Freud to unconscious wishes as a foundation of meaning, at odds with the Talmudic metaphor "all dreams follow the mouth," which emphasizes the active role of the interpreter. Freud seeks to pierce beyond the dream report to motivating contents. Certain Judaic sources show, in contrast, how meaning emerges through a grafting of text upon text, of dream upon Scripture and of Scripture upon dream. The meanings of texts always evolve through other texts, translations, associations, transformations. Freud's dream of interpretation is a method that denies its own place as a revision of Judaic traditions. Freud "feared for the future of his work; he feared that it would be known to posterity as a Jewish science."[58]

As the Talmudic interpretation of "Cappadocia" brings together Aramaic and Greek, Freud's interpretations of certain dreams pass through German, English, Yiddish, Latin, Greek, and Hebrew. In the Talmud, to

---

58. See Abram Kardiner, "Freud: The Man I Knew, the Scientist, and His Influence," in *Freud and the 20th Century*, ed. Benjamin Nelson (New York: Meridian Books, 1957), p. 52; compare Freud's letter to Karl Abraham of 3 May 1908.

the extent that the Hebrew Bible is considered the blueprint for reality, linguistic hybrids pose a potential threat. Nonbiblical languages and expressions, if they bear hidden layers of non-Hebraic contents, may challenge the priority of God's words. Freud's insistently secular interpretations powerfully pose this threat, in each case deciphering an individual dream code on the basis of the patient's free associations. Freud discerns virtually endless meanings in every dream or linguistic utterance, thus decentering the claims of Scripture. Only the operations of the dream work remain constant, forming the dream, deforming meaning, and informing interpretation. Freud's own dreams and methods of interpretation, when reinterpreted, express his own repressed position in Judaic culture.

Freud takes a step beyond Talmudic dream texts when he points to the overdetermined quality of signification and translates various linguistic codes. In retrospect, the Talmud places in question the scientific pretenses of modern psychology when it reveals the active power of the interpreter who, by offering meaning, casts himself in the role of prophet. Furthermore, the Midrashic narratives of rabbis and dream interpreters anticipate Freud's skeptical approach to dream prophecy.

Freud presumes to work objectively when he translates manifest contents into latent contents or dream thoughts. The Talmud recognizes a tendency toward arbitrariness in the processes of interpretation, which does not prevent prophetic interpretations from being fulfilled. The overdetermination of dream contents prevents Freud from claiming a definitive interpretation, yet he hesitates to admit that dream interpretation may follow arbitrary patterns. The dream work is ultimately indistinguishable from the interpreter's work.

CONCLUSION

1

This book brings together the disparate Freudian and ancient Judaic traditions of dream interpretation. While there is no purely or exclusively Jewish way of interpreting dreams, and no continuous line of influence runs from the biblical Joseph and Daniel to Freud, these shifting patterns of dream interpretation are themselves open to interpretation. The relationship between Freud and his forerunners is not one of direct influence, but of denied influence: Freud's dream book and later essays are marked by conspicuous gestures of avoidance.

Freud understandably renounced his forebears, since the dream interpreter faced nearly insurmountable prejudices in the late nineteenth century. Almost alone among scientific dream theorists, Freud insisted that dreams have an interpretable meaning; this linked him to ancient beliefs and popular opinion. Although Freud could have drawn from biblical and Talmudic precursors, prevailing biases led him to disavow them.

Freud was not the first authority to feel threatened by ancient dream interpretation. Early rabbis were also threatened by sectarian dream interpreters who claimed to know the meaning of dreams. To the extent that dream interpreters made such claims and exerted influence, they stood in competition with rabbinic interpreters of Scripture. Neither scriptural commentary nor dream interpretation is, as a result, entirely distinct from power struggle. Rabbinic authorities wish to maintain the privileged place of their commentaries and are challenged by the apparent successes of other interpreters. The rivalry between competing interpretive groups is especially obvious in the Midrash to Lamentations, when R. Ishmael ben R. Yose denounces a Samaritan who sets himself up as a dream interpreter.

Biblical and Talmudic traditions show that interpretation is never a neutral act. Much as the interpreter may wish to appear unbiased, his work always furthers or hinders particular interests. In general, the dream interpreter rises to power through his interpretations, even when the dreamer (as in the case of Nebuchadnezzar) does not benefit from them. Biblical and Talmudic dream interpretation also demonstrate that no commentary can be entirely purged of prophetic effects. Rabbinic traditions suggest that no dream is intrinsically prophetic; only interpretation, not dreams in themselves, can foretell future actions and events. This notion was an anathema to Freud, who resisted the prophetic dimension of dream interpretation and sought the meaning of dreams in their relationship to the past.

Freud challenged and was challenged by alternative forms of interpretation. Similar to Joseph and Daniel, he attained power as an interpreter; whereas his biblical precursors attributed their successes to God's assistance, Freud claimed to rely on scientific methods. In so doing, he underplayed the prophetic potential of interpretation. While Talmudic opinion does not uniformly support the idea that dreams or their interpretations predict the future, tractate Berakhot implies that interpretations, like language in general, can alter reality. Despite his own recognition of the potency of language, Freud was obliged to ignore such troubling messages.

Freud's interpretations reflected a tension between nineteenth-century philology, with its methods of textual commentary, and the more radical psychoanalytic approach. Freud began with the dream text—the dreamer's narrative report, which is essentially a literary document—and developed a novel mode of textuality, an associative genre that is as unusual as Kafka's dreamy fictions. Nevertheless, in his assumptions about textual meaning, Freud often relied on the prevailing hermeneutics. He separated the manifest content from the latent content of dream reports, viewing the manifest level as an external husk that concealed an inner sense, and suggested that by reading back from manifest dream contents he could arrive at the thoughts that motivated and explained them. Freud indicated that the meaning of a dream text stands behind it, in the unconscious impulses of the dreamer; his analytic procedure purportedly returned from the external facade of expression to the hidden realm of repressed materials, from the dream disguise to naked truth.

Freud's theories were more conventional than his practices, and free association was his most radical interpretive innovation. Rather than simply provide an interpretation based on the dream report, Freud set up conditions under which the dreamer could generate the interpretation. Yet Freud did not acknowledge the full consequences of this method: faithful to his scientific aspirations, he argued that the associations always revealed motivating thoughts. This implied a deterministic view, and turned attention away from the prospective component of dream analysis.

Freudian techniques were torn between study of the individual past and efforts to change the future. In his writings, Freud chose to make light of the latter aspect. He dissociated himself from anything resembling prophetic dream interpretation, although his therapy necessarily went beyond research into the past. Despite Freud's rejection of collective Judaic traditions, in this respect the repressed returned to haunt him. Even the psychoanalytic dream interpreter modifies the dreamer's future—by means of suggestive guidance.

Whereas nineteenth-century philology sought meaning behind the text, in authorial intentions or ideas, current theorists recognize the innumerable possibilities for meaning beyond the text. Authorial intent no longer has special privilege, in part as a result of Freud's own demonstration of unconscious meanings. Even the notion of unconscious thoughts and wishes is, however, insufficient. Meaning does not lie inside the text or psyche, like wine aging in a bottle. What is supposedly inside depends on what is beyond it.

With his practice of dream interpretation by free association, Freud was both ahead of his time and behind his time. He never acknowledged the disparity, but went on practicing this novel method. He was ahead of his time when he allowed virtually limitless meanings to emerge through the dreamer's free associations. Yet in other contexts he fell back on nineteenth-century philology, when he tried to validate the method of free association by claiming that it always revealed the repressed thoughts that produced the dream. Following the metaphor of an imaginary journey, Freud's analyses purported to reenter the tunnel of sleep, shedding light on the shadowy realm from above. Nevertheless, like prophetic interpretations in the Bible or Talmud, the patient's associations often pointed toward a future.

Both ahead of and behind his time, Freud anticipated contemporary literary theory and recapitulated some aspects of ancient Jewish dream interpretation. When he interpreted a patient's dream psychoanalytically, attending to wordplays and associations, his interpretations interacted with a possible future. Freud understood, but did not publicize, the risks that are so vividly portrayed in the stories of Bar Hedia and R. Ishmael. He acted as a modern prophet, influencing personal lives and intellectual history, at the same time that he argued against prophecy.

The founder of psychoanalysis opposed other forms of dream interpretation, as did R. Ishmael ben R. Yose when he disparaged a competing interpreter. Another milieu might have encouraged Freud to draw upon biblical and Talmudic models, since his own interpretations easily appeared prophetic to patients experiencing the transference neurosis. Freud sought to ground his interpretations in causal explanations, although every interpretation of the past interacts with the present and projects toward the future.

Freud was not overtly influenced by ancient dream interpretation, but had he allowed himself to submit to such an influence, the most forward-looking aspects of his method might have been in harmony with these repressed, prior models. In any event, Freud treated the dream report "as a holy text" (*Td* 493/*ID* 552), and in some respects he was of the rabbis' party without knowing it, or without wishing to let it be known.

2

Freud repudiated ancient traditions and the most radical implications of interpreting dreams. The two denials are interconnected: had he come to terms with the biblical and Talmudic texts on dreams, Freud might have found an unexpected context for his revolutionary interpretive methods. This was not, however, an affiliation he could accept. He sought the meaning of dreams in conscious, preconscious, and especially in unconscious thoughts, assuming that these existed prior to, and were responsible for, dreams. Yet his theory of secondary revision recognizes an element of dream formation that is analogous to waking mental processes. Associations, if indeed "free," also create new materials. Freud denied both Judaic traditions and the freedom of interpretation by which meaning exceeds the boundaries of an individual psyche.

The Interpretation of Dreams sets out to solve the riddle of dreams, leaving behind a scene of unresolved mysteries. Scrutiny of Freud's dream of interpretation reopens the dream book, showing that the dream continues: interpretation discovers hidden pathways between texts, adds dream upon dream, and never attains a realm of absolute clarity. Freud, by isolating himself from his precursors, blocked access to forbidden routes that remain obscure. Like Freud—when he explored the "unconscious of the dream"—we may reexamine what remains unresolved in the dream book and take tentative steps forward with the repressed traditions.

Freud's biblical precursors associated the interpreter of dreams with the prophet; Freud contradicted them when he asserted that dreams express past wishes and do not foretell future events. Freud could not develop a neutral method of interpretation, however, for the patient's associations link dreams to continuing dramas of life. Every interpretation in terms of the past has implications, and may change the meaning and making of the future. Turning away from such intimations, Freud nevertheless innovated when he substituted a text for a text and a dream for a dream.

In the shadow of nineteenth-century thought, we intuitively favor a philological view of interpretation, whether it seeks meaning as divine or human intentions, or even as an abstract content that subsists in relation to a text. Associations and displacements threaten reason, suggesting an endless re-creation of sense. Dream interpretations that explain determining causes may add little to the individual's particular self-understanding. Another style of interpretation, discussing possible consequences as revealed by personal associations, reveals a desired future that must be evaluated, sought, or rejected. Prophecy is not limited to prescience; there need be no exact correspondence between a prophetic statement and what later occurs. Prophecy provokes change, just as wishes, promises, projects, ambitions, and requests imply a future. Desire itself, the mythical libido, aims toward future events.

Future-oriented dream interpretation is both more problematic and more significant than diagnostic interpretation. An interpreter who recognizes his power over the future accepts an ethical burden; to the extent that Freud did not take responsibility for the future, he restricted or misrepresented his curative role. In order to ground his science of psychoanalysis, Freud claimed that recollection of the past facilitated a working-through of complexes. In practice, however, Freud exploited the transference relationship toward cure, aiming beyond the dream's manifest content with the help of the dreamer's free associations.

Freudian theory has been divided between its dual orientation toward a formative past and a future to be formed. Freud himself declined to interpret fully his own dreams of Irma and *Auf Geseres*, which attempted to resolve conflicts that had little connection to repressed childhood wishes. If psychoanalysis does not explain repeatable patterns, it cannot claim to be scientific, and if it does not promise to change the course of an individual life it cannot claim to be useful. Freud sought to determine underlying causes of dreams; on the other hand, he employed free associations and the transference to transform his interpretations into the talking cure.

Meaning is both cognitive and performative. Every dream sets a stage and enacts a play, while every interpretation produces further meanings as the interpreter oversees continuing performances. From the interpretation of dreams and the dream of interpretation there is no escape. The meaning of a dream, like the meaning of a word, depends on its use.

Where the dream was, there interpretation shall be. The interpreter assumes an active role in the creation of sense.

References

Abbreviations of Works by Sigmund Freud

AP   *Aus den Anfängen der Psychoanalyse: Briefe an Wilhelm Fliess, Abhandlungen und Notizen aus den Jahren 1887–1902*. London: Imago, 1950.

BWF   *Briefe an Wilhelm Fliess 1887–1904*. Ed. Jeffrey Moussaieff Masson and Michael Schröter. Frankfurt am Main: S. Fischer, 1986.

CC   *Character and Culture*. Ed. Philip Rieff. New York: Macmillan, 1963.

CL   *The Complete Letters of Sigmund Freud to Wilhelm Fliess 1887–1904*. Trans. and ed. Jeffrey Moussaieff Masson. Cambridge: Harvard University Press, 1985.

GPT   *General Psychological Theory*. Ed. Philip Rieff. New York: Collier, 1963.

GW   *Gesammelte Werke*. Vols. 1–18. London: Imago, 1940–68.

ID   *The Interpretation of Dreams*. Trans. James Strachey. New York: Avon, 1965.

ILP   *Introductory Lectures on Psychoanalysis*. Trans. James Strachey. New York: W. W. Norton, 1966.

NIL   *New Introductory Lectures on Psychoanalysis*. Trans. James Strachey. New York: W. W. Norton, 1965.

OD   *On Dreams*. Trans. James Strachey. New York: W. W. Norton, 1952.

OP   *The Origins of Psycho-Analysis: Letters to Wilhelm Fliess, Drafts and Notes, 1887–1902*. Ed. Marie Bonaparte, Anna Freud, and Ernst Kris. Trans. Eric Mosbacher and James Strachey. New York: Basic Books, 1954.

SA   *Studienausgabe*. Vols. 1–10 and Supp. vol. Ed. Alexander Mitscherlich, Angela Richards, James Strachey, and Ilse Gubrich-Simitis. Frankfurt am Main: S. Fischer, 1969–75.

SE   *The Standard Edition of the Complete Psychological Works of Sigmund Freud*. Vols. 1–24. Ed. James Strachey. London: The Hogarth Press, 1953–74.

SP   *Studies in Parapsychology*. Ed. Philip Rieff. New York: Collier, 1963.

Td *Die Traumdeutung.* In the *Studienausgabe.* Vol. 2. Ed. Alexander Mitscherlich, Angela Richards, and James Strachey, Frankfurt am Main: S. Fischer, 1972.

TT *Therapy and Technique.* Ed. Philip Rieff. New York: Collier, 1963.

UTT *Uber Träume und Traumdeutungen.* Frankfurt am Main: S. Fischer, 1971.

VEP *Vorlesungen zur Einführung in die Psychoanalyse.* In the *Studienausgabe.* Vol. 1. Ed. Alexander Mitscherlich, Angela Richards, and James Strachey. Frankfurt am Main: S. Fischer, 1969.

Freud, Psychoanalysis, and Dreams

Adler, Alfred. *The Practice and Theory of Individual Psychology.* Trans. P. Radin. London: Routledge and Kegan Paul, 1929.

————. *Praxis und Theorie der Individualpsychologie: Vorträge zur Einführung in die Psychotherapie für Ärzte, Psychologen und Lehrer.* 3d ed. Munich: J. F. Bergmann, 1927.

Anzieu, Didier. *L'auto-analyse de Freud et la découverte de la psychanalyse.* Vols. 1–2. 2d ed. Paris: Presses Universitaires de France, 1975.

————. *Freud's Self-Analysis.* Trans. Peter Graham. Madison, Conn.: International Universities Press, 1986.

Aristotle. *Prophesying by Dreams.* In *The Basic Works of Aristotle.* Trans. Richard McKeon. New York: Random House, 1941.

Aron, Willy. "Notes on Sigmund Freud's Ancestry and Jewish Contacts." *YIVO Annual of Jewish Social Science* 11 (1956/57), 286–95.

Artemidorus. *The Interpretation of Dreams.* Trans. Robert J. White. Park Ridge, N. J.: Noyes, 1975.

Bakan, David. *Sigmund Freud and the Jewish Mystical Tradition.* Boston: Beacon, 1975.

Balkanyi, Charlotte. "On Verbalization." *International Journal of Psycho-Analysis* 45 (1965), 64–79.

Basic Psychoanalytic Concepts on the Theory of Dreams. Ed. Humberto Nagera et al. London: George Allen and Unwin, 1969.

Beck, Aaron T. "Cognitive Patterns in Dreams and Daydreams." In *Dream Dynamics.* (*Science and Psychoanalysis.* Vol. 19.) Ed. Jules H. Masserman. New York: Grune & Stratton, 1971.

Bergmann, Martin S. "Moses and the Evolution of Freud's Jewish Identity." *The Israel Annals of Psychiatry and Related Disciplines* 14 (March 1976), 3–26.

Bettelheim, Bruno. *Freud and Man's Soul.* New York: Alfred A. Knopf, 1983.

Binswanger, Ludwig. *Dream and Existence.* Trans. Forrest Williams and Jacob Needleman. *Review of Existential Psychology and Psychiatry* 19, no. 1 (1984–85).

———. *Le rêve et l'existence.* Trans. Jacqueline Verdeaux. Bruges: Desclée de Brouwer, 1954.

———. "Traum und Existenz." In *Ausgewählte Vorträge und Aufsätze.* Vol. 1. Bern: A. Francke, 1947.

Blatt, David S. "The Development of the Hero: Sigmund Freud and the Reformation of the Jewish Tradition." *Psychoanalysis and Contemporary Thought* 11 (1988), 639–703.

Bloom, Harold. *Agon: Towards a Theory of Revisionism.* New York: Oxford University Press, 1982.

———. *The Anxiety of Influence: A Theory of Poetry.* New York: Oxford University Press, 1973.

———. *Poetry and Repression: Revisionism from Blake to Stevens.* New Haven: Yale University Press, 1976.

Boss, Menard. *Der Traum und seine Auslegung.* Bern: Hans Huber, 1953.

Bossard, Robert. *Psychologie des Traumbewusstseins.* Zürich: Rascher, 1951.

Cuddihy, John Murray. *The Ordeal of Civility: Freud, Marx, Lévi-Strauss, and the Jewish Struggle with Modernity.* New York: Basic Books, 1974.

Dalbiez, Roland. *La méthode psychanalytique et la doctrine freudienne.* Paris: Desclée de Brouwer, 1936.

Damstra, Marten N. "Telepathic Mechanisms in Dreams." *Psychiatric Quarterly* 26 (1952), 100–134.

Derrida, Jacques. *La carte postale de Socrate à Freud et au-délà.* Paris: Flammarion, 1980.

———. *L'écriture et la différence.* Paris: Editions du Seuil, 1967.

———. "How to Avoid Speaking: Denials." Trans. Ken Frieden. In *Languages of the Unsayable: The Play of Negativity in Literature and Literary Theory.* Ed. Sanford Budick and Wolfgang Iser. New York: Columbia University Press, 1989.

———. *Psyché: Inventions de l'autre.* Paris: Galilée, 1987.

————. *Writing and Difference.* Trans. Alan Bass. Chicago: University of Chicago Press, 1978.

Devereux, George, ed. *Psychoanalysis and the Occult.* New York: International Universities Press, 1953.

Edelson, Marshall. *Language and Interpretation in Psychoanalysis.* New Haven: Yale University Press, 1975.

Ehrenwald, Jan. "Presumptively Telepathic Incidents during Analysis." *Psychiatric Quarterly* 24 (1950), 726–43.

Erikson, Erik. "The Dream Specimen of Psychoanalysis." *Journal of the American Psychoanalytic Association* 2 (1954), 5–56.

Falk, Avner. "Freud and Herzl." *Contemporary Psychoanalysis* 14 (July 1978), 357–87.

Felman, Shoshana, ed. *Literature and Psychoanalysis: The Question of Reading: Otherwise.* Baltimore: Johns Hopkins University Press, 1982.

————. "Postal Survival, or the Question of the Navel." *Yale French Studies* 69 (1985), 49–72.

Ferenczi, Sandor. *Bausteine zur Psychoanalyse.* 2d ed. Vols. 1–4. Bern: Hans Huber, 1964.

French, Thomas. "Insight and Distortion in Dreams." *International Journal of Psycho-Analysis* 20 (1939), 287–98.

————. *The Integration of Behavior.* Vols. 1–2. Chicago: University of Chicago Press, 1952–54.

Fromm, Erich. *The Forgotten Language.* New York: Holt, Rinehart and Winston, 1951.

Gay, Peter. *Freud, Jews, and Other Germans: Masters and Victims in Modernist Culture.* New York: Oxford University Press, 1978.

————. *A Godless Jew: Freud, Atheism, and the Making of Psychoanalysis.* New Haven: Yale University Press, 1987.

Goldhammer, Leo. "Theodor Herzl und Siegmund [*sic*] Freud: (Träume)." In the *Theodor Herzl Jahrbuch.* Vienna: H. Glanz, 1937, pp. 266–68.

Gordis, Robert. "The Two Faces of Freud." *Judaism* 24 (1975), 194–200.

Grinstein, Alexander. *On Sigmund Freud's Dreams.* Detroit: Wayne State University Press, 1968.

Grollman, Earl A. *Judaism in Sigmund Freud's World.* New York: Appleton-Century, 1965.

Grunbaum, Adolf. *The Foundations of Psychoanalysis: A Philosophical Critique.* Berkeley: University of California Press, 1984.

Gutheil, Emil A. *The Handbook of Dream Analysis.* New York: Liveright, 1951.

————. *The Language of the Dream.* New York: Macmillan, 1939.

Habermas, Jürgen. *Erkenntnis und Interesse.* Frankfurt am Main: Suhrkamp, 1973.

————. *Knowledge and Human Interests.* Trans. Jeremy J. Shapiro. Boston: Beacon Press, 1971.

Hildebrandt, F. W. *Der Traum und seine Verwertung fur's Leben.* 2d ed. Leipzig: Reinboth, 1881.

Hook, Sidney, ed. Psychoanalysis, Scientific Method, and Philosophy. New York: New York University Press, 1959.

Hyppolite, Jean. "Commentaire parlé sur la 'Verneinung' de Freud." In Jacques Lacan's *Ecrits.* Paris: Editions du Seuil, 1966.

Isakower, Otto. "Spoken Words in Dreams." *The Psychoanalytic Quarterly* 23 (1954), 1–6.

Jakobson, Roman, and Morris Halle. *Fundamentals of Language.* 2d ed. The Hague: Mouton, 1975.

Jones, Ernest. *The Life and Work of Sigmund Freud.* Vols. 1–3. New York: Basic Books, 1953–57.

Jones, Richard M. *Ego Synthesis in Dreams.* Cambridge, Mass.: Schenkman, 1962.

Judovitz, Dalia. "Freud: Translation and/or Interpretation." *Sub–Stance* 2 (1979), 29–38.

Jung, C. G. *Dreams.* Trans. R. F. C. Hull. Princeton: Princeton University Press, 1974.

————. *Über psychische Energetik und das Wesen der Träume.* 2d ed. Zürich: Rascher, 1948.

————. *Wirklichkeit der Seele.* 4th ed. Zürich: Rascher, 1969.

Kanzer, Mark. "The Communicative Function of the Dream." *International Journal of Psycho-Analysis* 36 (1955), 260–66.

Kanzer, Mark, and Jules Glenn, eds. *Freud and His Self-Analysis.* New York: Jason Aronson, 1979.

Klein, Dennis. *Jewish Origins of the Psychoanalytic Movement.* Chicago: University of Chicago Press, 1985.

Kofman, Sarah. *L'enfance de l'art: Une interprétation de l'esthétique freudienne.* Paris: Payot, 1970.

Krüll, Marianne. *Freud and His Father.* Trans. Arnold J. Pomerans. New York: W. W. Norton, 1986.

————. *Freud und sein Vater: Die Entstehung der Psychoanalyse und Freuds ungelöste Vaterbindung.* Munich: C. H. Beck, 1979.

Lacan, Jacques. *Ecrits.* Paris: Editions du Seuil, 1966.

————. *Ecrits: A Selection.* Trans. Alan Sheridan. New York: W. W. Norton, 1977.

————. *Le Séminaire.* Vols. 1–2. Ed. Jacques-Alain Miller. Paris: Editions du Seuil, 1975–78.

Laplanche, Jean, and J.-B. Pontalis. "Fantasme originaire, fantasmes des origines, origine du fantasme." *Les Temps Modernes* 19 (1964), 1833–68.

————. "Fantasy and the Origins of Sexuality." *International Journal of Psycho-Analysis* 49 (1968), 1–18.

————. *The Language of Psycho-Analysis.* Trans. Donald Nicholson-Smith. New York: W. W. Norton, 1973.

————. *Vocabulaire de la psychanalyse.* 2d ed. Paris: Presses Universitaires de France, 1968.

Lauer, Chaim. "Das Wesen des Traumes in der Beurteilung der talmudischen und rabbinischen Literatur." *Internationale Zeitschrift für Psychoanalyse und "Imago"* 1 (1913), 459–69.

Leavitt, Harry C. "A Biographical and Teleological Study of 'Irma's Injection' Dream." *Psychoanalytic Review* 43 (1956), 440–47.

Lewy, Heinrich. "Zu dem Traumbuche des Artemidorus." *Rheinisches Museum für Philologie,* N. F. 48 (1893), 398–419.

Loewenberg, Peter. "A Hidden Zionist Theme in Freud's 'My Son, the Myops . . . ' Dream." *Journal of the History of Ideas* 31 (1970), 129–32.

————. " 'Sigmund Freud as a Jew': A Study in Ambivalence and Courage." *Journal of the History of the Behavioral Sciences* 7 (1971), 363–69.

Loewenstein, Rudolph M. "The Problem of Interpretation." *Psychoanalytic Quarterly* 20 (1951), 1–14.

Lowy, Samuel. *Psychological and Biological Foundations of Dream-Interpretation.* London: Kegan Paul, Trench, Trubner, 1942.

Luders, Wolfram. "Traum und Selbst." *Psyche* 36 (September 1982), 813–29.

McGrath, William J. *Freud's Discovery of Psychoanalysis: The Politics of Hysteria.* Ithaca: Cornell University Press, 1986.

Maeder, A. "Über die Funktion des Traumes." *Jahrbuch für psychoanalytische und psychopathologische Forschung* 4 (1912), 692–707.

————. "Über das Traumproblem." *Jahrbuch für psychoanalytische und psychopathologische Forschung* 5 (1913), 647–86.

Malcolm, Janet. *In the Freud Archives.* New York: Alfred A. Knopf, 1984.

Masson, Jeffrey Moussaieff. *The Assault on Truth: Freud's Suppression of the Seduction Theory.* New York: Farrar, Straus and Giroux, 1984.

Maury, Alfred. *Le sommeil et les rêves.* 2d ed. Paris: Didier, 1861.

Meitlis, Jacob. "The Last Days of Sigmund Freud." *Jewish Frontier* 18 (September 1951), 20–22.

Menninger, Karl. "The Genius of the Jew in Psychiatry." In *A Psychiatrist's World: The Selected Papers of Karl Menninger.* Ed. Bernard H. Hall. New York: Viking Press, 1959.

Nelson, Benjamin, ed. *Freud and the 20th Century.* New York: Meridian Books, 1957.

Pfrimmer, Théo. *Freud: Lecteur de la bible.* Paris: Presses Universitaires de France, 1982.

Politzer, Georges. *Critique des fondements de la psychologie.* 3d ed. Paris: Presses Universitaires de France, 1968.

Rassial, Adélie, and Jean-Jacques, eds. *La psychanalyse est-elle une histoire juive?* Paris: Editions du Seuil, 1981.

Ricoeur, Paul. *De l'interprétation: Essai sur Freud.* Paris: Editions du Seuil, 1965.

————. *Freud and Philosophy.* Trans. Denis Savage. New Haven: Yale University Press, 1970.

Rieff, Philip. *Freud: The Mind of the Moralist.* New York: Anchor Books, 1961.

Roazen, Paul. *Freud and His Followers.* New York: Alfred A. Knopf, 1975.

Roback, A. A. *Jewish Influence in Modern Thought.* Cambridge, Mass.: Sci-Art Publishers, 1929.

Robert, Marthe. *D'Œdipe à Moïse: Freud et la conscience juive.* Paris: Calmann-Levy, 1974.

————. *From Oedipus to Moses: Freud's Jewish Identity.* Trans. Ralph Manheim. Garden City, N. Y.: Anchor Books, 1976.

Robin, Régine. "Le yiddish, langue fantasmatique?" *L'écrit du temps* 5 (1984), 43–50.

Roland, Alan. "The Context and Unique Function of Dreams in Psychoanalytic Therapy: Clinical Approach." *International Journal of Psycho-Analysis* 52 (1971), 431–39.

Rosenfeld, Eva M. "Dream and Vision—Some Remarks on Freud's Egyptian Bird Dream." *International Journal of Psycho-Analysis* 37 (1956), 97–105.

Schafer, Roy. "Narration in the Psychoanalytic Dialogue." *Critical Inquiry* 7 (1981), 29–53.

———. *A New Language for Psychoanalysis.* New Haven: Yale University Press, 1976.

Scheidt, Jürgen vom, ed. *Der unbekannte Freud: Neue Interpretationen seiner Träumen.* Munich: Kindler, 1974.

Scherner, Karl Albert. *Das Leben des Traums.* Berlin: Heinrich Schindler, 1861.

Schönau, Walter. *Sigmund Freuds Prosa: Literarische Elemente seines Stils.* Stuttgart: J. B. Metzler, 1968.

Schorske, Carl E. *Fin-de-Siècle Vienna: Politics and Culture.* New York: Alfred A. Knopf, 1980.

Schur, Max. *Freud: Living and Dying.* New York: International Universities Press, 1972.

———. "Some Additional 'Day Residues' of 'The Specimen Dream of Psychoanalysis.'" In *Psychoanalysis—A General Psychology: Essays in Honor of Heinz Hartmann.* Ed. Rudolph M. Loewenstein et al. New York: International Universities Press, 1966.

Silberer, Herbert. *Der Traum: Einführung in die Traumpsychologie.* Stuttgart: Ferdinand Enke, 1919.

Simon, Ernst. "Sigmund Freud, the Jew." *Leo Baeck Institute Year Book* 2 (1957), 270–305.

Smith, Joseph H., ed. *Psychoanalysis and Language. (Psychiatry and the Humanities.* Vol. 3.) New Haven: Yale University Press, 1978.

Specht, Ernst Konrad. "Der wissenschaftstheoretische Status der Psychoanalyse: Das Problem der Traumdeutung." *Psyche* 35 (September 1981), 761–87.

Spence, Donald P. *Narrative Truth and Historical Truth: Meaning and Interpretation in Psychoanalysis.* New York: W. W. Norton, 1982.

Starobinski, Jean. "*Acheronta Movebo.*" Trans. Françoise Meltzer. *Critical Inquiry* 13 (Winter 1987), 394–407.

Stekel, Wilhelm. *Fortschritte und Technik der Traumdeutung.* Vienna: Weidmann, 1935.

———. *Die Sprache des Traumes.* Wiesbaden: J. F. Bergmann, 1911.

———. *Der telepathische Traum.* Berlin: Johannes Baum, 1920.

Strümpell, L. *Die Natur und Entstehung der Träume.* Leipzig: Veit, 1874.

Velikovsky, Immanuel. "The Dreams Freud Dreamed." *Psychoanalytic Review* 28 (1941), 508–10.

Ver Eecke, Wilfried. *Saying "No": Its Meaning in Child Development, Psychoanalysis, Linguistics, and Hegel.* Pittsburgh: Duquesne University Press, 1984.

Vitz, Paul. *Sigmund Freud's Christian Unconscious.* New York: Guilford, 1988.

Vogel, Léon. "Freud and Judaism: An Analysis in the Light of His Correspondence." Trans. Murray Sachs. *Judaism* 24 (1975), 181–93.

Volkelt, Johannes. *Die Traum-Phantasie.* Stuttgart: Meyer and Zeller, 1875.

Volochinov, V. [Mikhail Bakhtin]. *Au délà du Social: Essai sur le freudisme.* In *Ecrits sur le freudisme.* Trans. Guy Verret. Lausanne: Editions l'Age d'Homme, 1980.

Vološinov, V. N. *Freudianism: A Marxist Critique.* Trans. I. R. Titunik. Ed. Neal H. Bruss. New York: Academic Press, 1976.

Weber, Samuel. *The Legend of Freud.* Minneapolis: University of Minnesota Press, 1982.

Wittgenstein, Ludwig. *Wittgenstein: Lectures and Conversations.* Ed. Cyril Barrett. Berkeley: University of California Press, 1966.

Wollheim, Richard, ed. *Freud: A Collection of Critical Essays.* New York: Anchor Books, 1974.

Woods, Ralph L., and Herbert B. Greenhouse, eds. *The New World of Dreams.* New York: Macmillan, 1974.

Wyss, Dieter. *Die tiefenpsychologischen Schulen von den Anfängen bis zur Gegenwart.* 3d ed. Göttingen: Vandenhoeck & Ruprecht, 1970.

———. *Psychoanalytic Schools from the Beginning to the Present.* Trans. Gerald Onn. New York: Jason Aronson, 1973.

Bible, Talmud, and Midrash

Albeck, Chanoch. *Bereschit Rabbah.* Jerusalem: Wahrman Books, 1965.

Alter, Robert. *The Art of Biblical Narrative.* New York: Basic Books, 1981.

——. "Old Rabbis, New Critics." *The New Republic,* 5–12 Jan. 1987, pp. 27–33.

Berakoth. In *The Babylonian Talmud: Seder Zeraʿim.* Vol. 1. Ed. I. Epstein. Trans. Maurice Simon. London: Soncino, 1948.

Baldwin, Joyce. *Daniel: An Introduction and Commentary.* Ontario: InterVarsity Press, 1978.

Bilu, Yoram. "Sigmund Freud and Rabbi Yehudah: On a Jewish Mystical Tradition of 'Psychoanalytic' Dream Interpretation." *Journal of Psychological Anthropology* 2 (1979), 443–63.

Brown, Ronald N. *The Enjoyment of Midrash: The Use of the Pun in Genesis Rabbah.* Ph.D. dissertation, Brown University, 1980.

Buber, Martin. *Werke.* Vols. 1–3. Munich: Kösel, 1962–64.

Buber, Martin, and Franz Rosenzweig. *Die Schrift und ihre Verdeutschung.* Berlin: Schocken, 1936.

Das Buch der Frommen. 2d ed. Ed. Jehuda Wistinetzki and J. Freimann. Frankfurt am Main: M. A. Wahrmann, 1924.

Charles, R. H., ed. *The Book of Daniel.* Edinburgh: T. C. and E. C. Jack, 1913.

Clermont-Ganneau, Charles. "Maneé, Thécel, Pharès, et le festin de Balthasar." *Journal Asiatique.* Series 8. Vol. 8 (1866), 36–67.

Cohen, Abraham. *Everyman's Talmud.* New York: E. P. Dutton, 1949.

Cohen, B. "Über Traumdeutung in der jüdischen Tradition." *Imago* 18 (1932), 117–21.

Dommerhausen, Werner. *Nabonid im Buche Daniel.* Mainz: Matthias Grunewald, 1964.

Dougherty, Raymond Philip. *Nabonides and Nebuchadnezzar: A Study of the Closing Events of the Neo-Babylonian Empire.* New Haven: Yale University Press, 1936.

Driver, S. R. *The Book of Genesis.* 11th ed. London: Methuen, 1920.

Eissfeldt, Otto. "Die Menetekel-Inschrift und ihre Deutung." *Zeitschrift für die alttestamentliche Wissenschaft* 63 (1951), 105–14.

Erlich, Ernst Ludwig. *Der Traum im alten Testament. Beihefte zur Zeitschrift für die alttestamentliche Wissenschaft* 73 (1953).

Finkel, Asher. "The Pesher of Dreams and Scriptures." *Revue de Qumran* 4 (1963), 357–70.

Gros Louis, Kenneth R. R., and James S. Ackerman, eds. *Literary Interpretations of Biblical Narratives.* Vol. 2. Nashville: Abingdon, 1982.

Haddad, Gérard. *L'enfant illégitime: Sources talmudiques de la psychanalyse.* Paris: Hachette, 1981.

Handelman, Susan A. *The Slayers of Moses: The Emergence of Rabbinic Interpretation in Modern Literary Theory.* Albany: State University of New York, 1982.

Harris, Monford. "Dreams in the *Sefer Ḥasidim.*" *Proceedings of the American Academy for Jewish Research* 31 (1963), 51–80.

Hartman, Geoffrey H., and Sanford Budick, eds. *Midrash and Literature.* New Haven: Yale University Press, 1986.

Heineman, Isaac. *Darkhei ha-aggadah.* Jerusalem: Magnes Press, 1970.

In the Beginning: A New English Rendition of the Book of Genesis. Trans. Everett Fox. New York: Schocken, 1983.

Jacob, Benno. *Das erste Buch der Tora: Genesis.* Berlin: Schocken, 1934.

——— . *The First Book of the Bible: Genesis.* Ed. Ernest I. Jacob and Walter Jacob. New York: Ktav, 1974.

Kraeling, Emil G. "The Handwriting on the Wall." *Journal of Biblical Literature* 62 (1943), 11–18.

Kristianpoller, Alexander. *Traum und Traumdeutung.* In *Monumenta Talmudica.* Vol. 4. Pt. 2. Vienna: Harz, 1923.

Lacocque, André. *Daniel et son temps.* Geneva: Labor and Fides, 1983.

——— . *Le livre de Daniel.* Paris: Delachaux et Niestle, 1976.

Lauer, Chaim. "Das Wesen des Traumes in der Beurteilung der talmudischen und rabbinischen Literatur." *Internationale Zeitschrift für Psychoanalyse und "Imago"* 1 (1913), 459–69.

Levinas, Emmanuel. "Quelques vues talmudiques sur le rêve." In *La psychanalyse est-elle une histoire juive?* Ed. Adélie and Jean-Jacques Rassial. Paris: Editions du Seuil, 1981.

Lieberman, Saul. *Greek in Jewish Palestine.* New York: Jewish Theological Seminary, 1942.

——— . *Hellenism in Jewish Palestine.* New York: Jewish Theological Seminary, 1950.

Löwinger, Adolf. *Der Traum in der jüdischen Literatur.* Leipzig: M. W. Kaufmann, 1908.

Midrash Rabbah. 3d ed. Vols. 1–10. Ed. H. Freedman and Maurice Simon. London: Soncino, 1983.

Montefiore, C. G., and H. Loewe, eds. *A Rabbinic Anthology.* London: Macmillan, 1938.

Montgomery, James A. *A Critical and Exegetical Commentary on the Book of Daniel.* New York: Charles Scribner's Sons, 1927.

Prince, John Dyneley. *Mene Mene Tekel Upharsin: An Historical Study of the Fifth Chapter of Daniel.* Ph.D. dissertation, Johns Hopkins University, 1893.

Rad, Gerhard von. *Das erste Buch Mose: Genesis Kapitel 25, 19—50, 26.* Göttingen: Vandenhoeck & Ruprecht, 1953.

————. *Genesis: A Commentary.* 2d ed. Philadelphia: Westminster Press, 1972.

Rosenthal, Ludwig A. "Die Josephsgeschichte, mit den Büchern Ester und Daniel verglichen." *Zeitschrift fur die alttestamentliche Wissenschaft* 15 (1895), 278–84.

Sarna, Nahum M. *Understanding Genesis.* New York: Shocken, 1970.

Sefer Chasidim. Ed. Reuben Margulies. Jerusalem: Mosad ha-Rav Kook, 1957.

Silberman, Lou H. "Unriddling the Riddle: A Study in the Structure and Language of the Habakkuk Pesher." *Revue de Qumran* 3 (1961), 323–64.

Speiser, E. A. *Genesis.* New York: Doubleday, 1964.

The Talmud: Berakhoth. Ed. A. Zvi Ehrman. Vol. 4. Jerusalem: El-ʿAm, 1982.

Trachtenberg, Joshua. *Jewish Magic and Superstition.* New York: Behrman, 1939.

Velikovsky, Immanuel. "Psychoanalytische Ahnungen in der Traumdeutungskunst der alten Hebräer nach dem Traktat Brachoth." *Psychoanalytische Bewegung* 5 (1933), 66–69.

Zockler, Otto. *The Book of the Prophet Daniel.* Trans. James Strong. New York: Scribner and Armstrong, 1876.

Index of Names and Works

Abaye, 80–82
Abed-nego, 64
Abraham, 87
Abraham, Karl, 15n, 29n, 102n, 121n, 131n
Ackerman, James S., 52n
Adler, Alfred, 31–33, 98n, 140
Akiba, R., 83n
Albeck, Chanoch, 57n, 147
Alberti, Leon Battista, 35
Alexander, 117
Almoli, Solomon, 91n
Alter, Robert, 6n, 52n, 70n, 148
Anzieu, Didier, 11n, 13n, 116n, 121n, 140
Aristander, 117
Aristotle, 5, 17, 95, 98n, 140
Aron, Willy, 2n, 140
Artemidorus, 5, 17–20, 117, 140
Aue, Maximilian, 123n

Babylonia, 64, 70
Bakan, David, 1n, 74n, 140
Baldwin, Joyce, 66n, 148
Balkanyi, Charlotte, 36n, 140
Bally, Charles, 98n–99n
Banaᵓah, R., 78–79, 92
Bar Hedia, 79–82, 86–87, 91–93, 135
Bar Kappara, 83
Barrett, Cyril, 24n
Beck, Aaron T., 33n, 140
Bein, Alex, 120n
Belshazzar, 59, 66–68
Berakhot. See Talmud, Babylonian: Tractate Berakhot
Bergmann, Martin S., 1n, 123n, 141
Bettelheim, Bruno, 38n, 45n, 141

Bible, x, xi–xii, 2–3, 6–8, 47–71, 84, 101, 132, 133–36, 148–50
Bilu, Yoram, 73n, 148
Binswanger, Ludwig, 21n, 31, 141
Birdsey, Bruce, 86n
Blatt, David S., 1n, 141
Bloom, Harold, ix–x, xii, 6, 128–29, 141
Blumenthal, David, 86n, 123n
Boss, Menard, 22n, 141
Bossard, Robert, 115n, 141
Boyarin, Daniel, xii
Brenkman, John, 26n
Breuer, Josef, 13, 19, 41
Brisman, Leslie, xii
Brown, Ronald N., 83n, 148
Buber, Martin, 70n, 148
Budick, Sanford, 5n, 7n, 149

Cappadocia, 85, 118, 131
Casey, Edward, xii
Charles, R. H., 60n, 148
Childs, Brevard, xii
Chisda, R., 75–76, 80
Clermont-Ganneau, Charles, 67n, 148
Cohen, Abraham, 74n, 148
Cohen, B., 73n, 148
Cracow, 101–2
Cuddihy, John Murray, 1n, 30n, 43n, 127n, 141

Dalbiez, Roland, 28n, 141
Damstra, Martin, N., 106n, 141
Daniel, ix, 3, 47–48, 58–71, 131, 134
Daniel, Book of, 47, 58–71, 76n
Darius, 68–70
De Man, Paul, 22n, 129n

De Mauro, Tullio, 98n
Derrida, Jacques, xii, 6, 7n, 98n,
    108n, 110n, 113n, 129n, 141–42
De Saussure, Ferdinand, 98n
Descartes, Dreams of, 33
Deuteronomy, Book of, 84
Devereux, George, 97n, 98n, 109n, 142
Dilthey, Wilhelm, 6
Dommerhausen, Werner, 66n, 148
Don Juan, 37
Dougherty, Raymond Philip, 66n, 148
Driver, S. R., 56n, 148

Ecclesiastes Rabbah, 93n
Eckstein, Emma, 13–15. *See also* Irma
Edels, Samuel (Maharsha), 92n
Edelson, Marshall, 115n, 142
Egypt, 18, 58, 122, 124
Ehrenwald, Jan, 106n, 142
Ehrman, A. Zvi, 75n, 150
Eisenbud, Jule, 97n
Eissfeldt, Otto, 68n, 148
Eitington, Max, 98n
Eliezer, R., 56–57
Elon, Amos, 120n
Epstein, I., 75n
Erikson, Erik, 11n, 13, 142
Erlich, Ernst Ludwig, 51n, 53n, 148
Esau, 49
Esther, Book of, 70n

Falk, Avner, xii, 1n, 120n, 124n, 125n,
    142
Felman, Shoshana, xii, 11n, 26n, 142
Ferenczi, Sandor, 36n, 50n, 117, 142
Ferguson, Margaret W., 43n
Finkel, Asher, 70n, 148
Fliess, Wilhelm, 9n, 10, 13–15, 106n
Florence, 35
Foucault, Michel, 21n
Fox, Everett, 56n, 149
Franz Joseph, 118
Freedman, H., 57n, 87n, 93n
French, Thomas, 33n, 142
Freud, Anna, 128
Freud, Sigmund. Abbreviations of
    works, 139–40. Dreams: *Auf Geseres*

("My Son, the Myops" or "the
Passover Dream"), 119–26, 137;
Autodidasker, 117; Count Thun, 43–
44; Irma's Injection, 11–16, 137;
"R.," 42–43. Letters: to Karl Abraham, 15n, 29n, 102n, 121n, 131n; to
Wilhelm Fliess, 9n, 10–11, 13–15,
45n, 71, 106n, 120n; to the *Jüdische
Presszentrale Zürich*, 2n. Works:
"Address to the B'nai Brith Society,"
2n; *An Autobiographical Study (Selbst-
darstellung)*, 2n; "Dreams and Telepathy" ("Traum und Telepathie"), 32,
102–5; "A Fulfilled Dream Premonition" ("Ein erfüllte Traumahnung"),
99–100; *The Interpretation of Dreams
(Die Traumdeutung)*, ix, xi, 2, 10–46,
54–55, 95–100, 110–11, 113, 116–25,
129–31, 135–36; *Introductory Lectures on Psychoanalysis (Vorlesungen
zur Einführung in die Psychoanalyse)*,
16n, 25–27, 31n, 32, 35, 38n, 45n,
107–9, 111–13, 114–15, 117; *Jokes
and Their Relation to the Unconscious
(Der Witz und seine Beziehung zum
Unbewussten)*, 43n, 101–2; "Negation" ("Die Verneinung"), 126–28;
*New Introductory Lectures on Psycho-
analysis (Neue Folge der Vorlesungen
zur Einführung in die Psychoanalyse)*, 31, 35, 101n, 104n, 106n, 108;
"A Note on the 'Mystic Writing
Pad' " ("Notiz über den 'Wunderblock' "), 46n; "The Occult Significance of Dreams" ("Die okkulte
Bedeutung des Traumes"), 105–6;
On Dreams (Über den Traum), 16n,
18, 29; "On the Dynamics of the
Transference" ("Die Dynamik der
Übertragung"), 40–42; *On the History of the Psychoanalytic Movement
(Zur Geschichte der psychoanalytischen Bewegung)*, 31n; Preface to
the Hebrew edition of *Introductory
Lectures on Psychoanalysis*, 2n; Preface to the Hebrew edition of *Totem
and Taboo*, 2n; "Psychoanalysis and

Telepathy'' (''Psychoanalyse und Telepathie''), 100–102; *The Psychopathology of Everyday Life* (*Zur Psychopathologie des Alltagslebens*), 106n; ''Remarks on the Theory and Practice of Dream Interpretation'' (''Bemerkungen zur Theorie und Praxis der Traumdeutung''), 107, 111, 114; ''Remembering, Repeating, and Working Through'' (''Erinnern, Wiederholen und Durcharbeiten''), 4, 127; *Totem and Taboo*, v, 2n

Frieden, Joan Branham, xii

Frieden, Ken, ix–x, 7n

Fromm, Erich, 74n, 142

Gadamer, Hans-Georg, 7n

Gay, Peter, 2n, 9n, 142

Genesis, Book of, 47, 48–58, 62, 78, 87, 131

Genesis Rabbah, 52n, 56–57, 60n, 79, 85n, 147, 150

Gesenius, F. H. W., 122n

Goldhammer, Leo, 120n, 142

Gomperz, Theodor, 19

Gordis, Robert, 1n, 142

Green, Arthur, 119n

Grimm, Jacob and Wilhelm, 123n

Grinstein, Alexander, 11n, 44n, 117n, 121n, 123n, 124n, 142

Grollman, Earl A., 1n, 142

Gros Louis, Kenneth R. R., 53n, 149

Grunbaum, Adolf, 45n, 143

Gur Aryeh, 60n

Gutheil, Emil A., 32n, 37n, 143

Habermas, Jürgen, 21n, 143

Haddad, Gérard, 2n, 74n, 84n, 149

Handelman, Susan A., 1n, 74n, 149

Harkavy, Alexander, 123n

Harris, Monford, 90–91, 149

Hartman, Geoffrey H., 5n, 149

Hartmann, Eduard von, 115n

Heine, Heinrich, 28

Heineman, Isaac, 83n, 149

Herod, 124

Herzl, Theodor, 120–26

Hesiod, 62n

Hildebrandt, F. W., 98n, 115n, 143

Hook, Sidney, 45n, 143

Horowitz, Samuel, 119n

Howe, Irving, 43n

Huna, R., 77

Hyppolite, Jean, 126n, 143

Ibn Ezra, 56n, 63n

Irma, 11–16, 137. *See also* Eckstein, Emma

Isaac, 52

Isaiah, Book of, 84

Isakower, Otto, 36n, 143

Ishmael, R., 81, 85–86, 93, 135

Ishmael ben R. Yose, R., 86–88, 93, 133, 135

Jacob, 49–53, 125n

Jacob, Benno, 48n, 54n, 149

Jakobson, Roman, 22n, 143

Janus, 9, 44

Jastrow, Marcus, 85n

Jehoiakim, King, 59

Jochanan, R., 57, 83n

Jones, Ernest, 18n, 98n, 120n, 143

Jones, Richard M., 34n, 143

Joseph, ix, 2, 3, 17–18, 20, 47–58, 69n, 125n, 131, 134

Josephus, 52n

Judah, 49, 52

Judah, R., 86n

Judovitz, Dalia, 111n, 143

Jung, C. G., 4, 31, 33, 34n, 65, 96, 98n, 143

Kafka, Franz, ix, 134

Kanzer, Mark, 10n, 13n, 18n, 112n, 143

Kardiner, Abram, 131n

Klein, Dennis, 1n, 143

Kofman, Sarah, 36n, 110n, 144

Kraeling, Emil G., 67n, 149

Kristianpoller, Alexander, 74n, 78n, 83n, 149

Krüll, Marianne, 11n, 144

Kugel, James, 5n

Laban, 49
Lacan, Jacques, 13n, 23n, 108n, 110n, 126n, 144
Lacocque, André, 60n, 68n, 149
Laderman, Peter, xii
Lamentations, Book of, 88
Lamentations Rabbah, 83n, 85n, 86–88, 89, 93, 131, 133, 150
Laplanche, Jean, 97, 126n, 144
Lasker: dream about, 117
Lauer, Chaim, 2n, 73n, 144, 149
Leah, 49
Leavitt, Harry C., 11n, 144
Lemberg, 102
Levinas, Emmanuel, 74n, 149
Lewy, Heinrich, 19n, 144
Lieberman, Saul, 18n, 83n, 86n, 149
Livy, 111
Loewenberg, Peter, 1n, 120n, 125n, 144
Lorand, Sandor, 74n
Lowenstein, Rudolph M., 11n, 13n, 34n, 144
Löwinger, Adolf, 73n, 78n, 92n, 149
Lowy, Samuel, 22n, 23n, 25n, 32n, 144
Luders, Wolfram, 34n, 144
Lueger, Karl, 44n
Luther, Martin, 121n, 122n

McGrath, William J., 2n, 120n, 125n, 145
Maeder, Alphonse, 31–32, 145
Maimonides, 91n
Malcolm, Janet, 11n, 145
Margulies, Reuben, 89n
Masserman, Jules H., 34n
Masson, Jeffrey Moussaieff, 11n, 145. See also Freud, Sigmund. Letters: to Wilhelm Fliess
Maury, Alfred, 21n, 145
Meitlis, Jacob, 124n, 145
Menninger, Karl, 1n, 145
Meshach, 64
Midrash Rabbah. See Genesis Rabbah; Lamentations Rabbah
Miller, Jacques-Alain, 13n, 108n, 144
Mizrachi, Elijah, 60n

Montefiore, C. G., 74n, 150
Montgomery, James A., 60n, 61n, 150
Moses, 84

Nachman of Bratslav, R., 118–19
Nagera, Humberto, 21n, 140
Nancy, Jean-Luc, xii
Nebuchadnezzar, 59–69, 76n, 122n, 133; dreams of, 60–62, 64–65
Nelson, Benjamin, 37n, 131n, 145
Nietzsche, Friedrich, v

Ovid, 62n

Paul, Robert, 121n
Pfrimmer, Théo, 2n, 121n, 122n, 145
Pharoah: dreams of, 18, 53–55, 58, 60, 62
Philo, 58n
Picasso, Pablo, 3
Plato, ix
Politzer, Georges, 11n, 22n, 97n, 145
Pontalis, J.-B., 97n, 126n, 144
Potiphar's wife, 52–53
Prince, John Dyneley, 67n, 150
Proverbs, 84
Psalms, 121–23

Raba, 79–82, 93
Rabbi, 83
Rachel, 49
Rad, Gerhard von, 50n, 51n, 52n, 150
Rashi, 63, 75–77
Rassial, Adélie, 74n, 145
Ricoeur, Paul, xii, 20n, 97n, 145
Rie, Oskar, 13
Rieff, Philip, 20n, 145
Roazen, Paul, 1n, 120n, 145
Roback, A. A., 2n, 117n, 145
Robert, Marthe, 1n, 145
Robin, Régine, 2n, 118n, 146
Roland, Alan, 36n, 146
Rome, 82, 120–21
Rosegger, Peter, 27n
Rosenfeld, Eva M., 2n, 43n, 146
Rosenthal, Ludwig, A., 70n, 150
Rosenzweig, Franz, 70n

Samuel, R., 77–78
Sarna, Nahum M., 48n, 150
Schafer, Roy, 97n, 146
Scheidt, Jürgen vom, 11n, 146
Scherner, Karl Albert, 10n, 146
Schiller, Friedrich, 20
Schleiermacher, Friedrich, 6–7
Schönau, Walter, 38n, 146
Schopenhauer, Arthur, 4
Schorske, Carl E., 30n, 38n, 44n, 121n, 146
Schur, Max, 1n, 11n, 13n, 15n, 146
Sefer Chasidim, 89–91, 150
Shadrach, 64
Shakespeare, William, 3, 4, 5
Shengold, Leonard, 10n, 18n
Sholem Aleichem (Sholem Rabinovitsh), 43n
Silberer, Herbert, 31–32, 98n, 146
Silberman, Lou H., 67n, 150
Simon, Ernst, 1n, 146
Simon, Maurice, 75n
Smith, Joseph H., 97n, 146
Specht, Ernst Konrad, 107n, 146
Speiser, E. A., 48n, 150
Spence, Donald P., 20n–21n, 97n, 146
Starobinski, Jean, 38n, 146
Stein, Gertrude, 3
Steinthal, Chajim, 7
Stekel, Wilhelm, 22n, 31, 33, 98n, 147
Stockbridge, Patricia, xii
Strachey, James, 123n, 139
Strümpell, L., 16n, 112n, 147
Sully, James, 46, 119
Swartz, Michael, 86n

Talmud, x, xi–xii, 2, 4, 6–7, 8, 19n, 57, 73–93, 101, 102n, 131–32, 133–36. *See also* Talmud, Babylonian; Talmud, Palestinian

Talmud, Babylonian: Tractate Baba Kama, 83n, 84; Tractate Berakhot, 4, 73–93, 131, 134, 148, 150; Tractate Chagigah, 76n; Tractate Gittin, 91n; Tractate Horayot, 91n; Tractate Nedarim, 77n; Tractate Sanhedrin, 79n, 85n, 91; Tractate Yoma, 91n
Talmud, Palestinian: Tractate Maᶜaser Sheni, 57, 83, 85n
Tamar, 52
Trachtenberg, Joshua, 91n, 150

Velikovsky, Immanuel, 73n, 120n, 147, 150
Ver Eecke, Wilfried, 125n, 147
Vienna, 7, 120, 123n, 124
Virgil, 38
Vitz, Paul, 124n, 125n, 147
Vogel, Léon, 1n, 147
Volkelt, Johannes, 10n, 23n, 32n, 111n, 112n, 115n, 147
Volochinov, V. (Vološinov, V. N.), 38n, 147

Wahrig, Gerhard, 123n
Weber, Samuel, 31n, 147
Weidmann, Heinrich, xii
Weinreich, Max, 86n
Weiss, Frederic, 25n, 36n
Weizsaecker, Viktor von, 37n
Wistinetzki, Jehuda, 89n
Wittgenstein, Ludwig, 24n, 147
Wollheim, Richard, 25n, 45n, 147
Woods, Ralph L., 74n, 147
Wyss, Dieter, 21n, 147

Zechariah, 77
Zockler, Otto, 64n, 66n, 150

Index of Terms

Abbreviations: of Freud's works, 139–40
Aggadah, 56–57, 73–93
"All dreams follow the mouth," 57, 78–83, 89–93
Ambivalence, ix, xi, 2, 9, 14n, 51, 73, 97–98, 100–101
Anacoluthon, 57
Angels, 75–76, 89–90
Association, Free, ix, xi, 5, 9, 19–26, 36n, 47, 71, 84, 96, 110, 116, 127n, 132, 134–37. *See also* Association, Method of
Association, Method of, xii, 4–5, 7, 19–24, 26n, 33, 36n, 47, 71, 74, 84, 86, 89, 103, 108–9, 112–13, 118–20, 131. *See also* Association, Free

Battles, xi, 12, 37–44, 100, 124, 128–29, 133
Besetzung. See Occupation
Bipartite model, 22–26, 29, 36–37, 110, 116

Cathexis (*Besetzung*). *See* Occupation
Cognitive therapy, 33n–34n
Condensation (*Verdichtung*), 13, 17, 23, 28–9, 45, 114, 117, 119. *See also* Dream work
Content, latent, 19–24, 27, 32, 35–37, 105, 107, 109–11, 114, 132, 134. *See also* Dream thoughts; Bipartite model
Content, manifest, 8, 15, 19–27, 30, 32, 34–37, 44–45, 53, 79, 84, 104, 109–10, 114–15, 132, 134, 137

Correspondence: hermeneutics of, 3, 5, 19, 22–24, 27, 33, 47, 53, 109–11, 113–14
Countertransference, 37, 39, 106n

Davar: as key word, 50–51
Daydreams, 28–29
Day's residues (*Tagesreste*), 11n, 13, 21–22, 79, 89–90, 104, 115
Deconstruction, ix, 6–8, 129n
Decree (*g'zerah*), 62, 64–65, 69–70, 119–26, 130, 137
Denial (*Verneinung*), xi–xii, 1, 8, 14n, 47, 103, 107, 115, 123, 125–31, 133, 136
Diaspora. *See* Exile
Disavowal. *See* Denial
Disguises, 9, 13, 15, 26, 43, 45–46, 47–48, 52–53, 57–59, 69–70, 78, 116, 134
Displacement (*Verschiebung*), 4–5, 13–14, 17, 19, 22–25, 28–29, 33, 45, 47, 71, 88, 95, 104, 108–11, 113–14, 136. *See also* Dream work
Dream Facade. *See* Facade
Dream interpretation: "anagogic," 32–34
Dream interpretation: associative. *See* Association, Method of
Dream interpretation: symbolic. *See* Symbolism
Dream report, 3, 11, 24–25, 28n–29n, 30, 34, 36–37, 55, 78, 108, 110, 112–13, 134–35
Dream thoughts (*Traumgedanken*), 6, 17, 19–25, 28, 31n, 36, 71, 105, 110–11. *See also* Content, latent

Dream work (*Traumarbeit*), x, xi–xii,
16–17, 21–22, 24–31n, 35–37, 44,
46–47, 96, 98, 104–5, 107–10, 112,
114–17, 127–30, 132. *See also* Con-
densation; Displacement; Revision,
Secondary
Dreams: of children, 26–27, 105, 113
Dreams: of Joseph, 17, 49–50
Dreams: prophetic. *See* Prophecy
Dreams: telepathic. *See* Telepathy
Dreams: as wish fulfillments. *See* Wish
fulfillment

Economic model, 38–39, 41, 79–82,
85–88, 112, 127
Evasion, x, xi–xii, 104, 125, 131
Exile, 59n, 82, 86, 92–93, 121–24

Facade, 22, 34–35, 116
Figuration, 5, 22n, 26–27, 37–38, 42,
44–46, 65, 70, 75, 78, 83, 89, 92,
108, 115–16, 127–28. *See also* Metaphor, Rhetoric, Tropes
Free Association. *See* Association, Free

Geseres. See Decree
Greek language, 18n, 85–86, 88, 92,
117–19, 125, 131
G'zerah. See Decree

Halakhah, 74, 77n, 92–93
Hand: as key word, 59, 62–70, 89
Hebrew, v, 2, 50n, 59–60, 83, 86, 91,
93, 95, 119, 122–23, 131–32
Hermeneutics, 6–7, 9–10, 20–24, 36,
111, 116, 134–35
Hieroglyphics, xii, 109–13, 115–17
Hyperbole, 59–60

Intertextuality, ix, 1–2, 6–8, 16–19,
33, 60–63, 69, 74, 76n, 77–78, 83–
84, 87–88, 93, 95n, 121–22, 128–
32, 133–36
Introjection, 38, 43
Investment (*Besetzung*). *See* Occupation
Irony, 50–51, 60–61, 64, 69, 123n

Key words, 50–51, 70n, 122, 125. *See
also* Hand
K'tonet passim, 49, 51

Latent Contents. *See* Contents, Latent;
Dream thoughts

Manifest Contents. *See* Contents, Mani-
fest; Dream report
Masks, 4, 9, 37, 39–41, 43, 59, 104,
116. *See also* Disguises
Metaphor, ix, 4–5, 10, 16–17, 22n, 23,
26, 34–35, 38, 40–42, 44–45, 47,
78, 81, 91, 93n, 109, 111–12, 115,
127, 129n, 131, 135
Metonymy, 22n, 112, 114
Midrash, 6, 56–57, 73–93. *See also*
Genesis Rabbah; Lamentations Rab-
bah; Talmud, Babylonian; Talmud,
Palestinian
Military model. *See* Battles

Narration, 3–4, 20, 21n, 22n, 29n, 30,
34, 46, 48–52, 54–56, 62, 64–68,
71, 74, 82, 91, 96–97, 107n, 110,
114, 128n, 134
Negation. *See* Denial

Occupation (*Besetzung*), 37–42, 112.
See also Battles; Economic model
Overdetermination, x, 8, 23, 27, 114,
116–17, 132

Palimpsest, 46, 119
Paronomasia, 18n, 68. *See also* Word-
play
Passover, 120–26
Postmodern criticism, xii. *See also*
Deconstruction
Poststructuralism, 6–7. *See also*
Deconstruction
Power, 3–4, 37–38, 41–43, 47–53,
55–66, 68–70, 73, 77–82, 85–89,
98, 101, 104, 107, 133, 137

Precursors, 8, 10–11, 16–20, 31, 44, 46, 47, 73–74, 95, 98n, 101, 113–14, 116–17, 119–20, 126, 128–31, 133–36
Prophecy, ix, xi–xii, 3–4, 9, 47–48, 50–51, 54–60, 62–63, 65–66, 68, 70, 73–74, 76, 78–83, 87–88, 92, 95–106, 119, 130, 132, 134, 136
Prophecy, Self-Fulfilling, xi, 44, 56–58, 66, 68, 70–71, 73–74, 79–82, 89, 92, 97, 101, 109
Providence, 52–53, 55, 58–60, 64
Puns, 7, 74, 83–85, 96. *See also* Paronomasia; Wordplay

Repression, x–xi, 8, 13, 15, 27, 32–33, 38, 46, 86, 95, 98n, 99, 104, 107, 116, 118, 126–30, 132, 134–37
Resistance (*Widerstand*), 12–13, 26, 37–41, 100
Reversal, 26, 39, 64, 99–100, 114, 117, 129n
Revision, Secondary, 27–31, 110, 136. *See also* Dream work
Rhetoric, ix, 3, 25, 37, 39, 44, 46, 50–51, 53, 64, 69–70, 96, 115–16
Rhetorical criticism, 6, 8. *See also* Deconstruction

Samaritan, 86–88, 93
Secondary Revision. *See* Revision, Secondary

Seduction, 10, 11n, 37, 41–42, 52
Sefer Chasidim, 89–91
Simile, 34–35, 75, 100
Substitution, 25–26, 33, 39, 61, 88, 100, 112, 136
Suggestion, xii, 34, 47, 74, 79, 82, 97, 105–8, 114, 135
Symbolism, 18–20, 32, 47, 54–55, 62, 64–65, 82, 85, 87, 96, 105, 107–8, 113, 116–17

"Talking cure," 4, 37, 126, 137
Telepathy, xi, 96–106, 130
Transcendence, ix, 76, 91, 96, 98, 105
Transference, ix, xii, 9–10, 14, 37, 39–42, 44–45, 79, 96–97, 101, 105–9, 112, 126, 130, 135, 137
Translation, xii, 4, 27, 36n, 40, 45, 49n, 56, 59, 62, 75, 82, 92–93, 106, 108–14, 116, 124, 130–32
Tropes, x, 25, 27, 44, 78. *See also* Figuration, Metaphor, Rhetoric

Wish fulfillment, 10–11, 12n, 13, 15–16, 19, 26–27, 32n, 39, 48, 95n, 99–101, 104–5, 126, 130–31
Wordplay, 7, 18–19, 67n, 68, 76n, 83–85, 116–18, 122–24, 135. *See also* Puns

Yiddish, 2, 43n, 101–2, 117–26, 127n, 131

Zionism, v, 120–26